North Vietnam:

POPULATION: 16 million.

TOPOGRAPHY: Jungle-covered mountains in the hinterland, with a densely populated deltaic plain and a narrow coastal plain.

CAPITAL: Hanoi.

POLITICS: Communist. Ho Chi Minh is President of the Democratic Republic of Vietnam. Authority rests with Ho and the Politburo of the Lao Dong (Communist) Party of North Vietnam.

South Vietnam:

POPULATION: 14 million.

TOPOGRAPHY: A deltaic plain in the south. In the north the Annamite Chain separates the narrow coastal plain from the High Plateau. Much of this region is sparsely populated, or populated only by primitive tribesmen, and largely unexplored.

CAPITAL: Saigon.

POLITICS: Anti-Communist. Ngo Dinh Diem is President of the Republic of Vietnam, and has absolute power.

Thailand:

POPULATION: 27 million.

TOPOGRAPHY: A rich and fertile central plain, with mountainous jungles in north and south; unproductive plain in the northeast.

CAPITAL: Bangkok.

POLITICS: Anti-Communist. On the framework of a constitutional monarchy Field Marshal Sarit Thanarat leads a military dictatorship.

Laos:

POPULATION: Perhaps two million to three million, but no one really knows.

TOPOGRAPHY: A narrow plain along the north bank of the Mekong River. Elsewhere the land is rugged and mountainous.

CAPITAL: Luang Prabang, seat of the Royal family, is generally known as the Royal capital. Vientiane is the administrative capital.

POLITICS: Under the terms of the 1962 Geneva Agreement, Laos is officially neutral and unaligned. The King reigns as a constitutional monarch, while neutralist Prime Minister Souvanna Phouma leads a coalition government of neutralists, rightists, and Communists.

Cambodia:

POPULATION: About four million.

TOPOGRAPHY: Fertile river plains and jungle-covered mountains.

CAPITAL: Phnom Penh.

POLITICS: Unaligned. Under a constitutional monarchy, Prince Norodom Sihanouk, who at times has been both King and Prime Minister, strives to preserve a neutral balance while feuding with his pro-Western neighbors in Thailand and South Vietnam.

THE
LAST
CONFUCIAN

DENIS
WARNER

The
Last
Confucian

The Macmillan Company, New York
Collier-Macmillan Limited, London

First Printing

The Macmillan Company, New York
Collier-Macmillan Canada, Ltd., Toronto, Ontario

Printed in the United States of America

Library of Congress catalog card number: 63-14185

DESIGNED BY RONALD FARBER

CONTENTS

Introduction

A quarter of a billion people live in South-East Asia. There are more South-East Asians than there are Americans and Canadians, or Latin Americans, or Africans, or Russians. That is one of the reasons why South-East Asia matters: there are many others.

In a continent of hungry people many South-East Asians are not hungry. Most live from hand-to-mouth on ill-balanced diets and are frequently stricken by disease: but almost every country in the region is either a food exporter or close to self-sufficiency in food production. Burma, Cambodia, South Vietnam, and Thailand are Asia's rice bowl. They grow more rice than they can eat, and could grow much more. This is important to the people who live in these hot and wet lands and also to predatory neighbors, who do not grow enough food, and, faced with continuing population explosions, may never be able to grow enough.

Sparsely populated Malaya is the world's greatest producer of rubber and tin: it earns 14 percent of the sterling area's annual crop of dollars. In known natural resources Indonesia ranks third to the United States and the Soviet Union. Scrape away the mud in Central Sumatra and there is oil, sometimes only four hundred feet below the surface. Indonesia is also well supplied with tin, bauxite, coal, manganese, iron ore, asphalt, phosphate, copper, nickel, tungsten, sulfur, iodine, gold, silver, platinum, and diamonds. It has a huge hydroelectric potential. The forests of Kalimantan (Borneo) are largely trackless jungle filled with teak, ironwood, bamboo, and rattan. Yet, despite such natural wealth, South-East Asia is both underdeveloped and, in comparison with other parts of Asia, underpopulated. Virgin jungle covers half of Vietnam, three-fifths of Malaya, and almost all of Laos.

Centuries before European seamen set off in little ships into the unchartered waters of the world to "discover" the mysterious lands and peoples of the Orient and to seize for themselves a share in its rich trade, South-East Asia was a great commercial center. The Indians called it Suvarna-dvipa, which means "islands of gold."

As early as the fourth century after Christ, the Arabs, who had learned the secret of the monsoons, traveled to South-East Asia in their dhows. Four-masted Chinese junks came along the Indo-China coast to the Malayan port of Malacca, where the silks and brocades and tea and porcelain of China were exchanged for the cloves, nutmeg, mace, and sandalwood of the Indies, the opium of present-day Laos and Burma, and rugs from Persia.

Separated by the great Himalayan mountain ranges, India and China met by sea in Malacca and the other ports and marketplaces of South-East Asia. Great Hindu kingdoms flourished and died. Arab traders came not only to buy and sell but also to implant the Muslim faith in the Malay Peninsula, the Indonesian archipelago, and the southern islands of the Philippines. Hinayana Buddhism, which looks on Buddha as a human teacher, spread from Ceylon to Burma, Thailand, Laos, and Cambodia. China left such a mark on Vietnam that through the centuries the mandarins at the Imperial Court at Hue took examinations in the Chinese language and the Chinese Classics. Confucianism, Mahayana Buddhism, which regards Buddha as a deity, and a provincial system similar to China's are some of the legacies of Chinese domination of the "Lesser Dragon," as Vietnam is sometimes called.

The Europeans came in the first twenty years of the sixteenth century. Like the Indians, the Chinese, and the Arabs before them, they came first for trade. Although territorial conquest was the least of their objectives, for protection, and the defense of their trading interests, they quickly expanded their control. On the eve of the Second World War all the countries of South-East Asia, with the exception of Thailand, were European colonies. The British had Burma, Malaya, Singapore, and a slice of Borneo. The Dutch had the rest of Borneo, and the great arc of islands stretching for three thousand miles from northern Sumatra to West New Guinea; the small island of Timor they shared with the Portuguese. The Philippine islands were American. The French ruled over Tongking, Annam, and Cochin-China, the three component parts of Vietnam, and two other Associated States of Indo-China, Laos and Cambodia.

To help them in their colonial tasks the Europeans made extensive use of Chinese labor. The discovery of tin in Malaya and the development of Singapore as a big entrepôt encouraged the migratory movement, especially from South China. Singapore became a Chinese city under British rule, and a clearinghouse for Chinese migrants into the rest of South-East Asia, where their diligence, industry, and thrift soon won them a disproportionate share of the wealth of all these lands.

The Japanese shattered the complacency of these colonial domains in 1941. By the mock freeedom they granted to the dependent peoples of South-East Asia, they spurred the demand for genuine independence. Master was suddenly coolie and coolie, master.

In the early postwar years the United States and Britain bowed gracefully to the winds of change. India, Pakistan, and Ceylon in South Asia and Burma and the Philippines in South-East got their independence. The move toward independence began in Malaya, Singapore, and even in the much more primitive territories of British Borneo.

The Dutch and the French chose to resist. Against the background of the cold war and the fall of China to Mao Tse-tung and his Communist forces, bloody revolts broke out in South-East Asia. Where the colonial Powers resisted indigenous demands for independence, true nationalists were often driven into the arms of the Communists. In the Philippines, Malaya, and Burma, where the colonial Powers had responded to nationalist pressures, Communist revolts failed. Dutch intransigence, first in Indonesia and subsequently over the disputed territory of West New Guinea, contributed to the rise in Indonesia of the largest Communist Party outside the bloc and to the rapid Soviet buildup, in 1961 and 1962, of the Indonesian armed forces, which are now equipped with a heavy cruiser, submarines, destroyers, long-range jet bombers, MIG 21's with a speed of 1,200 miles an hour, ground-to-air missiles, and a wide range of other modern Russian weapons. That Indonesia is not yet another, much larger, Cuba is not due to any lack of effort on the part of Moscow. In Indo-China the Communists prevailed against the French at the battle for Dien Bien Phu and at the Geneva conference table in 1954, and thereafter became locked in a politico-military struggle with the remnant, United States–backed Right-wing nationalists of Laos and South Vietnam.

With the withdrawal of the European colonial Powers through the fire exits and following the rise of Communist China, the

United States inevitably became drawn deeper into the struggle for South-East Asia. It was not from choice. President Roosevelt had no patience with European colonialism in Asia, and advocated some sort of international control, preferably Sino-American, to supplant the French administration in the then Associated States of French Indo-China while the local peoples prepared themselves for independence. Yet, under President Truman, Washington began large-scale military assistance to the French in Indo-China, and, in 1954, under President Eisenhower, once moved to the brink of war.

Each year since has seen the deeper involvement of the United States. Following the visit of General Maxwell Taylor to Vietnam in October, 1961, Washington set up a Military Assistance Command under General Paul D. Harkins. American military advisers flowed into South Vietnam, and by the end of 1962 there were more than ten thousand in the field. Technically they were only advisers, but often they were called on to fight—and to die. In all, a billion and a half dollars in "economic" aid has gone to South Vietnam since 1955; most of it has been used to pay the army, which the United States raised and trained.

This is only one of many American commitments in the area. American aid financed the Royal Laotian government and paid for the Royal Lao army. Thailand gets substantial quantities of American economic and military aid; and the South-East Asia Treaty Organization, which was created on American initiative after the fall of Dien Bien Phu, and is heavily dependent on the deterrent power of the United States 7th Fleet, throws what Mr. Dulles used to call a "mantle of protection" over Pakistan, Thailand, the Philippines, and South Vietnam. Laos and Cambodia were also covered for several years. Laos slipped out under the terms of the second Geneva Agreement in 1962, while Cambodia, afraid of offending its powerful Chinese neighbors, and at daggers drawn with Thailand and South Vietnam, has chosen to regard SEATO as a dangerous foe.

The region is filled with discord. Thailand regarded the 1962 Geneva Agreement, which recognized the "neutrality" of Laos, as another Munich. It directed most of its hostility toward Britain and France, two of its SEATO allies, which had invoked the treaty organization's unanimity rule to veto military action in Laos; but the United States did not escape its censure. Cambodia and Thailand have broken off diplomatic relations. Cambodia and South Vietnam maintain relations which are constantly strained by border incidents. Small, Muslim, and economically successful Malaya is threatened by big, Muslim, and economically unsuccessful Indonesia. The Philippines claims North Borneo, part of the new Federation of Malaysia, which embraces Malaya, Singapore, Sarawak, and Brunei, an arrangement that caused Brunei's eighty thousand inhabitants, who have seen their tiny country grow rich on oil royalties, rise in revolt in December, 1962. The Portuguese, fearful of the Indonesians, cling desperately to their part of Timor. Burma, despairing of the West and awed by Communist China, has pinned its hopes of survival on peaceful coexistence.

This is the background against which the Communists are making their bid for the human and material resources of South-East Asia. As Tillman Durdin, the hardest working and best informed of all reporters who have covered the postwar South-East Asian scene, wrote in the *New York Times* on October 21, 1962: "The American stake in South-East Asia is immense. The region is the communications crossroads between territories in the Pacific basin and South Asia. Hostile forces in domination of the area would be in a position to control, or, if they wished, to block for the United States and its allies a key round-the-world route for air and sea lanes. The trade and products of South-East Asia, if not basic to the American economy, are highly important to us and even more so to allied nations, notably Japan and Australia and countries in Europe. If Communist Powers were to gain domination of South-East Asia, this would not only be strategically damaging to the United States but would constitute a severe political and psychological reverse. Such a development would make Communism and the Communist Powers the chief force in Asia, and the United States would become, at best, peripheral."

What are our chances of winning in South-East Asia? The overt struggle is concentrated largely in South Vietnam at the moment. This is, therefore, largely a book about South Vietnam, and, in a much less detailed way, about the related struggle in Laos and the coming struggle in Thailand. The campaign in Laos, which halted with the Geneva Agreement in 1962, did not have a separate identity: it was part of the battle for Vietnam, in the same way that the second Indo-China War (1959–   ) is merely a continuation of the first (1946–1954). Since the initiative in both cases has been with the Communist forces, it would be misleading to discuss the second without also considering the first. Circumstances and the cold war have made President Kennedy a sort of latter-day Gustavus Adolphus in this South-East Asia war, which, now in its seventeenth year, is likely to drag on for a long time yet and to become much more difficult in the process.

Divided at the 17th parallel by the Geneva Agreement in July, 1954, Vietnam consists of the Democratic Republic of Vietnam, under the leadership of Ho Chi Minh, and the Republic of Vietnam, under the leadership of President Ngo Dinh Diem. Roughly sixteen million people live under Ho's Communist rule in North Vietnam, which is about the size of Georgia, and about fourteen million under Diem's anti-Communist rule in South Vietnam, which is slightly smaller than North Dakota. The Vietnamese often think of their country as looking like a carrying pole, with rice baskets on each end. It is an apt description. The Red River delta in the North is a sea of rice, as is the much larger Mekong delta in the South. In between is a narrow coastal plain and the Annamite Chain, or Truong Son, a sparsely populated, largely unexplored, jungle-covered range of mountains. The twin cities of Saigon-Cholon in the South have two million inhabitants. Hanoi, under Communist rule since 1954, has doubled in size, and now has a population of some 600,000.

Though these are large cities, and, in the North, especially, attention has been devoted to industrial development since the defeat of the French, about 80 percent of the Vietnamese people are peasants. They are mostly poor, but not in comparison with the Laotians, with whom they were once associated under French rule.

No one knows how many Laotians there are, though two or three million is the usual guess. For many years their "Land of a Million Elephants" was the neglected patch at the bottom of the South-Asian garden. Opium poppies grown on the mountain slopes by Meo tribesmen provided its only worthwhile cash crop. Then came American aid. It not only failed to shore up the defenses of Laos against the Communists but even hastened its decline, which, in turn, has inspired some serious doubts as to the worth of their Western alliance among twenty-five million neighboring Thais.

✓ This is not an attempt to write a history of recent events in South-East Asia. I am a reporter, not a historian, and all I hope to present is a general picture of the events leading up to and including the current fighting in which American soldiers, British advisers, and a handful of Australian jungle-warfare experts are involved. I break the specialists' rules about the use of proper names, but since this is not a book for the specialist I make no apologies. Ho Chi Minh is mostly known in Vietnam as Ho, and Ngo Dinh Diem as Diem: in this book they are Ho and Diem. I am indebted to many colleagues, friends, and officials for assistance and information. One very good friend helped particularly with the biographical material about Diem. For reasons that will be obvious to the reader, it would be impolitic to mention many of these sources by name. I thank them best by preserving their anonymity.

Several chapters contain material that appeared in shorter form in *The Reporter* magazine, and I am grateful for permission to use it here. My thanks are also due to the publishers of *The New Republic* for permission to reproduce part of my article, "Have We Forgotten the Lessons of the Indo-China War?" which appeared on December 12, 1959.

DENIS WARNER
April, 1963

CHAPTER 1

War
In
The
Delta

WE HAD BEEN going for twenty-one hours when we sat down to dinner in the official residence of Colonel Le Van Phuoc, chief of Vinh Long Province in South Vietnam. It was now long after midnight and we were very tired.

"You think now that we are brutal," said my Vietnamese host. "With your softer Western standards you did not care for what you saw today."

It was a statement, an accusation, not a question. It was also slightly offensive.

"You extracted information by brutality and did not act on it," I said. "That was purposeless."

"I think we were not brutal at all," said my host at whose request Colonel Phuoc had arranged the operation. "Our soldiers were very gentle. They did not kill while they were doing it."

"Only once the *coup de grâce*," said Colonel Phuoc, a solemn

1

thirty-six-year-old, loyal servant of the government, and one of the best province chiefs in Vietnam.

"Only once."

The American said all his knowledge of war had been in Asia—against the Japanese in the Second World War, in Korea, and now here. Did I remember, he asked, how the Koreans had used torture? Did I remember the execution of civil prisoners? He had become used to Asian brutality, he said.

The night before, talking about such things, we discovered that we had met in the first days of the Korean War. He was then a junior officer with the 21st Regiment of the 24th Division, which I had joined as a correspondent in time for the first day's fighting south of Osan. Now he held field rank, and, as chief adviser to Colonel Phuoc, a position of considerable importance in the Mekong delta. His name was Major Robert M. Campbell.

His question took me back, as it was meant to, to that first Sunday night in Korea. Colonel Richard Stephens, of the 21st Regiment, had set up his command post in an abandoned bank in the poverty-worn town of Chochiwon. We all knew when we turned in that it was a one-night stop at best. Disaster had telegraphed itself to the people as we came in on the Saturday afternoon. Everyone knew instinctively that the North Koreans were at our heels, and from the meager shops and houses women came with their bedding and their children, and men with loads they couldn't possibly carry and soon abandoned.

Late Saturday night the town seemed deserted. It was—except for Stephens' headquarters, the police, and the jail with its political prisoners.

Chochiwon, with its soiled tatami matting and bedbugs and lice, was not good for sleeping. Dawn on Sunday morning, I came out, hungry, hoping that I might find some fruit in an abandoned shop. Instead, I found myself alongside a group of thirty men and women roped together with their hands behind their backs. I counted seven girls, mostly in their late teens to judge by their appearance, but battered and dirty.

South Korean military police, with white armbands, and civil police were there. Both seemed dissatisfied with the way the prisoners were boarding a waiting truck. The boot and the butt were used a good many times before one policeman went off for a box for them to step on; and the chain struggled aboard.

In the afternoon, retreating before the North Koreans, we went out across the fields, and there, only a chain or so from the road, found an open grave, semicircular in shape and about three feet deep. In it were the remains of the truckload I had seen drive off in the dawn, their hands still tied, and seventy others, all of them murdered by the South Koreans.

"Maybe I'm used to it, too," I said, bringing my thoughts back from Korea, and Campbell's question, to Vietnam, "but surely the terrible mistake here is that we should be winning people over, and we will not do it by the methods we saw today."

"They were not innocent people," said Colonel Phuoc. "You saw their documents. They were not innocent people. They were Viet Cong" (simply, Vietnamese Communists).

Yes, they were Viet Cong, or under Viet Cong orders, or at least had been frightened into going with the Viet Cong. But now, over the white napery and the red Algerian wine, it all seemed so futile, so much a repetition of the blunders that cost the French and the Vietnamese troops of their day the backing of the people in the phase of the war that ended at Dien Bien Phu in 1954.

In the new M113 9-ton aluminum-alloy armored and amphibious troop carriers we had broken into a Viet Cong sanctuary. Traveling at speeds of twenty miles an hour or more across the flooded rice paddies, protected by .50-caliber machine guns and with six infantrymen in each of the fifteen carriers, we had brought terror to a region that once considered itself all but immune from attack. In many ways it was a highly successful operation with grim portents for the Viet Cong's future in the open rice and swamp country of the Mekong delta. In many ways, also, it was a ghastly blunder.

We started the day in Vinh Long at 3:00 A.M., and headed west past the town of Sadec and through the blacked-out villages that lined the way. At each bridge a light glimmered from the top of the Boa An (Civil Guard) post tower. A flickering oil flame cast a pale gleam as far as the barbed wire that surrounded each post. Here, behind mud and concrete walls and barbed-wire entanglements, the Civil Guard lived, and often died, with their families, just as their predecessors had lived, and often died, in French days. Together with the An Ve (Self-Defense Corps) they are the primary target of Viet Cong attacks: in the first six months of 1962 their combined losses in killed were sixteen hundred, compared with only four hundred for the army.

Just after daylight a girl of about seventeen came to the door of one post as we labored our nine tons across a bridge restricted to loads of six tons, with no more than half an inch to spare on either side. She was combing her long black hair, which stretched well below her waist. She wore only long black trousers. She was good looking and totally unembarrassed.

This was an ambush road, and the farther we traveled in the hour or so of daylight before we arrived at our starting point, the less friendly the people became. We were driving through fairly heavily wooded country, with patches of vegetables and occasionally a neatly cared-for paddy plot between banana, papaya, and other fruit trees. The houses were primitive and mostly made of saplings with atap roofs and dirt floors. Almost the only attempt to provide more than shelter was the latticework that sheltered the open living room from the road. The smallest houses were only ten feet by ten feet, the largest perhaps twice that size.

"You see some men around here," said Major Campbell, "but wait until we get inside. You won't see any." Even so, there were very few men. People coming out to work in the fields were mostly women, wearing their conical straw hats tied under their chins and sometimes with babies carried in slings across their backs. Small boys guarded the lumbering gray water buffalo munching at the grass by the wayside. Small girls cared for even smaller children.

At 7:15 A.M. we lurched off the road into the vegetable fields and then on into the rice, through water about a foot deep, our tracks clawing a wide swath through the half-grown shoots. Patches of dien dien, a quick growing plant widely used for fuel in the delta, with here and there fruit trees on higher ground and an occasional banyan of imposing size and spread created a parklike effect of considerable beauty. The finest of early-morning mists softened the scene, giving it a tranquillity that was soon lost in the heat and violence of the day.

Quite close to the road we passed a man using a long billhook to cut the dien dien, which a woman bundled up and carted off to a nearby hut. Neither paid any attention as the fifteen M113's roared and clattered their way past. Nor did they appear concerned when from the right flank came the first sound of gunfire.

By radio an infantry company reported having seen a full Viet Cong company moving across our front. Along the sides of this corridor of rice we were now entering a reinforced regiment of the Army of the Republic of Vietnam (Arvins to their American advisers), Civil Guards, and Self-Defense Corps troops had been moving in since dawn, sealing off an area roughly fifteen miles long and five or six miles wide.

The only normal means of access to the villages in the center of this zone is by small boat along the canals that irrigate the rice fields. Since the canals are small and easily defended, the region, like many others in remote parts of the delta, had become a Viet Cong sanctuary, complete with Communist combat villages. Troops in the past had been able to enter the area by plowing their way on foot over the rice fields; but they were too slow ever to be effective against the Viet Cong, who stayed and fought only if they felt they could cope, and took to the rice fields and remained there if they were outnumbered.

This day it was like a big-game hunt, with the beaters on the side driving the prey into the center for the guns. In this case, the "guns" were our fifteen amphibious carriers. Intelligence reports said that companies of Viet Cong, or perhaps two hundred men, were in the area.

Air and artillery support were available if we needed them. We had an L-19 spotter plane for guidance, and three platoons of infantry aboard to engage the Viet Cong if they elected to stand and fight.

The going was slow at first. The drivers of the carriers lacked experience and confidence. They found it difficult to get accustomed to driving in a bog. They were often too cautious when approaching the deep canals which irrigated the rice fields. We got caught many times on embankments. The infantry had to strip off to their blue, red, and yellow parachute-silk underwear and help to dig, or pull, us out.

It was while we were negotiating a quite large stream that we got the news we had been waiting for. The L-19 came in a few feet above the command carrier and dropped us a message that two companies of Viet Cong troops were assembled in a village only six or seven miles ahead.

By half-past nine we had begun to make high speed across the rice field. Ahead, the spotter plane showed us the way. It circled and dived on the village, marking the target with small smoke bombs.

As we approached the village the Viet Cong abandoned their original plans to fight. The sheaves of rice and the branches with which they had camouflaged their fortifications and trenches outside the village had been left in obvious haste. The Viet Cong were still in the village, however. The spotter plane indicated their position no more than a hundred yards from us.

On our part now there was much indecision. The M113's had stopped immediately outside the fortifications with their .50-caliber machine guns trained on the village. Neither the troops nor their officers were keen to move. Campbell was impatient. He jumped off our carrier and waded thigh-high to the edge of the village, made a brief inspection, and came back.

"Aren't you sending the troops in?" he asked Colonel Phuoc.

"I've asked for air support," the colonel replied.

"Air support? Hell, they'll be gone," replied Campbell.

Ten minutes later, however, we did go in, with Campbell showing the way. But the troops were cautious, and moved only after the .50-calibers had sprayed the village.

The Viet Cong had gone, of course, and the spotter plane lamented that they were scattering through the rice on the far side of the village. Every man had gone. Only the women and children remained, and not very many, either.

The village itself was desperately poor. It was built around a twisting but quite fast-flowing canal, with small side canals branching off, a sort of paddy-field Venice. The bridges were the single width of a slender tree trunk with a flimsy handrail of bamboo above.

Many of the houses contained nothing that had not been made locally. The houses themselves were made of bamboo, thatched with rice straw. The beds were of wood, covered with rush matting. Cooking utensils were homemade earthenware.

Curiously, the troops made no attempt to search the village, or even to question the villagers. They seemed to be anxious to get out of it in case the Viet Cong returned. With the exception of one old woman, who was sweating with fright, most of the others seemed calm enough. A young woman sitting cross-legged on the floor of a house went on weaving cloth when I entered. A smaller girl could even be coaxed into a grin.

Just before noon we left and went on a long trek north to find a way around the canal that flowed through the village. All along it was a forest of almost jungle thickness. Every inhabited area had been prepared as a defensive position by the Viet Cong, with spikes and earthworks and trenches.

It was long past noon when we turned the corner and began

to make our way back along the far side of the canal toward the village. We were now in the middle of a vast rice field, thousands of acres of it, and unbroken except for occasional canals and haystacks perched on dry ground.

We made our first capture here. A soldier on the next carrier fired into the water, and a man dressed in black but camouflaged with bunches of green rice hung around his shoulders shot out of the water with his hands up. The troops bound his hands behind his back. I did not concern myself with him again, since now all the troops were in the rice field, probing and shooting into every conceivable underwater hiding place. Before we moved off again, a soldier came across with the prisoner's documents. They established quite definitely that he was Viet Cong.

We buttoned up for lunch in torrential rain. This was the command vehicle, and we ate well—chicken, bread rolls, and some acid Algerian wine.

Midafternoon, and we met a more difficult barrier, another heavily wooded canal, with no apparent crossing place. Eventually, however, we got across, and after that the going was easy. The Viet Cong had grown careless. In the vast expanse of rice that lay ahead of us, scores, perhaps even hundreds, of figures were moving about.

We came from the canal in formation and fired warning bursts from the .50-calibers at the nearest figures. Our first kill was accidental. We went into a deep, well filled ditch at speed, and the wash brought a black-clad man to the surface. The soldier next to me fired, and the body disappeared, leaving a well stocked army medical kit floating on the water.

We stopped and began a water hunt. Sometimes fifty yards away, or more, there would be a movement in the water. A shot occasionally brought out a man with his hands up, but the ratio of killed to captured ran two to one during the afternoon.

None had guns. In the past, when the troops came, the Viet Cong always buried their guns near the villages and simply waited underwater in the rice fields until they had gone away. Since the only means of communication in these remote areas is by small boat, there was no danger of surprise until the helicopter and the M113 appeared on the scene.

Undoubtedly some of those we killed or captured were innocent men who had fled in fear with the Viet Cong. But most were not. Their papers gave them away, even when they did not confess. One even had a Viet Cong code giving passwords for the month of April, 1962, on notepaper bearing the printed heading "United States Military Advisory and Assistance Group, Headquarters, Saigon."

Captives got uniform treatment. After their hands were tied behind their backs their questioners would kick and punch them, dragging them from the water to knock them down again. Presumably this failed on all occasions to produce satisfactory replies to questions, and all went through the second stage. This involved three soldiers who forced the man underwater and held him there until he was on the point of drowning. A minute or two at a time and spread repetitively over ten or fifteen minutes was routine for this performance, the final act of which was to hold the prisoner's mouth open while another man poured water down his throat from a helmet. When he could hold no more, he was thrust back under the water.

Once, either in deference to my feelings, or Campbell's, or because the tormentors disapproved of my camera, we moved some fifty yards from the interrogation.

Campbell had been looking away from it. "Have they drowned him yet?" he asked.

I replied that he still seemed to be alive.

"What are they trying to get?" said Campbell in disgust. "He probably doesn't have a weapon. All the times I've seen them do this not once have they ever got a gun, or gone to look for one."

As the afternoon wore on, the troops forgot their inhibitions. The chief interrogator was a chunky man from Colonel Phuoc's bodyguard. He wore a gold cross on a fine chain around his neck. It swung loose and dangled in front of the prisoner's face each time he stooped to plunge his victim under the water.

Many times I expected a prisoner to die. But none did. All were well enough after the ordeal to stagger into the troop carriers, which suggested that the purely physical aspects of the torture were less damaging than they appeared to be. There was no question about the mental stress, however. One man who had been through the treatment clasped his hands together as if in prayer, and shook with terror and shock while another was interrogated in front of him. I noticed that his right thumb was split in two, forming two separate upper joints with two nails. His deformity was irrelevant and unimportant and the result, I suppose, of village inbreeding: but it added another small detail to a squalid scene.

The troops knew all the tricks of elementary torture. Once a soldier marched off his captor through the rice and threatened to shoot him with his .45, which he held next to the prisoner's ear. Every time he fired it the prisoner sank on his knees. Other prisoners hidden behind one of the carriers were sure that it was their turn next to be shot, though this happened, in fact, only to a badly wounded man who was finished off before interrogation. He was too far gone to be questioned about his gun. Some prisoners denied they were Viet Cong, or had guns, and the latter statement, at least, was probably true enough, since in many areas such as this not every guerrilla has a gun but must rely on a knife or billhook, or on recovering a gun when a comrade is killed or wounded in action.

Those who said they had guns always insisted they had buried them back at the village. But no one thought of going back to look. It was too far, or too late, or perhaps just not worthwhile, which made the torture not only brutal but pointless, also.

The quarry were usually hidden like fish deep in the water, breathing through their bamboo tubes. Like fish, also, they tended to seek the safety of the deepest pools, the lotus ponds, and the irrigation channels. Sometimes they were so deep that though the spotter plane could see them, we could not.

Many were not too deep to hear and to see, however. After searching one area, where we had taken two or three Viet Cong and were about to push on, a man suddenly jumped to his feet ahead of us and ran. He did not get very far before he was cut down. Just before dusk, and at least a mile from us, another man took off into the setting sun. The water in the paddy field mirrored the fading light and his splashing run. The long-range shots that followed him in the water were more clearly visible than the man himself. He got away. For once in the day I felt glad.

It does not require an imaginative flight of fancy to guess the tale he told when he got back to his hamlet that night. He went with death at his heels, and, because of it, he must also have gone with fear and hate in his heart.

"Bad news, troops come," used to be a saying in the Chinese villages in the early days of the Communist uprising in Malaya. The British learned quickly, and sent policemen instead of soldiers.

Their task was to establish, to maintain, and to extend the government writ. The army kept out of administrative tasks of this sort, except in the defense of the established authority.

There was no thought of establishing anything out here in the paddy fields. This was simply an armed raid into a Viet Cong area. Its intention was to break up Viet Cong companies which had been harassing and hitting Civil Guard posts and strategic hamlets. In this it was undoubtedly successful. But, on balance, the Viet Cong certainly won the day. They want the people to learn war by war, to identify themselves with the struggle against the "My-Diems," their expression of contempt for the Americans and Diem, and to think that they have no alternative but to fight against them. Beyond doubt, on this day, they succeeded. When unarmed men are shot without question and without chance, the innocent inevitably suffer with the guilty, and soon, because of the need for self-defense, there are no innocent, and every man's hand must be turned against those who come with blazing guns, as we had come on this day.

Something like eight or nine million people live in the Mekong delta. Theirs is a flat world, a hot world, a wet world, a world of green and yellows by day, a world of darkness and fear by night. Out near Tay Ninh, where the Cao Dai have their temple of dragons and purple plaster, and get messages by planchette from Victor Hugo, one of their favorite saints, there is a hill, a Viet Cong hill. There are two other hills—in Ha Tien Province, hard against the Cambodian border, and by the Bay of Rach Gia. These are the only hills in the delta, and they are all Viet Cong. The rest of the delta is flat, all flat. The French built watchtowers along the roads, and the Vietnamese are rebuilding them, a kilometer apart. High above the buffalo, the automobiles, the buses, and the military convoys, the sentries watch the black-clad figures moving below and try to tell bootless friend from bootless foe. It is easy to tell only when it is too late.

Every military convoy that goes from Saigon to Ca Mau, at the southern tip of Vietnam, is ambushed. The Viet Cong hit it going or they hit it coming: but they hit it. Some roads are said to be safe enough, but nothing is really safe. Viet Cong mobile checkpoints hold traffic at will almost anywhere and on any of the main roads. Things are much worse on the secondary roads, or where there are just tracks, or no roads at all. Saigon makes a major effort to preserve its main lines of communication. The rest must care for themselves, which means that the Viet Cong's control over a large part of the area is disputed only occasionally.

The Viet Cong themselves expect loyalty and obedience. When they get what they regard as disloyalty, they are savage and brutal. They take their eye for an eye and tooth for a tooth.

They pick their targets and they hit hard. One of their targets is the hamlet of Phu Long, what the Vietnamese government now calls a strategic hamlet, which means that it is surrounded by two booby-trapped and pointed bamboo palisades with numerous watchtowers, and looks like a cross between a medieval fort and something out of a space-travel comic strip. There is a deep ditch between the two fences, and in the mud are razor-sharp spears embedded in boards and poisoned with human excreta. The Self-Defense Corps mans the defenses, and mans them very well, too, much too well to suit the Viet Cong.

Phu Long is not a rich hamlet. It is a poor one, and it is also out in the twilight zone of divided Viet Cong and governmental authority. Colonel Phuoc claims it: but he has to fight for it. Twice a week he runs supplies through to the hamlet, always at different times and always on different days. It takes two platoons of infantry to get them there. The road is often mined, or even carted away, by the Viet Cong. But somehow, until now, Phu Long has held out. Everyone works and everyone fights. The lights go out at dusk in the hamlet. People do not talk in terms of "if" an attack comes but "when." They know where to go and what to do. They are desperately afraid—but always they fight. The day the Viet Cong break through, they know their men will be crucified and disemboweled. They have to fight. There is no alternative.

In one attempt to break into Phu Long, the Viet Cong made a contraption of large poles mounted on wheels and fitted with a long piece of thick bamboo pipe filled with gasoline. It looked like a heavy-caliber antiaircraft gun, with the barrel pointing in the air at an angle of about seventy-five degrees.

Under cover of fire the Viet Cong got the weapon in position outside the hamlet, tilted the barrel downward, and spilled the gasoline on the peasant cottages on the far side of the fence. Other Viet Cong troops hurled grenades at the gasoline-soaked huts, trying to set fire to the hamlet. On another occasion, when the Self-Defense Corps at Phu Long were almost out of ammunition and feared they would be overrun, Major Xinh, the district chief, who was personally leading the defense and had been twice wounded, ordered a counterattack. With their antiquated guns and almost no bullets left to fire, the home guards broke through their bamboo fence, and put the Viet Cong to flight.

This sort of thing does not happen often in the Mekong delta. But it happens more often than it happened in the past. That is progress in this grim, unspectacular war.

No one can say how much each side controls of the delta. There are some Viet Cong in every village and hamlet, in every street of every town. They may not be known to all, or any, of their fellow villagers. It is better for the villagers not to know such things.

In Vinh Long Province about a third of the land area is under general Viet Cong domination, and much more of it is partly under their control. It is not a "bad" province in any sense of the word, however. It is, on the contrary, a model province. Colonel Phuoc is one of the régime's favorite sons, and Vinh Long is a favorite province. The colonel's budget is relatively elastic, and his means available to carry out the palace wishes are the envy of other province chiefs. He was presented on his arrival in Vinh Long in 1959 with the body of his predecessor, slain in a Viet Cong ambush, on a palanquin. He has survived three ambushes himself, capturing along the way his Viet Cong counterpart, the Communist province chief.

Like his fellow province chiefs, Colonel Phuoc is much more than a governor. In Vinh Long he is king. He has the power of life and death over his half-million subjects, who live in nine districts, eighty-one villages, and some two hundred hamlets sandwiched between the Mekong and Bassac rivers. Most people in Vinh Long are subsistence peasant farmers, who grow rice, fruit, and vegetables. Snakes provide a small cash crop, and the inhabitants of the snake-infested island of Cho Lac in the Mekong are regarded as fortunate. Snake soup is a delicacy, and sales of snake bring in about $7,000 a year. The current crop of snakes was very good when I was there, and Colonel Phuoc was pleased.

Colonel Phuoc rules through his district chiefs, all of them, like himself, now army officers. Three are majors and six captains. The town of Vinh Long, with a population of about twenty thousand, has a school of rehabilitation for fallen girls, an orphanage, and a technical school with boardinghouses for boys and girls. The orphanage and the school are impressive. The fallen girls seem only to have another fall in front of them. "We teach them how to sew and cook," said a motherly Catholic sister, with a rich Irish brogue, "but when they are free to go there is no work for them. We hope some will go back to their homes and some will get married, but the others . . ." She did not complete the sentence. The sister told Colonel Phuoc that they were expanding and that another fifty girls were due to arrive from Saigon.

"Why go to Saigon?" asked the colonel. "Give me half an hour and I can give you fifty here."

For a time Colonel Phuoc also had in Vinh Long the régime's only training center in Personalism, the country's official ideology. Here Catholic priests instructed cadres (the approved word) in the Confucian-Catholic-Hindu-Buddhist philosophy created by Ngo Dinh Nhu, the President's youngest brother, political adviser, and brain truster, to persuade the people of South Vietnam that they should look beyond the Viet Cong in search of an ideology suited to their Vietnamese environment.

On the right bank of the brown waters of the Mekong, Colonel Phuoc has built a hotel and restaurant, neat, modern, and tidy. He has set up a scrupulously clean cafeteria for civilians where five cents buys a bowl of rice and a choice of three hot dishes. The army is even better off in its canteen. The often neglected paramilitary forces are not neglected here. A Civil Guard off duty can even have his ears cleaned for three cents.

Atap huts have been pulled down and replaced with houses and shops of plaster and cement. The streets are clean and paved and lit by electricity. People even have electricity in their homes. Of all this, and many other things, also, Colonel Phuoc is justifiably proud.

"People were afraid to come into the streets when I came here two years ago," he said late one evening as we drove back to his home by the side of the Mekong. "Just look at them now." It was as peaceful a scene as one might have expected to see anywhere in South-East Asia. The night was hot and stifling, and men, women, and children were sitting outside their homes. Here and there a coffee shop was open. Nowhere could one see men with guns. The colonel had pushed out his defenses and now it was safe enough not only in town but also for several miles beyond.

Not far from the town of Vinh Long is the model strategic hamlet of Phuoc Nguon. It has a population of nearly two thousand people, and is surrounded by its twin fences of spiked saplings and bamboo, and deep ditches. There is some barbed wire, but not much. "We were supposed to get fourteen tons of barbed wire for each hamlet," said Colonel Phuoc. "Instead we got ten tons for 163 hamlets." This meant, of course, that the villagers had to provide a substitute for barbed wire, cut down the trees and bamboo, and build the fences.

I inquired whether the people were paid for their work. Phuoc replied that the people provided the manpower and the province the piasters. When I pressed him, he said the government had been able to contribute only a million piasters (or not much more than $13,000), which had to be spread among all the 163 hamlets already built in the province. Phuoc Nguon had had the lion's share. The other hamlets were made by the sweat and labor of the villagers.

Forced labor? "Well," said the colonel, "how can you call it forced when it is in the people's own interests?"

Life is regimented in Phuoc Nguon. As in every other strategic hamlet, those who know what is good for them join the régime's National Revolutionary Movement, the only political organization permitted in the hamlets. Phuoc Nguon has 529 members. Membership involves the payment of monthly dues, four or five hours of indoctrination each week, and a disproportionate share of the corvée labor. But it also carries priority in rice, in agricultural credits, in schooling, in medical care, when and if available, and the right to express an opinion when the district or province chief calls a meeting.

As in villages under Viet Cong control, there are both vertical and horizontal controls. Across the National Revolutionary Movement and interlocking with it are official organizations such as the Women's Solidarity Movement and the Republican Youth, all of which carry their responsibilities and privileges.

Colonel Phuoc has introduced his own land-reform campaign. In Viet Long families with sons or husbands known to be fighting with the Viet Cong, or to have gone north in 1954 with the Viet Minh, are given three months to get them back. "I take half their land and say to them that if after three months they have not got their men back I will take their homes and property," he told me as we sheltered from torrential rain in a mud-bound hamlet. "At the end of that time I give them another three months. If their men are not back then, they go to a concentration camp and lose their property, which we divide up among those who are for us."

"How on earth do you expect them to get their relations back from North Vietnam?" I asked.

"That's their business," replied the colonel. "In this province the men who are willing to fight for us, their families, and those who support the National Revolutionary Movement are those who will do well."

But how well is well?

The lack of democratic rights exercises the villagers only to the point that they rarely appreciate the appointed village chiefs. But the evidence suggests that they do resent the demands made on their time and labor. The average peasant today is required to spend almost as much time on unproductive and unpaid government work as he spends in the fields. His basic freedoms may be no less than they were in the past: but he is now obliged to suffer an almost commune-like regimentation.

Province chiefs speak with pride about the greater controls they are able to exercise over the people because of the strategic hamlets and of such things as the much improved tax collections. No doubt this is good for State revenues. It is not always good for the peasant's state of mind.

Out in the more remote villages of mud and wattle, the government is identified as the man in uniform who comes on a punitive raid, or with a heavy bodyguard, and who always wants something —money, labor, or even those suspected, sometimes incorrectly, of working for the Viet Cong. The Viet Cong cadre, on the other hand, is barefooted and dressed in black like every other peasant. He makes tax demands, but they are not excessive. He is meticulous about paying for food and lodging, and scrupulous, also, in his relations with village girls and with the villagers' property. To begin with, he does not talk Communism or Marxism, but exploits local grievances, and is at pains to implant the idea that the Vietnamese have thrown off French colonialism only to be saddled by President Diem with American colonialism. It is simple propaganda, but effective.

Communism, Personalism, Viet Cong cadres, Diem cadres, Viet Cong combat villages, Diem strategic hamlets . . . even the terminology is the same. The ideology is different. Personalism stands for freedom, and Communism is the negation of freedom. But what point is there in teaching freedom only to deny it? The practice of Personalism mocks the principle. The peasants need permits to leave the hamlets. They are watched, spied on, dossiered, and either favored or ill-favored. Like the peasants in Viet Cong villages they are required to listen to hours of political indoctrination each week. The rice they grow fetches a low price and is sold by the government for a high price. Supplies cannot be harbored against a rainy day. Many of the controls are necessary for security; but many others are needless irritants.

Everything, in theory, is taken care of by the strategic hamlet. All over the delta bamboo groves are toppling, and millions of peasants, under orders from the provincial, district, and village chiefs, are at work digging ditches, sharpening bamboo spears, and making booby traps. The cultivation of rice and vegetables, the day-to-day business of growing enough food and spinning and weaving enough cloth just for basic needs have been put aside as lesser priorities. There must be strategic hamlets.

Basically, the concept is not new. All over Asia, and in many other parts of the world, people have sought security by huddling together behind fences, moats, and walls. Faced with a deteriorating security situation in 1958, and in search of a way to provide both security and control, Ngo Dinh Nhu proposed the resettlement of scattered peasant families and groups in "agrovilles." The intention was strategic, economic, social, and political.

Shortage of funds and peasant opposition prevented the agrovilles, which were much larger than the strategic hamlets, from moving much beyond the experimental stage. Late in 1961, however, Diem appointed as an adviser an Englishman named Robert Thompson, who had served as Secretary for Defense under General (later Field Marshal) Gerald Templer in Malaya. The key to the defeat of the Malayan Communist insurgents was the "new villages." Half a million Chinese peasants were resettled in them and isolated from contact with the guerrilla groups in the jungle. By providing the villages with medical help and schools and other social services, and with quite formidable defenses in the way of barbed-wire fences, floodlighting, and weapons, and by paying handsomely for information, the Templer administration gradually involved even the Chinese people in the war against the Communists, who were also Chinese. Needing food, money, and information, the Communists were forced to come to the villages. When they came, they died.

Thompson found the situation in South Vietnam much worse than he had expected, or had been led to believe. He saw that though the food situation was much more complicated here, there were enough similarities in other fields to warrant an urgent experiment on the Malayan lines. His plan was welcomed by Nhu and by General Maxwell Taylor. Though some Americans on the spot warned against giving guns to the villagers, an essential part of the Thompson scheme, Taylor accepted the risk. The United States gave the guns and the know-how to use them. Nhu busied himself on the ideological side. While Thompson aimed at security, medical help, schooling, and the promise of a rising living standard, however, Nhu thought in terms of control, regimentation, political indoctrination, and organization.

The result has often been unhappy. "Too many lessons are being copied from the Communists in the strategic hamlets," said one Westerner who had come to Vietnam to help Diem win the war. "It makes it difficult for the peasant to find a criterion by which to discriminate between the Communists and the government. The difference should be unmistakable to the peasant, and patently to the Communists' disadvantage." It has not been in the immediate past. It is not, even now.

Go quietly, was Thompson's advice. Start in the white areas and work out through its disputed zones into the Communist territory. Make the hamlets worthwhile and worth the inhabitants' while to defend. Clear a main base around Saigon, then establish yourself in the Mekong delta.

Instead of going slowly, South Vietnam went into mass production. Instead of concentrating on white (or Viet Cong free) areas, the government went for the red (or Viet Cong dominated). Operation Sunrise, which was intended to separate the Maquis D, the Viet Cong's main base in the rubber, jungle and swamps immediately north of Saigon, from the capital and the Maquis D itself from the Cambodian border by the resettlement of the peasants, was almost Operation Sunset for the strategic-hamlet concept. Without warning, preparation, or consent, peasants saw their homes, and often their belongings, burned behind them. They were uprooted at bayonet point and planted down in new areas which had not been prepared to receive them. It was the worst of starts for the strategic hamlet. To add to their misfortunes, the villagers were not settled in their own localities but were often moved considerable distances. This meant that they lost not only their homes but also their land. In Malaya where such drastic action was necessary it was done cautiously, and the villagers were also compensated for their loss of land.

Fortunately, the Vietnamese officials learned by error, and the results everywhere were not bad. In many areas they were extremely good. Many guns passed quickly into the hands of the Viet Cong. Many more did not. All over South Vietnam small teams of American instructors arrived and went out into the hamlets to teach the people how to fight. They slept with guns and grenades by their sides and they built their own defenses around them— among the people they taught.

They became marked men. The Viet Cong sentenced them to death and posted rewards for their execution, sometimes in the agrovilles and hamlets where they were working. They were ambushed and stalked and sometimes killed. Sometimes their nerves broke. The strain was too much. But they taught well and they taught widely. Their contribution to the Vietnamese effort was rapid and effective. Officer for officer and sergeant for sergeant, these ten thousand Americans who flowed into South Vietnam during 1962 were superb, an élite of unprecedented quality and dedication. They knew their job as soldiers and they were equally effective in their relations with the Civil Guard, the Self-Defense Corps, and the people themselves—though they were significantly less successful with the army, and were openly, and sometimes unwisely, contemptuous of the government.

For the first time ever in this war it was possible to report that many of the right things were being done in the right way. It was also true that the full value of the Americans' effort, especially the training program, had not yet been felt and would not be felt until well into 1963. But for their effort South Vietnam would have fallen. It may still fall. The war is not being won, only lost more slowly. All the experience of the war before, that struggle between the French and the Viet Minh, which ended at Dien Bien Phu in 1954, suggests that there are bitter days ahead.

CHAPTER 2

They
Call
Him
Uncle
Ho

Ho Chi Minh
History —
War with France
British

Until the summer of 1962, when fear of Viet Cong attack pushed the outdoor bars and restaurants off the streets, it used to be the agreeable custom for foreigners in Saigon to meet under the awnings of the Hotel Continental in rue Catinat for a noonday drink, a Pernod or a *citron pressé* in the days of the French, a coke in the new American era.

Vietnamese girls in their long colored smocks split to the thigh and their graceful ankle-length, and often diaphanous, trousers flitted past like butterflies. The bookstore and the Indian shops banged their steel shutters for the noonday siesta. The bicycles and automobiles went from the streets, and only the peddlers

19

with their water colors, lacquer boxes, books, and filthy pictures remained.

Only the peddlers and, of course, the newsboys, who fought for custom as newsboys fight nowhere else in the world. They punched and kicked and tore. These were not talking fights, but blood and knuckle battles. The bigger boys hit the smaller boys, and always the smaller boys fought back. These fights did not happen once or twice. They were an everyday event.

Sometimes a softhearted foreigner seeing a fight for the first time might incautiously intervene. Nothing closed the ranks quicker. The toes of Saigon's urchins are bare but horny, and their aim is keen.

"Now I know why the Viet Minh beat the French," said a bruised and reeducated American as he ordered a cognac soda to restore his nerves after one such encounter with the newsboys. It was not a really serious observation: it was a penetrating one, nevertheless. The Vietnamese are the toughest people in South-East Asia. For the past twenty-one years there has been almost nothing but war, or preparations for war, in Vietnam. For almost two thousand years the Vietnamese people have resisted, and revolted against, alien control.

Close to the banks of the Saigon River a twin statue dedicated to the Trung sisters, Vietnam's Joans of Arc, commemorates the first known revolt against Chinese domination in A.D. 43. The statue, which was built under Diem's rule, is cast appropriately, but to the irritation of many in Saigon, in the shapely image of Madame Nhu, Diem's sister-in-law and official hostess. The Trung sisters led their armies in a brief and glorious revolt against the Chinese after the execution of one of their husbands. When their armies were finally put to flight, the sisters plunged to their death in the Day River in North Vietnam. Ever since, the Vietnamese have regarded them as symbolic of Vietnam's resistance to foreign domination. Three times the Mongols invaded Vietnam and three times they were cut to pieces. Vietnam absorbed Chinese culture, Mahayana Buddhism, Confucianism, and the emperor system: but it was an always turbulent tribute State.

The French found it even more turbulent. They came first as missionaries and stayed on as colonizers. Emperor Tu Duc in 1851 described them as "barking like dogs and fleeing like goats." He ordered them to be seized and thrown into the sea with stones around their necks. This displeased the French. Eight years later they captured Saigon and brought the Emperor to heel in Hue: but the spirit of Vietnamese resistance never died. The French controlled through the Sûreté, the Foreign Legion, and the political prison on the penal island of Poulo Condore, while Vietnamese of all walks of life and political persuasion planned and plotted, like Emperor Tu Duc, to throw them into the sea. It was the aim alike of those steeped in the Confucian traditions of the mandarinate and of peasants from the paddy fields.

The Russo-Japanese War, the fall of the Manchus in China, the rise of Sun Yat-sen, the Pacific War, and the occupation of Vietnam and the other States of Indo-China by Japanese forces all had their part in shaping the ultimate, inevitable uprising against France. But it remained for a wisp of a man with great capacity for leadership and the "thoughts" of another to bring the French to final defeat.

"There are no mysteries whatsoever in the strategy of defeating superior forces," Mao Tse-tung once said. "This is how it is done. In this way, and only in this way, can armed revolutionary forces succeed in destroying an enemy twenty times their number."

President Ngo Dinh Diem, who is now up to his ears in fighting the Maoist tactic, learned it bitterly and puts it simply. "For the man in the street the cities come first," he says, "then the countryside, then the mountains. The Communists work entirely in reverse. In their strategy, the mountains come first, then the countryside. After that, the cities can be isolated."

Standing in his map room in Saigon one evening in the summer of 1962, he quickly sketched how the Viet Minh had used this technique against the French, working from the mountain ranges north of the Red River delta and fanning out, with guerrillas in the Red River delta and mobile war in the mountains, until they brought the French to defeat at Dien Bien Phu. "These are very simple notions," he added, "but few people understand them."

Among those who do are Che Guevara, Mao's Cuban disciple, who believes that a nucleus of thirty to fifty men is sufficient to initiate a successful Maoist armed revolt in any country in the Americas. Another is a former cook's helper, photographer's retoucher, artist, poet, linguist, senior Comintern official and revolutionary, who between 1946 and 1954 cost the lives of more than 94,000 French and French Union soldiers in Indo-China and now, in the sunset of his life, is embarked on a war by proxy in South Vietnam which challenges not only the authority of President Ngo Dinh Diem but also that of the United States. The world will remember him as Ho Chi Minh, but this is only the last of a score of aliases used by Nguyen Tat Thanh, better known for many years as Nguyen Ai Quoc, who was born in Nghe An Province, North Vietnam, on May 19, 1890.

Ho's career has been remarkable in many ways. For the first twenty-eight years of his life he was a nonentity. He lacked almost everything—physique, education, appearance. For a vital decade he was divorced not only from his own country but also from revolutionary associates. Mao Tse-tung found his path to revolution in the library of the Peking University: at a similar age Ho wore a chef's hat and was diligently rolling pastry in a London kitchen. Later, as he matured and became involved with the Communists, his primary role was that of an internationalist. For more than thirty years he did not even set foot on Vietnamese soil. Yet time after time his capacity to rally support as a nationalist leader prevented the Vietnamese revolutionary forces from disintegrating.

Like Mao Tse-tung, who has been built up by the Peking propagandists as a gentle and kindly old man who likes nothing better than to drop in for a chat and a cup of tea in a commune cottage, Ho's propagandists portray him as a lover of children. "Uncle Ho," they call him. Most Westerners who know him also like him. There is no language barrier with Ho. He speaks English and French in an idiomatic way.

He is neither an innovator like Mao nor a ruthless dictator like Stalin, neither a great thinker nor a man of action. Mao led his men against Chiang Kai-shek. Ho has never fired a shot in action, nor given a command in battle.

He will not be remembered so much in Vietnam for his own contributions to revolutionary theory, though forty-two years ago they were important, as for his translations of Mao Tse-tung. Some of his lieutenants were much better educated and much more brilliant than Ho, yet always in times of crisis they accepted him as the decision-maker.

As in the Chinese Communist Party, the top five in the Viet Minh politburo have held their places for many years. There are pro-Soviet wings and pro-Chinese wings of the Lao Dong (Communist) Party, but even the tendency to edge closer and closer to the Chinese position has not yet caused a major upset in Ho's inner ranks.

He came from poverty. His father was a minor official in the mandarinate, a bully who eventually lost his job because of drunkenness: he passed on to his children his own learning and much of his own bitterness. He taught them to read and write Chinese characters and the use of the brush and got them involved in the revolutionary activities of the times. This was almost the extent of Ho's early education. Though for a time he attended the Quoc-Hoc school at Hue, the Imperial capital, he did not complete his secondary schooling.

Ho's father lost his job in 1910 and turned automatically to the rebel movement, then led by two intellectuals, Phan Boi Chau and Phan Chau Trinh, who had begun to campaign for independence. French repressive measures led to a flight of young nationalists from Vietnam. Some went to Japan, where Prince Cuong De, a claimant of the Annam throne, was living; others followed Phan Boi Chau to South China, where he had formed the Association for the Restoration of Vietnam. Ho's elder brother and sister remained with those who continued the struggle as best they could in Vietnam.

Ho himself got a job as a galley hand aboard the Messageries Maritimes steamship *Latouche-Tréville*, and in July, 1911, at the age of twenty-one, he sailed for France. Nothing at this stage of his career suggested that he might develop as a leading Vietnamese and Asian revolutionary. He seems to have left Vietnam for no other reason that that it was becoming unhealthy, even for such minor figures in the nationalist movement as himself, to remain there. His departure was more an act of weakness than a gesture of defiance.

On the eve of the First World War he was in London, and unemployed. His knowledge of French and his experience at sea got him a job at the Carlton Hotel as a kitchen help to Escoffier, the prince of French chefs, who grew to like the tiny, unobtrusive little Vietnamese and eventually promoted him to the cake-baking department. For six years he lived in London. He was shy, sensitive, and retiring, and for entertainment liked to write poetry.

It is still his hobby. For preference he writes in Chinese, finding double pleasure in the artistry of the brush and the music of the words:

> "Planning the campaign deep into the night.
> I stretch myself into a pool of leisure.
> The autumn wind outside and the autumn rain
> bring with them the autumn chill.
> Suddenly I hear an autumn's pipe sounding
> Coldly like a signal on the screened hillside,
> The patrol returns
> and warm still is the awaiting wine."

or,

> "Reading . . . a mountain bird alights on my windowsill.
> In the ink-stone I see reflected a spray of spring.
> As reports of the campaign's success
> Crowd in with straining horses,
> Thinking of you and touched by this living scene of strange
> beauty,
> I am moved to present you with this freshly attempted poem."

After the First World War he moved from London to Paris. Here, after ten years as a kitchen hand, he now became a photographer's retoucher. With his deft brushwork, he also earned spare-time money as an artist, specializing in Oriental scenes.

Great international meetings inevitably attract men with causes. And Ho had now become a man with a cause. Letters from home told of his sister's sentence to nine years' hard labor by the provincial court at Nghe An for revolutionary activities and his brother's sentence by the same court for a similar offense. Calling himself Nguyen Ai Quoc, or Nguyen the Patriot, Ho decided to lobby for Vietnamese independence at the Versailles Peace Conference. He wrote an eight-point petition, calling for an end to arbitrary political arrests and other abuses in the colonies, which he distributed among the various delegations. It had no impact on the peace treaty, but it brought him to the notice of men like Charles Longuet, Karl Marx's son-in-law, who was editing *Le Populaire*.

Longuet asked Ho to become a political contributor to the

paper. Ho's French and his writing were not at this time up to the task. Within a year, however, he had improved enough to contribute articles and short stories to *L'Humanité*. His political satire, *The Bamboo Dragon*, was performed at the Left-wing Club du Faubourg. It was described by his friends as witty and subtle and a deadly attack on colonialism, and by his critics as dull and hackneyed. It won him attention, however, which is what he needed, and in 1920 he was invited to attend the Tours Congress of the French Socialist Party. When the party split into two wings, Ho went Left with the group that joined the Third International and became the French Communist Party. A founder member of the Party in 1921, he was now accepted as an expert on colonial affairs, and, as such, became the editor of the newspaper *Le Paria*, which was financed by a group from the French colonies living in Paris and calling themselves the League of Colonial Countries. *Le Paria*, and his pamphlet "French Colonialism on Trial," were both banned in Indo-China, but crews on French ships smuggled them home, where they created a sensation among Vietnamese nationalists. Ho's star was rising.

In June, 1923, he went to Moscow as a member of the French Communist Party's delegation to the Peasants' International Congress. Under the name of Song Man Tcho, he remained in Moscow for two years as a colonial delegate on the standing committee of the Peasants' International, learning Russian and studying revolutionary techniques at the newly established University of the Toilers of the East. French Communist leaders in Moscow to attend Lenin's funeral in 1924 introduced him to Stalin and others, and early in 1925 he was sent to Canton in South China as an interpreter to the Russian delegation led by Michael Borodin.

He was no mere interpreter. Under a new alias, Ly Thuy, he became one of the Chinese Communist Party's principal propagandists and a rallying point for Vietnamese nationalists. In June, 1925, he created an organization known as the Association of the Annamite Revolutionary Youth. Through Ho and the Revolutionary Youth, the Whampoa Military Academy under Chiang Kai-shek and Chou En-lai became a training ground for Vietnamese revolutionaries, including Pham Van Dong, now Prime Minister of the Democratic Republic of Vietnam, and one of Ho's earliest followers.

Pham Van Dong, like President Ngo Dinh Diem, comes from

senior mandarin stock. Both their fathers held high office at the Imperial Court at Hue. While Diem was scaling the mandarinate ladder, however, Dong was still a student in Hanoi—under close surveillance from the French Sûreté. In 1925, at the age of nineteen, he went to Canton, met Ho, and enrolled in the Whampoa Military Academy. By 1926 he was back in Indo-China, with the Sûreté close at his heels. Caught after only a few months, he was sentenced to six years of hard labor at the penal settlement of Poulo Condore. When he got out in 1933, he left for Moscow, joined the Communist Party, and ever since has been one of the more defiant and forbidding figures associated with Ho.

The long-held theory that Ho was a nationalist and not a Communist dates from his Canton days. In a speech in 1927 he said that no one would understand Communism in Indo-China. This was widely taken to mean that he was not for Communism, especially since his Revolutionary Youth Movement, though provided with Russian funds, was nationalist and Marxist but not Communist.

In addition to his other duties in Canton, Ho edited a Vietnamese-language newspaper and busied himself with the training and indoctrination of larger groups of Vietnamese, who, after a few months in Canton, went back to Indo-China to organize revolutionary cells. Several hundred had passed through his hands before April 6, 1927, when the Right wing of the Kuomintang turned on the Communists. The Borodin delegation was in Fukien Province on its way to Hankow to attend the Pan-Pacific Labor Union Congress when Chiang Kai-shek struck. After many difficulties, the delegation, including Ho, escaped from China and got back to Moscow.

After a temporary arrangement with Chiang Kai-shek that they could continue to use Canton as the headquarters for the central committee, the Revolutionary Youth moved to Hong Kong, thereby losing their close links with their cells in Indo-China. This soon precipitated a crisis. The Indo-China groups declined in 1929 to accept the orders of the Hong Kong executive and set up their own Indo-Chinese Communist Party. Not to be outdone, the Hong Kong committee then announced the formation of the Annamite Communist Party.

These divisive actions angered both the Comintern and Ho. The Comintern recognized neither, and Ho himself took off from

Moscow and went to live with the Vietnamese minority in Thailand, where he founded a new association, the Overseas Vietnamese Association in Thailand and Laos for the Liberation of the Fatherland, and published a newspaper, *L'Humanité*, which, like his Canton publication, was intended also for circulation in Indo-China. It circulated to such effect that on October 10, 1929, the provincial court of Vinh in North Vietnam sentenced him to death in absentsia.

According to his Communist biographers, Ho adopted many disguises in Thailand, sometimes appearing as a barefooted peasant, or as a Buddhist monk with shaven head and begging bowl, or as a peddler selling cigarettes on a street corner.

Publication of his death sentence led to the discovery of his whereabouts by the Annamite Communist Party in Hong Kong, which sent him a message asking him to restore unity to the revolutionary movement. At a conference which was held either in Hong Kong or at Kweilin in Kwangsi Province, or possibly in both, Ho, early in 1930, urged representatives from the three main dissident groups to regroup either under the old name of Revolutionary Youth or as a single Communist Party. His appeal succeeded, and all Communist organizations in Indo-China now united under the new Indo-China Communist Party.

All except Ho himself went back to Indo-China, where nationalist feelings against the French had already passed the crisis point. A non-Communist nationalist group, backed by wealthy Indo-Chinese and with widespread support both within the civil service and the army, had risen in revolt at the post of Yen Bay on the Red River. This was the signal for a general uprising, which the nationalists were in no position to carry through. The French put down the revolt with great brutality. The Communists had few contacts with the Nationalist Party, which had led the revolt, but drew on the hardship and discontent of a calamitous famine in 1930–1931 to press their own plans for revolt. In Ho's home province, Nghe An, and in adjoining Ha Tinh province, they organized several small and for a time autonomous Soviets. Overconfident and ill prepared, they led mass demonstrations of starving peasants, established people's courts, and hoped to pose a serious challenge to the French administration. Their key men came from Ho's cells in Thailand.

The French reacted predictably, brutally, and successfully. Communists and nationalists who had escaped the guillotine now found themselves in the same jails and united by the determination not to rest until the French were driven from the land. Among the recruits who moved to Ho from the ranks of the nationalist detainees was Vo Nguyen Giap. The son of poor peasants, Giap joined the New Revolutionary Party at the age of fourteen, and earned himself a dossier with the French Sûreté at the same time. He was a brilliant, precocious student who fought his way through school with energy and brilliance, topping every class. His youth saved him from the guillotine when he was eighteen, and he was released along with large numbers of other nationalists and Communists in 1933.

By this time, however, the French had made a bitter enemy. Giap went from jail to the University of Hanoi, and took his doctorate in political economy. As a lecturer during the period of the Popular Front in France, he had unusual license. By 1939, when the Popular Front collapsed and the Indo-China Communist Party was outlawed, and the French once again began to imprison Communists and nationalists, he had won many friends and supporters among the young intelligentsia of Hanoi. Their efforts failed to save Giap's family, however. The French seized his wife, his young son, and his sister. His sister was executed in 1940, and his wife died in prison about the same time. Giap, who had fled to China, never forgot or forgave.

But what, meanwhile, of Ho? A French Communist leader who fell into the hands of the British Special Branch (police intelligence) in Singapore in 1931 disclosed that Ho, now permanently based on Hong Kong, was the Comintern's ambassador-at-large in South-East Asia and that, on a visit to Singapore, he had played an important part in the creation of the Malayan Communist Party. He was arrested and held for eighteen months. For a time the British considered putting him on a French ship and sending him to Indo-China, where the French were demanding his extradition. Since there was no evidence that he had plotted to overthrow the Hong Kong authorities, however, he was eventually allowed to go.

What his activities were during the next few years remains vague. He says he used various influences to get Pham Van Dong and others out of jail. It seems likely that he was ill, and living in at least semiretirement.

Every now and then during the Indo-China War the French used to report that he had died of tuberculosis. The inference that he suffered from the disease is apparent in much of the writings of his lieutenants. Pham Van Dong, who wrote a book entitled *The Private Life of President Ho*, says, for instance, that "Ho rarely used medicine, and this only when he felt that his own strength was unable to resist the disease." Dong makes other references to Ho's ill-health, but usually to point up his moral strength.

In any event, Ho was on hand when he was most needed. Just as he had brought the Communists together in 1930, he was ready early in the Pacific War to unite the nationalists and the Communists, the Vo Nguyen Giaps and the Pham Van Dongs and the others who had fled from renewed French repressions into South China, in a new and wider united front. At a conference in the South China town of Chingsi, near the Indo-China border, in the spring of 1941 many of the Indo-China refugees under Ho's appealing guidance made common cause. The Viet Minh, the League for Independence for Vietnam, was formed on May 1st.

It was to be against the Japanese and against Vichy and for the allies. Ho Chi Minh became its secretary-general. One of his first acts was to send two of his most promising lieutenants, Vo Nguyen Giap and Dang Xuan Khu, to Mao Tse-tung's headquarters at Yenan for military and political training. Dang, who had spent the years 1930 to 1936 in a French prison and was again jailed by the French in 1939, returned calling himself Truong Chinh, which means Long March, and so completely dedicated to the Chinese Communist cause that sometimes he was thought to be Chinese. In fact, he was born in Nam Dinh in the Red River delta, and is pure Vietnamese. Like Giap, he began to interest himself in revolution even before he was in his teens. He was expelled from primary school for rioting, and soon joined the staff of the Vietnamese Revolutionary Youth's underground newspaper, *Hammer and Sickle*. Author of numerous books, he is the theoretician of the Viet Minh movement.

Unlike Truong Chinh, who leads the Maoist faction in the North Vietnam politburo, and, as chairman of the standing committee of the National Assembly of Vietnam, seems likely to succeed Ho, Giap absorbed the Maoist revolutionary theories, but developed no particular love for Mao or for the Chinese Communist Party. His book *People's War, People's Army* is studded with acknowledgments to Chinese Communist tactics, as it ought to be, but makes no acknowledgment of any sort to the debt he owes to Mao.

While his two lieutenants were away learning the secrets of revolutionary warfare, Ho himself had run into trouble again. The Kuomintang were familiar enough with his activities to regard him and his followers as extremely dubious assets to their cause. According to Viet Minh accounts, Ho decided to go to Chungking to meet Kuomintang leaders, and was actually on his way when he was arrested and jailed. After eighteen months in prison, he changed his alias for the last time, and now calling himself Ho Chi Minh, the Enlightened One, was released to return to North Vietnam, where Giap, Truong Chinh, and Pham Van Dong had established themselves in the mountains around Thai Nguyen, immediately north of the Red River delta.

One story is that the local Kwantung commander, knowing the need both for intelligence and for guerrilla agents in Tongking, and equally aware that the Kuomintang's own efforts to create their network had been unsuccessful, suggested to Ho that, if he would cease calling himself Nguyen Ai Quoc, Chungking could be persuaded in their ignorance to accept him as a militant (but unknown) Annamite revolutionary who would be glad to accept Chiang's subsidies and American arms in exchange for intelligence reports about the Japanese.

The story may be a fairy tale, but this is roughly how it worked out. Late in 1944, after an absence from his country of thirty-three years, Ho Chi Minh crossed the China border and joined up with the guerrillas in the mountains. Outside the town of Cao Bang, on December 22, 1944, Vo Nguyen Giap formally created the first platoon of the Viet Minh army. It consisted of twenty-seven men. At the same time, Ho created a propaganda unit of similar strength. With assistance from the Office of Strategic Services the small guerrilla bases around Cao Bang, Bac Kan, and Lang Son, which had hitherto concerned themselves primarily with espionage and intelligence, and with the extension of the underground apparatus through the rest of Vietnam, began to devote themselves to guerrilla work. According to Giap, within weeks these original forces had multiplied and became several thousand strong.

In March, 1945, the Japanese ousted the French from nominal control of Indo-China. This left the way open for the Viet Minh to extend their authority through the rural regions of the North, where the French had hitherto exercised control. During the closing days of July and early August, when rumors of a Japanese surrender were widespread, the Viet Minh guerrillas grew bolder. Several towns and many villages north and west of the Red River delta passed into their hands. They were received with delight by the local population. The French had always been unpopular, and the Japanese, who had commandeered the rice supply as soon as they assumed full power, were now hated. According to Ho, two million Vietnamese died of famine at this period. The figure is probably overstated; but in any event the climate was favorable for the rebels.

There were now Viet Minh agents throughout North and Central Vietnam and the organization had contacts in the South. The Japanese, while alarmed at the events, were unable to do much about them. Indo-China had been only a staging area for their forces; and the French, under the Vichy leadership of Admiral Decoux, had been useful in maintaining order in the countryside. Japanese attempts to enlist the support of the Emperor Bao Dai and his puppet government in a campaign to liquidate all known Viet Minh agents leaked before it could be put to the test.

Time was running out for the Japanese. In expectation of their early surrender Viet Minh groups had begun to close around Hanoi, the North Vietnam capital. A hurried congress in the mountains appointed a National Liberation Committee to lead the coming revolution under the presidency of Ho Chi Minh. The Viet Minh guerrillas became the Vietnam Liberation Army under Vo Nguyen Giap. The call went out for a general uprising. "The hour has struck for an offensive on all fronts," Ho ordered. Bao Dai's puppet government collapsed, and the Vietnamese people, lacking any other leadership, rallied to the rash of Viet Minh revolutionary committees, which had spread through the country, and extended even into neighboring Laos, where Prince Souphanouvong, a member of the younger branch of the Royal family of Luang Prabang, and, among other things, a notable Greek scholar, had appeared with ten young officers from Ho's headquarters.

Giap entered Hanoi in the vanguard of his troops on August 17, 1945. The following day a Viet Minh provisional committee took over. Faced with a spontaneous and popular uprising, Bao Dai abdicated and took office as supreme counselor under the provisional government led by Ho. The Communists held all the key posts.

To the French, disarmed by the Japanese and fuming in their hotels, afraid almost everywhere to be seen on the streets, this was all a monstrous joke. No one had ever heard of Ho Chi Minh before, which was reasonable enough since the bearer of the name had scarcely grown familiar with it himself. It was inconceivable, they thought, that this fragile little man with a wisp of a beard, and who liked to be addressed as "Uncle Ho" and wore an open-necked white shirt and khaki shorts, could seriously challenge the authority of France. Ho's matchstick legs were scarred with jungle sores. He had the broad and calloused feet of a coolie, and his handshake was like the grip of an eagle's claw. Like most other things about him, this iron grip was deliberate. Pham Van Dong has said that when things were quiet in the mountains Ho would sometimes sit for the whole day throwing stones in order to strengthen his hands. His resolution needed no strengthening.

For Ho it was now a race against time—and against European colonial solidarity—and he lost. That most Vietnamese in the North were with him at this time was beyond doubt, but in Saigon, where the British occupation forces arrived to take the surrender of the Japanese, and where the French first made their come-back, his men were not fully in control. Their authority was challenged by religious sects and other dissident nationalist groups. Initially, the British lacked the troops to keep order, and called on the Japanese to do the job. This was bad enough. In the eyes of the Vietnamese, however, the British then compounded their felony by bringing in French troops in British uniforms. General Douglas Gracey, the British commander, had no patience with, or understanding of, the deep anticolonial emotions of the Vietnamese people. He had not come to Indo-China to preside over the liquidation of the French colonial empire, or to put a barefooted coolie in the palace. With his approval French troops took over control of Saigon on September 23rd.

It was now the French turn. Thousands who had sat in fear and outrage in their homes poured into the streets. They punched and kicked the Vietnamese and arrested all who tried to resist.

After one day of quiet and shock, and against the orders of the Viet Minh, who feared that an outbreak of violence would damage their interests, the Vietnamese took the law into their hands. This was much more than an eye for an eye and a tooth for a tooth. Several hundred French men, women, and children, including both metropolitan Frenchmen and Eurasians, were killed in revolting and brutal ways.

Subsequently, Colonel Dewey, a nephew of the governor of New York, and head of the O.S.S., which had been friendlily disposed toward Ho and his followers ever since one of their teams had joined his guerrilla headquarters some months earlier, was shot in the back and killed. The Vietnamese blamed the French for his death. There is nothing to suggest that they were responsible. Dewey's death was nevertheless symbolic of local French and American animosities which continued to the end in 1954, and after.

Shaken by this French and Vietnamese violence, the British reassumed responsibility for preserving law in Saigon. Their shock did not in any way cause Gracey to modify his plans to return power to the French, however. French forces pushed out to regain the southern towns and lines of communication while Gracey protected their rear. The countryside they never fully regained. No road was completely safe. Snipers lurked in the paddy fields. Every week brought its new crop of shootings.

Events in the North moved even less well for the French. Members of a French mission, which had parachuted into Hanoi, lived virtually as prisoners. They got no encouragement from the Japanese, and no help, either, from the small group of American O.S.S. officers, who had little sympathy for the French colonials.

About the middle of September Chinese Nationalist forces arrived in the North to take the surrender of the Japanese. By an arrangement reached earlier with Washington, their area of responsibility covered all of Tongking and extended well south of Hue, on the Central Vietnam coast. The French received none of the cooperation from the Chinese that General Gracey had extended to them in the South. Although the Viet Minh carried guns, all returning Frenchmen arriving in the North were immediately disarmed.

To broaden his popular base, Ho formally dissolved the Indo-China Communist Party and hastily organized elections, which were held openly in the North and Center and clandestinely in the South. They resulted in a sweeping victory for Ho, and, though their validity was open to serious question, they strengthened his position with the Chinese, who were, in any case, more concerned with looting than with the local political scene. They removed, among other things, the greater part of the Hanoi-Kunming railway line and all the plumbing fixtures in Hanoi and Haiphong.

Early in 1946, however, the French made a breakthrough. In return for the relinquishment of French extraterritorial rights in China and the promise of special conditions for Chinese living in Indo-China, the Nationalists agreed to withdraw their forces and to hand over control to the French. Because he felt he could not fight France and at the same time expedite the departure of the light-fingered Chinese, Ho reached a preliminary agreement with the French under which he gained some measure of independence.

The agreement did not satisfy any of his real aspirations. He signed it, he subsequently admitted, only because he had no alternative. He knew that he could not survive a joint French-Chinese offensive against him. The Vietnamese people were surprised: but at this time in the eyes of many of his countrymen Ho could do nothing wrong. Communist or not, he was a hero. Some Catholics even professed to see double pupils in his eyes, which they interpreted as signifying that he was a saint. To take advantage of this popular support, Ho announced the formation of an even wider national organization to be knows as the Lien Viet Front, or the League for the National Union of Vietnam. The idea was to conceal the hard-core Communists under a liberal coating of nationalism. It worked with many, but not with all. Men like Ngo Dinh Diem refused to join the Front. Bao Dai, an uncomfortable bedfellow, was soon exiled. In the South, the alliance with the sects was uneasy.

Meanwhile, Ho and Pham Van Dong led a delegation to France, leaving real control of affairs in the hands of Vo Nguyen Giap, who continued to eliminate opponents and to make prudent preparations for war. He reactivated his old guerrilla bases in the mountains and created new ones.

On their side, the French were equally guilty of bad faith. The French administration in Indo-China had passed into the hands of Admiral Georges d'Argenlieu, a Carmelite monk who had served with the Free French navy during the Second World War. Like Gracey, he saw his duty to save Indo-China for the French and to outsmart the Viet Minh "bandits" and Communists. Thus, while negotiations went on in France, both sides in Indo-China maneuvered for positions of political and military advantage.

Neither in Paris nor in Indo-China were the French prepared to bend before the winds of change. Negotiations broke down, and the main part of the Vietnamese delegation in France left for home. Ho stayed on in Paris for a few weeks, continuing to plead for something in the way of an agreement to appease his more extremist followers. He got a *modus vivendi* and the promise of another conference not later than January, 1947.

The conference was never held. Giap's men clashed repeatedly with the French forces, and widespread incidents, some of them minor, but several quite serious, were reported from various parts of the country. By November relations had passed almost to the point of no return. The French, in the mistaken belief that a show of force would bring the Viet Minh to heel, used their navy and air force to bombard and bomb the Vietnamese quarter of the densely populated port of Haiphong. It was a monstrous act. The cruiser *Suffren*, firing at point-blank range, poured broadside after broadside into the port. Six thousand Vietnamese lay dead in the ruins when the order was given to cease fire.

The French followed the attack with military demands which the Viet Minh at first seemed ready to accept. Gunboat diplomacy had worked again, the French thought. They were wrong. Giap issued his first Order of the Day on December 7th. This was merely an instruction to prepare for action. Troops were to be ready by December 12th. In a final effort to avoid war, Ho cabled Léon Blum, an acquaintance of his Paris days, whose election as premier of a Socialist Government in France appeared to offer some slight hope. But his cable lay for days in the French censor's office in Saigon. When at last it was sent and a reply came back, minor incidents in Hanoi had flared into all-out fighting. Ho Chi Minh and his government had fled to Giap's mountain bases north of the Red River delta, and Indo-China was at war.

CHAPTER 3

The
War
Before

FOR THE NEXT three years Ho Chi Minh tried to win the war by appealing to the nationalist sentiments of the Vietnamese people. Having dissolved the Indo-China Communist Party, he now dropped both Pham Van Dong and Giap, widely regarded at this time as the more extremist of his Communist followers, from his Cabinet. (Truong Chinh, then editorial writer for the Viet Minh journal *La République*, had not been included in the original Cabinet.) Buddhist, Catholic, and Socialist ministers all joined with him. Viet Minh propaganda played up their national aspirations and played down their Communist affiliations.

To the extent that the French, who rushed in heavy reinforcements of troops, were unable to crush the revolt, Ho's tactic succeeded. There was enough nationalist opposition to, and suspicion of, the Viet Minh, however, to encourage the French in their efforts to create a rival, more amenable, and less revolutionary pole of nationalist attraction around the former Emperor Bao Dai.

Even now, however, they were unwilling to make the concessions that might have drawn many nationalists away from Ho and united the fence-sitters. Bao Dai knew this; but in the end he went back to Vietnam as a French puppet, and an inactive one at that.

It was apparent within months that the Bao Dai experiment was a failure. Yet it also seemed unlikely that the Viet Minh would win the war. French Union casualties by the end of 1949 totaled about a hundred thousand. Rice exports had fallen from more than a million tons a year before the Second World War to less than a hundred thousand tons now. Where once there were roads there were now green overgrown tracks on which vehicles never ran. Almost all rail traffic had been brought to a halt. In the pacified areas of the Mekong delta and the Red River delta, watchtowers like pylons strode along the highways, providing some protection for the courageous traveler. Beyond the pacified areas guerrillas mobilized the peasants to destroy the roads, thereby preventing the movement of French trucks and tanks.

The war was still a guerrilla war, a war of attrition. It had effectively crippled the economy of the country; but the Viet Minh forces lacked a main striking force. Though they could harass small units, they were no match for the regular French military formations. The French claimed at this time that one good battalion, supplied from the air, could move anywhere with impunity. A military standoff seemed the most likely result.

Beyond the borders of Indo-China, however, other events began to have an urgent bearing on the course of the war. Across the great plain of China the Chinese Communists under the leadership of Mao Tse-tung were making history.

On paper, the Chinese Communists were heavily outmatched. Against Chiang Kai-shek's five million men, Mao could pit 2,700,000. Of these 1,200,000 were the tough élite of the Eighth Route Army and the New Fourth Army, both well blooded against the Japanese. They were reasonably well equipped with Japanese and American weapons, the latter captured from the Nationalists, but neither numerically nor materially comparable with Chiang's forces. They had no planes, no tanks, and their artillery formations were small. Their superiority, Marshal Chu Teh claimed later, lay in political quality and their ties with the people.

His patience exhausted and increasingly disturbed by the widespread evidence of Communist penetration, Chiang Kai-shek, in

July, 1946, decided to act. In a first sweep half a million men cleared the Communists from around Nanking and north along the coast from Shanghai. Two hundred thousand men plunged into North China. There were attacks against the Communists in the Shansi-Chahar-Hopei area, in the Shansi-Siuyen area, in the Shansi-Kansu-Ningsia area, and even on Hainan Island, off the southeast coast.

Chiang's three armies rolled, the cities toppled, and the Communists fell back, swooping to hit and destroy isolated columns, fighting only when victory was certain, running when they were outnumbered. In angry retaliation, the Nationalists struck at the only targets they could find, the villagers and the peasants suspected of providing the Communist armies with food and information. But razed villages, indiscriminate shootings, and mass reprisals only drove the people deeper into the Communist camp.

For the Kuomintang it was a period of seeming victory and concealed defeat. To the outside world Chiang's campaigns seemed to be paying off. The winter of 1946–1947 settled over China, and still the Nationalist armies marched on. In March, 1947, General Ho Tsung-nan led his forces into Yenan, the very heart of Mao's territory. But the caves were empty. There was no resistance. Mao and the central committee of the Chinese Communist Party had slipped away.

After eight months of fighting, Chiang could tick off a striking list of cities captured: but the cost was crippling. The Communists estimated they put out of action 710,000 Nationalist troops during this period. Of Chiang's original force of 117 divisions, only 85 remained battleworthy, and these were flung across the face of China, overextended and especially vulnerable to Mao's mobile and guerrilla tactics.

Committed to defend the cities he had acquired at such cost, Chiang lost all mobility. He had no reserves to blunt the Communist counteroffensive which began in June, 1947, when Mao's field army in the Shansi-Hopei-Honan area crossed the Yellow River into Shantung. In the ensuing months all North China burst into flame. The Great Plain between the Yellow River and the Yangtze became a "liberated" area, and General Lin Piao demolished the Nationalists in Manchuria. The Communists' regular forces had grown in strength to 2,800,000, while the Nationalists' total dropped to 3,365,000.

Now the Communists were taking cities and towns in order to annihilate the Nationalist troops defending them. Groups of Communist forces concentrated to provide local numerical superiority, and thousands of soldiers changed sides and joined Mao's victorious men. While remaining numerically inferior on the strategic level but numerically superior tactically, the Communists developed the "human wave" tactic, swamping the Nationalist defenses time after time. By the end of 1948 victory was clearly in sight. Four great campaigns of encirclement and annihilation thereafter wiped out another 1,600,000 Nationalist forces and sent the red flag to the masthead in Peking. The Nationalist defenses along the Yangtze crumpled under the amphibious assault of the Communist Second and Third Field armies on April 20, 1949. Three days later Nanking fell. In the closing months of the year the Communist armies rolled southward to the borders of Indo-China where Ho Chi Minh was locked in his battle with the French.

The West quickly made some agonizing reappraisals of the situation. In the hope that it might save some of its large financial investments in Shanghai, while bolstering up the French position in Indo-China, Britain elected to recognize both Bao Dai and Mao Tse-tung. The United States also recognized Bao Dai and began an aid program to the French in Indo-China which grew from a contemplated $23 million in 1950–1951 to a commitment of more than a billion dollars three years later.

At no stage, however, were the French ready to give the Vietnamese nationalists any incentive to fight. They were fearful even of the effect that dominion status for Indo-China might have on their African colonies. Within weeks of British and French recognition of Bao Dai, Nguyen Phan Long, his Prime Minister, told me that French officials were "fighting foot by foot to delay the transfer of power in the departments of police and justice."

His reign was predictably brief. He was followed into office by a succession of more amenable puppets, who, while enriching themselves, were unlikely to prove an embarrassment to the colonial power.

Ho Chi Minh fared better with his friends. Mao Tse-tung's statement of policy on July 1, 1949, "On People's Democratic Dictatorship," written to commemorate the twenty-eighth anniversary of the Chinese Communist Party, promised in unequivocal terms full support of such revolutions as Ho's. "Our dictatorship must unite with all international revolutionary forces. This, then, is our formula, our main experience, our main program," he said.

By Mao's standards, however, Ho was going about his revolt in the worst possible way. A revolution in which the Communist Party appeared to play a subordinate role to the national bourgeoisie was doomed to fail, he believed. He believed, also, that the purely guerrilla tactics that Giap had adopted were in themselves inadequate for the military task.

At a conference in Peking in November, 1949, at which members of the Viet Minh and Communists from other South-East Asian countries were present, Liu Shao-chi presented Mao's blueprint for conducting successful wars of national liberation. General Ho Lung, the former commander of the 120th Division of the Eighth Route Army, led a military mission to Ho's headquarters, and Giap subsequently went to Peking for discussions with Marshal Peng Teh-huai.

The Viet Minh wasted no time in falling into step with the Maoist formula, which received Moscow's imprimatur by publication in the *Cominform Journal* and also in *Pravda*. Giap was back in Vietnam by the New Year with two basic plans: to issue an order for general mobilization and to change from purely guerrilla warfare into mobile warfare. During his stay in China, Giap had also arranged for Viet Minh guerrillas to be trained as regular forces in Kwantung. Early in 1950 thousands packed their belongings and headed north into China. Their way of life, their military and political thinking all had to change. Instead of fighting a war of attrition against the French, they now had to learn the Maoist techniques of annihilation.

At the same time, Ho introduced sweeping political changes, again based on Mao Tse-tung's "thoughts." He now emphasized the need for long-term struggle. He personally translated Mao Tse-tung's *On Protracted War* into Vietnamese, while Truong Chinh, who, even at this early stage, seemed to have been designated as Ho's successor, wrote a series of articles entitled "The Long-Term Resistance Will Be Victorious," which put down the Chinese theories in terms the Vietnamese peasants could understand.

In March, 1951, the Viet Minh publicly abandoned all pretense at being a nationalist organization. Now the emphasis was on rallying all who could be rallied under the Communist banner. "All our people want democracy, genuine democracy," said Truong Chinh in an address to the leaders of all major political parties, forces, and organizations in the Viet Minh zone. "But only under the leadership of the working class can Vietnam's resistance and revolution be victorious. This is a historic truth. . . . The right to leadership of the revolution must be obtained through bloody sacrifice built on achievements and adorned with self-sacrificing spirit. This right to revolutionary leadership must be guaranteed by a vanguard revolutionary theory and a correct line of policy. Only a party that has a vanguard theory can lead the revolution. A vanguard theory is like a compass. Without a compass, there can be no skipper. The Lao Dong Party is the vanguard and general staff of the working class and the working people of Vietnam."

The Indo-China Communist Party was back in business under a new name. Full authority and power passed to the politburo of the Lao Dong Party. Both on the military and political levels the Viet Minh began to employ the tactics that had won victory for Mao Tse-tung in China.

Agrarian reform began to receive urgent attention. As early as 1927, in his "An Analysis of the Classes in Chinese Society," Mao Tse-tung had declared that "several hundred million peasants will rise like a tornado or tempest, a force so extraordinarily swift and violent that no power, however great, will be able to suppress it." The Viet Minh, with the repressive aid of the French, now began to stir up their volcano. "In a backward colonial country such as ours, where the peasants make up the majority of the population, a people's war is essentially *a peasants' war under the leadership of the working class*," said Giap, underscoring the final phrase. "The problem of land is of decisive importance."

Just as Mao had declared war on the landlords and rich peasants in South China in his earliest guerrilla days in the mountains, the Viet Minh now linked the "overthrowing of imperialism and the defeat of the feudal landlord class." By reducing land rents and interest rates and distributing land belonging to landlords, they began to rally support.

Weapons mattered less to Giap than tactics and people. His men used sticks, spears, scimitars, bows, and flintlocks in the early days. The regular forces, the élite, uniformed, battle-tried veterans, got the pick of the weapons. The regional troops, full-time and paid for their services but kept within provincial boundaries to support and supplement the regular forces, or to carry out local ambushes and attacks on posts, got what was left over. The village guerrilla units, even at the end, had to make their own. Most weapons came from the French. That was the primary source. While Chinese arms were vital in the buildup for Dien Bien Phu, for the rest small-scale arms factories, which were inadequate to meet their needs, and captured equipment, were what the Viet Minh had to depend on.

Until close to the end the Viet Minh had no trucks. A bulldozer, which was used to build the road to Dien Bien Phu, was their only tracked vehicle. The army moved on its own feet, with tiny ponies from the Thai Country in northwestern Tongking, bicycles, trishaws, and porters to carry supplies. A division of 10,000 men used up to 40,000 porters.

Recruits swore to "sacrifice themselves unreservedly" for the fatherland. A nine-point code of honor laid down the relations the troops were required to have with the civil population. Such practices as rape and the theft of pigs and poultry carried penalties including death. In return, the peasants were required to work for the army. They had to assist the guerrillas and the cadres to build defenses around their villages, to cart away the French roads, and to serve as porters.

Mao Tse-tung had forseen that to be effective guerrilla war had to change into mobile war. Giap made his first experiments in this quick concentration and rapid dispersal in the Mekong delta early in 1950. It was only on a small scale; but it was effective. The French fought to defend their towns and lines of communications, the Viet Minh to defend nothing but only to harass and then to annihilate the enemy forces.

Any mountain track over which a man or a pony could walk was a line of communication. Victories were always possible because the French, though strategically superior, could always be made tactically inferior: whatever the size of the French force employed in static defense, the Viet Minh could raise a larger one. A fifty-man post guarding a railway bridge could stand off an attack by fifty men but not by a battalion. Sixteen French Union battalions at Dien Bien Phu would have been enough to hold against a similar force; but they could not prevail against the fifty battalions the Viet Minh threw against them.

Giap, like Mao, often had to curb his commanders' impatience.

"Fight when you can win, run away when you cannot," said Mao. "Is the enemy strong? One avoids him," paraphrased Giap. "Is he weak? One attacks." On other occasions, Giap found the revolutionary change from guerrilla warfare to the breath-taking concepts opened up by mobile warfare beyond his officers' grasp. It was one thing to use a force of half a dozen men in a roadside ambush, but altogether a different matter to coordinate a regimental force to smash a French battalion, or a division to destroy a regiment. They learned war by war, as Mao Tse-tung put it.

With military discipline went Party control. The commissar system operated down to the section level. Giap distributed two books, one entitled the *Political Commissar's Book* and the other *Political Work in the Army*. They were required reading, for this was now a Party war. The Party committee gave the direction, and the military commander allotted the work. Both were equal heads of a unit. Platoons had political commissars, Party groups and branches. Political work became the "soul" of the army. From 35 to 40 percent of all troops were members of the Lao Dong Party. More than 90 percent of officers were members.

Everywhere the army went it established local cells and political groups. Thus, even in an area where the fighting had passed, political preparation, and the recruiting and training of guerrilla and regional troops, went on. "In the enemy's rear the guerrilla units in coordination with the regular army scattered and wore out the enemy, nailed them to their bases so that our regular army could launch mobile fighting to annihilate them," Giap wrote later. "They turned the enemy rear into our front line and built guerrilla bases as starting points for our regular army's offensive right in the heart of the enemy. In the free zones the guerrilla units effectively fought the enemy and kept watch on traitors."

The futile Viet Minh use of terror tactics in the cities came to an end. Saigon now became as peaceful on the surface as any city in Asia. Only the sound of gunfire beyond the city at night and the troops in the streets reminded one of the war in Hanoi. But the Viet Minh were everywhere. Every street had its party cell. There were shadow platoons and battalions, with nothing more than a waiting and watching brief. When it was all over and the Viet Minh were about to enter Hanoi, they put on white sun helmets and for the first time appeared quite openly in the streets.

Beginning in September, 1950, the Viet Minh moved from the

strategic defensive to the strategic offensive. Not once thereafter did they lose the initiative. By the end of 1950 their forces based in the mountains north of the Red River delta, and reinforced by divisions trained and equipped in China, had smashed the whole chain of French posts guarding the strategic Tongking-China border and sent thousands of French troops reeling in bitter defeat.

The first battle lasted for two days, the incredulous French resisting to the end in the fort at Dong Khe on the Lang Son–Cao Bang border road. Its fall split the main border garrisons and prevented both effective reinforcement and withdrawal by the French command. A French column, with orders to fight its way to Cao Bang, the provincial capital, was ambushed and destroyed. Cao Bang fell after a week. And the French, long accustomed to the sniping mortar and the twenty-man ambush, suddenly found in this new war that they had lost three thousand of their best troops.

Sweeping southeast along the frontier highway, the Viet Minh reduced fort after fort. Lang Son, a second provincial capital, was in Viet Minh hands by October 1st, and Dinh Lap ten days later. In six weeks a hundred vital miles of the most strategic highway in Indo-China had been secured by the Viet Minh. The porte de Chîne, border gateway into China, was now wide open, and the Viet Minh "sanctuary" at Bac Kan, in the high wild mountains north of the Red River delta, had a direct link with the Chinese Communists. From this main base, Giap marched south in preparation for what his Chinese advisers overoptimistically had told him would prove the decisive battle of the war.

"Hanoi for Tet" (the Buddhist New Year), and the greatest Vietnamese festival of the year, was the slogan. Along the roads leading to the Red River delta villagers broke out red banderoles and Viet Minh flags. The political cadres whose job it was to stimulate and excite the local peoples had little difficulty now. Ngo Van Chieu, a young Viet Minh soldier, in his *Journal d'un Combattant Viet Minh* (Éditions du Seuil, Paris) told how women young and old rushed from their houses with presents for the soldiers, and of the gaiety as accordions, guitars, and harmonicas were brought out and troops and villagers alike celebrated the victories that had been won and those which lay ahead. It was "Ho Chu Tich Muon Nam" (Ten Thousand Years for Ho Chi Minh), whose portrait, flanked by those of Stalin and Mao Tse-tung, decorated every house along the road to the war.

For three days the battle hung in the balance. General de Lattre de Tassigny took personal command of the French forces. He rushed in reinforcements and drenched the attacking Viet Minh with napalm, breaking their drive near Vinh Yen, a village of mud and thatch near the northwestern apex of the <-shaped French perimeter on the Red River delta. Giap suffered heavily, but did not persist when he saw the battle was lost. His main forces dispersed. Giap was beaten but not destroyed.

The battle has often been described as the one great French victory of the war. It gave a much-needed stimulus to French spirits after the drop in morale caused by the loss of the China border forts late in 1950, and provided General de Lattre de Tassigny with an opportunity to regroup, and to reorganize and to push on rapidly with the construction of blockhouses, fourteen hundred of which were built in the Red River delta during the following year.

In the longer view, however, the lessons the French assumed from the battle led only to catastrophe. French officers were sure they were more than capable of beating the Viet Minh when and if they got a set piece of battle, and it was this complacency three years later that led to disaster at Dien Bien Phu.

The French also began to attach far too much importance to weapons such as napalm. The sight of the khaki-clad Viet Minh regular troops running like rabbits under napalm attacks suggested that here was the sure means of breaking up any serious assault. In a clear-cut war, where lines are demarcated and the fighting is between soldier and soldier, napalm is often more effective than any conventional bomb, especially if the troops under attack are in open country. This was not that sort of war. As Mao Tse-tung puts it, the people were to the Viet Minh what water is to fish; or, as Giap described it, "the front was nowhere, it was everywhere." It was in a sea of flooded rice paddies, with the Viet Minh hiding under water with their bamboo snorkels. It was in a cave under a village among innocent people who did not care to speak out for fear of reprisals. The uniformed troops, the élite battle corps, were identifiable: but no one could tell whether the black-clad peasant went home to his family at night, or dragged out a gun and went hunting the French. Eventually, the French did not care. They thought the people did not count. French truck drivers in Hanoi used to play tip and run with Vietnamese civilians, and roar with laughter when they sent an old man spinning and at the curses and hatred their behavior involved. Napalm and artillery became French prophylactics. They used them "just in case." Through the mountains and plains of Indo-China villages became funeral pyres, killing many Viet Minh "fish" but only making it easier for their commanders to find willing helpers in the "ocean" of peasants. Punitive raids into Communist-dominated areas, where friend and foe were indistinguishable, and all, therefore, could be regarded as hostile, and vast mopping-up campaigns that killed hundreds of men, women, and children, merely drove more people into the arms of the Viet Minh.

General Chassin, the French air-force commander, thought the war could be won by air power. He conceded that the people were hostile and likely to remain so. "The Viet Minh get all the information," he told me once. "We get none. The Viet Minh troops are about as efficient as ours. Our numbers are similar. If we can get more planes, especially jets, we will turn the tables."

Chassin blamed Washington for not giving him Sabrejets and delayed-action fuses for his bombs, just as President Ngo Dinh Diem now blames it for failing to provide him with enough artillery. "The Americans first said they couldn't give us jets because the airfields were not good enough," said Chassin. "Now we have 8,000-foot concrete runways and still they don't give us jets." He must have wondered since how the Viet Minh won without a single plane.

In the months following the battle for Vinh Yen, the Viet Minh infiltrated their regular units into the vital Red River delta, and, from well prepared village bases, began to expand the areas under their control. While the French built their blockhouses and planted their mines and put out their barbed wire, the Viet Minh went to work on the local population. They infiltrated from both north and south, operating under cover of darkness when the French had retired to their forts. At this time, the Viet Minh strength in Tongking totaled about 220,000 men—about 120,000 regulars grouped into six infantry divisions and one heavy-weapons division. The rest were provincial troops and guerrillas.

The regulars had four main objectives: to gain access to the manpower of the densely populated Red River delta region, where the predominantly Vietnamese were more friendly than the mountain tribesmen; to protect their already established lines of communication inside the delta; to obtain food, principally rice and salt; and to bolster the morale of the often hard-pressed regional troops and guerrillas living in the delta.

De Lattre hoped to pacify the rice lands with his vast chain of interlocking blockhouses, thus securing a firm base from which to attack the Viet Minh lines of communication beyond the delta. With his rear secured he planned to use his élite mobile groups to smash the Viet Minh north-south supply route. The need was urgent. Less than two months after the Vinh Yen battle, in which the French claimed to have killed six thousand of Giap's élites, the Viet Minh had maneuvered south of the delta. Supplied by a road that skirted the western end of the delta through the village of Hoa Binh, they attacked, and for a time held, the Catholic town of Ninh Binh on the right bank of the Red River, fifty miles from Hanoi.

French troops had occupied the town early in 1950 and fortified its two commanding hills. The town garrison consisted of a mixed company of commandos and French marines. A second company of Vietnamese troops had its headquarters on one of the hill positions, where their three blockhouses, dug into limestone cliffs and protected by three feet of masonry and barbed wire, seemed almost impregnable.

French forces in the town resisted for only a few minutes when the Viet Minh attack began at dawn on May 29, 1951. Three hours later the French reinforced by river. The reinforcements included a newly formed Vietnamese company under Lieutenant Bernard de Lattre, son of the commander in chief. After heavy fighting during the day, the reinforcements withdrew for the night into the two hill positions. At dawn the following day the Viet Minh opened the second phase of their attack with a mortar barrage. Lieutenant de Lattre was killed and the position overrun.

After more than two weeks' continued hard fighting, which involved most of the 308th Viet Minh Division and fifteen French Union battalions, the Viet Minh pulled back into the limestone caves beyond the delta. Once again Giap had bitten off more than he could chew. But, as he described it in the magazine *People's Army*, the battle had taught him some valuable lessons. This was the first time he had engaged major French forces on a battlefield complicated by numerous rivers and marshlands. In place of the frontal assault, he now directed a strengthening of local organizations. "In order to attain our goal we must carry out the following works," he wrote: "Develop guerrilla warfare and strengthen local armies, destroy puppet administrations and extend the liberated areas in the enemy's rear. Intensify propaganda among draftees in order to make them realize that by serving in the French aggressive army they are guilty not only of treason against the people but also doomed to certain annihilation. Carry on this propaganda simultaneously with the fighting on the front. Speed up the consolidation of the people's bases in the area. Organize timely harvesting and make preparations for opposing the enemy's forthcoming mopping-up operations. By doing so the troops will carry out President Ho Chi Minh's order for a great political victory on the basis of a great military success."

The exhausting summertime heat of Tongking brought the usual military lull. The Viet Minh were especially busy restocking their larder from the delta harvest. For Marshal de Lattre, however, it was a time of intense reorganization and planning. Intensive bombing by the French air force had not succeeded in stopping the movement of considerable Viet Minh supplies, and, as the battle for Ninh Binh had indicated, he now faced the threat of serious attack from Viet Minh regulars to the south, as well as to the north.

The village of Hoa Binh, seventeen miles west of the delta, was, he felt, the key. With this effectively held he could break the north-south Viet Minh link, cut off the southern Viet Minh division from the main source of supply, and reestablish a firm hold over highly populous, largely Catholic, and therefore anti-Communist, areas of the southern and southeastern delta.

French difficulties began soon after their virtually unresisted paratroop capture of Hoa Binh on November 14, 1951, and the establishment of a succession of strong posts along the Black River. The Viet Minh mounted heavy machine guns on the hills overlooking the small airstrip at Hoa Binh. Planes bringing in supplies were obliged to fly low through a defile where they came under accurate and intense fire from light and heavy machine guns. Planes on the field itself were attacked by mortar fire. And the Black River flowed with French blood as the Viet Minh lashed out against French attempts to reinforce and supply by water.

Like so many subsequent operations, the Hoa Binh campaign was self-defeating. De Lattre set out to cut the Viet Minh lines of communication. To protect his own he had to draw off so many reserves from the delta that by the time General Raoul Salan, who took over after de Lattre's death, was able to extricate his forces, the French had suffered more than five thousand casualties, and the Viet Minh had infested the rice lands north and east of the southern delta town of Thai Binh. Salan's first task was to direct the evacuation of Hoa Binh, the second to endeavor to restore the situation in the southern delta.

Ten miles east of Thai Binh, where battered mud and plaster houses roughly thatched with straw clustered around the huge Catholic church, was a French fort. From its brick tower the lookout could see the neighboring forts, the one behind and the one in front, and what remained of the road that ran between. Beyond these there were others and others again in the great Red River rice and vegetable garden that fed the roughly seven million Vietnamese who lived in what was then officially described as the French perimeter.

The commander of this fort in the first months of 1952 was a young French officer who had completed his two years' service in Indo-China and was due to sail for France. Under him he had two sergeants, one French, the other Vietnamese, three Vietnamese corporals, and a total garrison strength of thirty-five.

For some months the commander's job had been more a matter of routine than of war. Patrols went out each day and made contact with the patrols from the neighboring forts. Twice a week there was a trip to Thai Binh for supplies. That was about it.

In December, 1951, the lieutenant realized that something was amiss. His daytime patrols were fired on by snipers. The road was mined and ambushed, and soon there was no road at all, or nothing that could be identified as a road. By night the Viet Minh mobilized the villagers to cut up the road and cart it away. It was a good, sealed, all-seasons road, raised some six to eight feet on a levee above the level of the paddy fields. The peasants took it in chunks. They would carve out a section that reached slightly more than halfway across the road and went all the way down to the paddy fields. Then, on the opposite side of the road, a yard or so farther on, they would remove a similar section, carrying off the rocks and dirt far across the rice field. It was a long and tedious job, but, since the only quarries were in undisputed Viet Minh territory in the hills and mountains beyond the delta, the finished task was worthwhile: the road was beyond repair.

By January, 1952, the commander knew not only that something was amiss but also that it would be something of a miracle if he ever left the fort alive. He could no longer travel to Thai Binh. His supplies, which now had to come by air drop, were erratic.

A fort far on the east coast was the first to fall. The Viet Minh crept through the paddy fields at night and blasted its tower with a bazooka. The walls crumbled and collapsed. With submachine guns and grenades the Viet Minh moved in. A week later another fort fell. This time it was much closer, and this time, also, the Viet Minh used a 75-millimeter gun to do the job. They wheeled it into position from a nearby village, and over open sights and at point-blank range blew a hole in the fort wide enough for the assault party to walk in. Then the forts on either side fell, both of them clearly visible along the road that no longer was a road but a barrier to all movement, whether by vehicle or on foot.

The attack on the fort opened from a village eight hundred yards to the south. Machine guns raked it and drew heavy fire in return. The commander knew that his fort was well designed, but also that it was no better, if no worse, than others whose fate he had seen marked by smoldering piles of rubble. It stood on an island in a narrow stream and was linked to the banks by two bridges heavily protected by booms and blocks.

The running waters served as a moat. On both banks and on the island itself were rows of barbed wire festooned with tin cans that rattled in the wind, or whenever anyone touched the wire. The tower was vulnerable. Its bricks were not stout enough to withstand artillery or bazooka fire. But the thick bunkers beneath the tower were provisioned with enough food and ammunition to withstand several weeks' siege.

Each dawn the Tricolor waved defiantly from the tower. Each night the Viet Minh surrounded it. They fired at any sign of movement, chipping the walls of the fort with their bullets. Everyone in the fort knew that the climax would not be long delayed.

Then, across the delta, the French forces came back from Hoa Binh. About the middle of March big military convoys began to move toward Thai Binh. The Viet Minh mined the road, sniped at the French forces moving by day, and kept them off the road at night. They were not enough, however, to stop preparations for what was obviously going to be a major French offensive.

Operation Mercury, the code name for the campaign, pushed

off from Thai Binh in the last week in March. Salan and his Tong-king commander, General de Linares, threw in almost all their mobile reserves, five reinforced *groupes mobiles*, in all, sixteen infantry battalions, with tank, artillery, and air support, moving in a big semicircle extending from the banks of the swollen Red River to the coast.

In principle, the 320th Viet Minh Division was trapped and had no way of escape. Cushioned by a screen of snipers and delaying troops, it fell back toward the sea by day and at night slipped through the French lines. Cowards, said the French, who had not read their Mao Tse-tung and did not appreciate therefore that the Viet Minh fought by rigid instructions to fight only when they could win and to run away when they could not. "Don't fight when the enemy force is larger, can call quickly for reinforcements, or is capable of continuing the action for a protracted period of time," Mao had laid down.

This was such an occasion. On the third day of the operation the French troops reached the isolated fort. The bearded commander, with his eyes bloodshot and his voice hoarse, kissed the advancing infantry officer on both cheeks. Everybody shook hands with everybody else. There were congratulations, tears, stories, and smiles. "I had a boat to catch in January," the commander kept saying. "I am very late."

He left the following day, homeward bound. His place was taken by another young lieutenant, who gave me a Pernod in the compact little cell that served as his mess. We climbed the rickety wooden ladder in the tower to see the ruins of the neighboring fort, a mile or so across the paddy field.

"I shall pull down the tower and put more concrete, much more concrete, round the sides," he said. "We have cleared the delta before, you know. Perhaps we shall have to do it all again."

This time, however, the French did not clear the delta. They smashed down the villages that lay in their path and used tip trucks to spread the rubble across the paddy fields. Since the villagers had carted off the roads, what was wrong with using the villages to make new roads? Back at General de Linares's headquarters the bottles of wine danced on the white tablecloths as the 155-milli-meter Long Toms fired their lunchtime salvos into suspect villages along the line of advance. When there was resistance the planes came in with bombs and napalm.

Napalm is a fireball, a furnace that scatters its sticky and lethal fire over a wide area before mercifully blanketing itself in a cloud of black smoke. One does not expect to find friends in villages that have been hit by it. The French found no friends here.

The wise took to the rice fields ahead of the French advance. Far off across the rice, well beyond the effective range of rifle or machine-gun fire, they watched the mainstream of the advance go past. Sometimes a tank would loose off a round or two from its main armament in their general direction. Sometimes the French used artillery against them—perhaps on the theory that bombs are good for fishing. Sometimes a fighter plane came over and strafed.

And so for a time, a very brief time, the southeastern corner of the Red River delta seemed secure. The hard-worked *groupes mobiles* pulled out to plug other holes in other dams. The Viet Minh returned. Despite the Viet Minh preoccupation with mobile warfare outside the delta, and the fourteen hundred French forts which covered this sea of rice, the deterioration was constant and rapid. At the end of September, 1952, the delta, by day and by night, was more in Viet Minh hands than in those of the French. Of the 6,492 villages, the Viet Minh held 2,292, the French 2,187, and the rest were in no-man's-land, controlled by those who happened to be there at the time. The situation was worst of all around Thai Binh. The French held the town, and nothing else.

CHAPTER 4

Defeat
At
Dien
Bien
Phu

DURING THE CAMPAIGNING season at the end of 1952 it became obvious to many that unless the French changed their tactics a major military defeat was only a matter of time. Complacent assurances by political observers such as Malcolm Macdonald, Britain's Commissioner-General in South-East Asia, that no amount of material aid short of intervention by Chinese Communist troops could disturb the balance in Indo-China had been shattered by Giap's autumn offensive.

Using three regular divisions, he launched a series of attacks on the French posts west of the Red River delta. Some of the posts were big and, in principle, well defended. One of these was

Nghai-Lo, where the French defenders were of battalion strength. Its main defenses fell in an hour on October 17, 1952, to an attack by a Viet Minh division which had been plotted by French intelligence as safely at rest in its home base north of the delta.

The French had looked for a small attack and were entirely unprepared for the vigor and weight of the Viet Minh assault. In a matter of days almost all the Thai Country, as northwestern Tongking is known, had fallen, and the surviving French forces, under repeated and bitter attack, were struggling back through the jungle to the Black River.

In an effort to take the pressure off the retreating French forces in the Thai Country, where the tribesmen were still friendlily disposed toward the French and mostly unsympathetic to the Viet Minh, General Salan committed his mobile forces northwest of the delta in another Hoa Binh–type operation to cut the Viet Minh supply route. The Viet Minh immediately increased the pressure on the southern delta and by a staggering forced march across the mountains brought the 308th Division into attack. It fell on the 4th Mobile Group under Colonel Louis Kergaravat as he shepherded the rest of the French force back into the delta line.

The column was making its slow way along the narrow jungle road when the Viet Minh, using six battalions of troops, smashed into the center of the column. They went for the Foreign Legion, hoping by knocking out the strongest unit to capture the weaker. After a day of furious fighting, the French, using tanks, aircraft, and artillery, succeeded in reopening the road, leaving several hundred dead behind.

The French called it a victory, but the threat to the Viet Minh supply route had been effectively eliminated, and the 308th Division, trundling their fieldpieces and supplied by an army of 30,000 porters, turned again to the Thai Country. There the 316th Division had now collected all the minor French forts west of the Black River and had a considerable force bottled up at Na Sam, an airfield near Son La, the abandoned capital of the Thai Country, and seventy-five miles through Viet Minh territory from the delta.

A dirt strip torn into the finest powder by nonstop daylight flights of Dakotas rushing reinforcements and supplies; sad little groups of Thai tribesmen with their possessions wrapped up in colored cloths waiting in the dust in the hope of a plane to take them to Hanoi; the headquarters dug in at the side of the airfield; a collection of bare knolls, where French battalions awaited attack. This was Na Sam.

By comparison with Dien Bien Phu, where the French conceded the high ground to the Viet Minh and concentrated on the plain, Na Sam was a good position. In every other way, it was hell. Every night, with bugle calls and using flares to light their way, the Viet Minh probed and tested.

A preparation of Viet Minh mortar fire began to fall at dusk on the night of November 30th. It continued without respite during the evening. Toward midnight it grew heavier. Battalions of Thai tribesmen and Moroccans manning the western hills saw the Viet Minh forming up for the assault. The garrison opened fire on fixed lines. The Viet Minh, ignoring casualties and in great strength, charged up the hill. Their bamboo bangalore torpedoes gapped the wire around one post, and the troops flooded through the breach, overwhelming a company of Thais. The Moroccans put up a more effective resistance, but they, too, were overwhelmed.

With several hours remaining before daylight and any hope of French air support, the Viet Minh appeared to be in a commanding position. Their intention clearly was to reinforce heavily, and, while they overlooked the airstrip, dominating it with small arms and machine-gun fire, they might yet succeed in destroying the garrison.

More than anything else, French artillery saved the battle. The entire fortified area was not more than about a mile long by a mile wide, but despite the obvious difficulty in sighting the guns, the French succeeded in bringing down heavy fire on the Viet Minh line of supply. Cut off by this heavy fire, the Viet Minh were unable to reinforce, and pulled out from one post. In the second they repaired the damage caused by their own attack and cut new positions in the undergrowth.

At daybreak the fighter-bombers came with napalm, and until noon they drenched the hilltop. A battalion of French paratroopers with fixed bayonets regained the position. The French counted a thousand Viet Minh dead against four hundred killed and wounded in their own ranks. Once again, as at Vinh Yen, the cry was victory. "Just give us a set-piece battle," the French said. "We'll beat them every time."

Before the late spring rains put a stop to campaigning, the Viet

Minh had swept far beyond Na Sam. With four divisions they drove through northern Laos, established Prince Souphanouvong at the head of his Pathet Lao "government" at Sam Neua, and directly threatened the Royal capital of Luang Prabang. The French built a new Na Sam on the ancient burial ground called the Plain of Jars, and Royal elephants dragged logs to build the defenses at Luang Prabang.

At the limits of their supply line, however, the Viet Minh were not looking for major and risky military engagements. Their aim was to sow the war in wider fields and to keep the initiative away from the French mobile forces. They succeeded all too well.

After seeing the long lines of ambulances plowing to the rear and battle-weary soldiers with their feet up along the wayside, too exhausted even to smoke, but feverishly digging in for their lives with the approach of night, I cabled my newspapers in London and Australia that the end was predictable. "It is clear that the French no longer have any real hope of defeating Ho Chi Minh and his Communist forces," I reported. "Worse, there is little doubt now that the Viet Minh by maintaining the offensive will inevitably precipitate a complete French withdrawal.

"Even more serious in its implications is the internal political-military situation. While the Viet Minh were content with a slow war of attrition the French set about building up a local Vietnamese army, which one day, it was planned, would be strong enough to take over the main burden of the war, paving the way for a reduction in French Union forces.

"On paper today this Vietnamese army is a formidable force. Commanded by General Hinh, son of Prime Minister Nguyen Van Tam, it consists of fifty-five operational battalions. By the end of the year it will have 150,000 men under arms. Mixed with the French, many of these troops have given a good account of themselves in paratroop battalions and other front-line units. Had the Bao Dai experiment worked, and had his government become a government in fact and not merely in name, the Vietnamese army might have proved a genuinely formidable force. Today, uncertain in loyalty and infiltrated by Communist agents, and weakened by doubt that it might yet be possible to do business with the enemy, it is of use only in the static defense of inactive areas. Nineteen of its battalions are in Tongking. The rest are all beyond the battle proper in the South. General Hinh is pressing for complete Viet-

namese control of the delta, a request that one may only pray the
French will not grant."

For this, and for the following comments on Bao Dai, I was
banished from Indo-China, and for many months refused permission to return. "For years," I wrote, "it was considered impolitic to suggest that one cause of the Vietnamese failure to make
headway as an 'independent' State lay at the top. Criticism of
Bao Dai, it was said, merely prejudiced his chances of success.
After four years of non-achievement, however, it is too much to
hope that Bao Dai, whatever chances he is given, will emerge as a
great patriot, capable of rallying the true nationalists to his standard. Bao Dai gathered around him Parisian Vietnamese who were
more French than the French. They came primarily from Cochin-
China, the southernmost state in Vietnam, which, as a pre-war
colony, enjoyed special privileges denied the Tongking protectorate. If they represented anybody, it was not the men and women
most intimately concerned with the Northern war. When the war
was a stalemate, the political situation also hung fire. The real political decline began with the military reverses. One speeds the
other. Defeat on the battlefield is defeat also in every peasant
cottage."

A little Vietnamese named Nguyen Van Huong, who looked
like a beardless Ho Chi Minh, was head of the Vietnamese Sûreté
in Hanoi at this time. We had been friends for several years, and
I had always found him a reliable source of information. He was
now greatly distressed. "At this moment we have been told to cut
by two-thirds the number of agents in the Viet Minh areas," he
told me. "At this very time when we know the first anti-aircraft
guns and field pieces are coming in from China."

General Henri Navarre, who succeeded Salan, was given an impossible assignment. With little knowledge of, or interest in, Asia
and its wars, he soon found that he had inherited a woefully inept
intelligence organization. Instructed to avoid casualties, he was
also committed, under pressure from the United States, which was
now paying for a third of all war costs, to a more vigorous and
aggressive campaign. In addition, he was required, for political
reasons, to defend Laos.

Since the opium-smoking Salan and General de Linares, his
Tongking commander, were scarcely on speaking terms, any
change at this time seemed a change for the better. General René

Cogny, who had taken over the Tongking command, was an outstanding man and an outstanding soldier. Navarre himself radiated optimism. Though he has since denied that there was anything like a "Navarre Plan," his briefing officers referred to it constantly and deliberately. Official Western observers who lived in Saigon and rarely bothered to push their way through the French red tape to look at the war were enthusiastic. The tide, it was said, had turned. With the Navarre Plan the French would win the war.

As Giap understood it, the plan called for a concentration of forces in the Red River delta during the autumn and winter of 1953 to destroy the Viet Minh's guerrilla bases, coupled with a major attack in the less firmly held Viet Minh zones in South Vietnam. If this proved successful, Navarre then intended to move his main forces back to the North for the set-piece showdown with the Viet Minh battle corps.

By the summer of 1953 Navarre had eighty-four mobile battalions under his command, more than half of which were concentrated in the Red River delta, where the mopping-up offensive had begun. On July 17, 1953, in the middle of the wet season, three battalions of paratroops occupied the border town of Lang Son and destroyed several thousand tons of Giap's military supplies freshly arrived from China. Navarre followed this on November 20th with a paratroop drop on Dien Bien Phu, the Thai Country's road junction and rice bowl, an hour and a half's flight from Hanoi by Dakota, and in the heart of the territory captured the previous year by the Viet Minh. Giap believed that Navarre's intention was to use Dien Bien Phu as a means of blocking the Viet Minh's way to Laos and, subsequently, as the second base for a major northern offensive.

On the Viet Minh side November came and passed. Campaigning weather was running out. Word trickled into Hanoi that Giap had called up hundreds of thousands of men and women to serve as porters. But there was more talk of Viet Minh land reform than there was of war. Puzzled at first by Giap's failure to react to their moves, the French soon became complacent and overconfident.

If Giap had been a conventional soldier, he would have countered the French moves. But he was not a conventional soldier, and this was the critical moment of the war. By meeting the French challenge in the delta he knew that he would run the grave risk of defeat. By an immediate attack on Dien Bien Phu with his main forces he would have left the way open for the mobile forces to invade his own free zones.

He therefore decided to keep the initiative by wide-ranging attacks in overwhelming strength against the maximum number of French positions, while he painstakingly prepared for the battle of Dien Bien Phu.

The Viet Minh battle corps was about to take off. Lai Chau, one of the two remaining French positions in the Thai Country, was the first target. Navarre got word that the Viet Minh regulars were moving on the town, but there was little he could do about it. After ten days the French had nothing left in northwestern Tongking but the plain of Dien Bien Phu. Their appreciation now was that the entrenched camp would be next on Giap's list. Navarre decided that it should be held at all costs.

Giap had many tasks to perform, however, before he was ready to accept the French challenge. Lai Chau had been in his hands only ten days when other Viet Minh forces, working in conjunction with Souphanouvong's Pathet Lao, struck in Central Laos and seized the Mekong River town of Thakhek. The French pulled back on their first-class airfield at Seno, reinforcing here with mobile forces originally scheduled for mopping-up operations in the Red River delta.

Another Viet Minh task force headed south in secrecy through the region controlled by a Kha tribesman named Sithone, who in 1950 had freed most of southeastern Laos from French control. These troops were the first to use what has become known as the Ho Chi Minh trail, a series of mountain tracks running through the jungles of Laos and linking up with the Annamite Chain and now providing the Viet Cong with cover all the way from the 17th parallel to the outskirts of Saigon. Without warning, the Viet Minh emerged from the jungle on the night of December 30-31, overran a French Union battalion, and marched on toward the town of Saravane.

In mid-January Navarre gambled with an offensive of his own. He launched an amphibious operation against the Viet Minh coastal provinces in Central Vietnam. He saw the Communist forces here as a threat to the naval base at Tourane, to Cochin-China itself, and to the sparsely populated but strategically important High Plateau. Seven days after his forces had landed at

Nha Trang, however, Viet Minh forces which had come down the Ho Chi Minh trail launched an attack against the High Plateau from the north, seizing the entire province of Kontum and threatening the town of Pleiku. Once again Navarre had to draw on his depleted Red River delta reserves.

The news from all fronts was bad. The coastal operation which had absorbed seventeen battalions of Navarre's troops had bogged down, and Viet Minh forces, which had been gathering around Dien Bien Phu since December, suddenly took off for northern Laos. Now the Royal capital of Luang Prabang was threatened. Desperately Navarre threw in more reserves for an action that was never joined. Giap was not looking for fights, however, but only to dissipate the French battle corps while he prepared his own set-piece battle. What he wanted was time, time to build a road across the mountains to Dien Bien Phu, time to place the new fieldpieces and antiaircraft guns in position around the French entrenched camp, time to prepare and plan every detail of the action that was soon to end this first phase of the Indo-China War.

In Hanoi, Nguyen Van Huong shook his head in despair. "The Viet Minh have new roads and a thousand trucks," he said. "They will attack and capture Dien Bien Phu." Others feared he was right. General Cogny had his desk stacked with reports about scores of thousands of coolies and troops with bicycles, all laden with ammunition, fording the streams and following the tracks, scuttling for cover when the French planes came overhead, moving by day and by night, always moving, with only one object: Dien Bien Phu. But Cogny did not direct the war.

At Na Sam the French had at least held the high ground. At Dien Bien Phu they surrendered it to the Viet Minh. The British military attaché went to Dien Bien Phu and reported that the French defenses were the closest he had seen in Indo-China to a conventional European defensive position. Americans looked at it and did not disapprove. In Saigon I asked Navarre whether he thought the Viet Minh would attack. "I hope so," he replied simply.

It was not a hope expressed very often in Dien Bien Phu itself.

In December, 1953, Giap visited the hills above the entrenched camp. What he saw was a plain about twelve miles long and four or five wide. The village of Muong Thanh in the center of the plain had been demolished to make way for the French defenses. Two-thirds of Colonel (later General) Christian de Castries's forces were concentrated here. Several connecting defense centers protected the command post, the artillery and commissariat bases and the airfield. Away to the south was a secondary defensive position which the French called Isabelle. Equipped with its own artillery, its object was to hold the line against the attack from the direction of the Laotian border. To the north the strong posts Beatrice and Gabrielle blocked the Lai Chau road.

Except for flat-chested Isabelle, the strongpoints were sited on bare knolls which gave Dien Bien Phu an odd, many-bosomed appearance. Elaine, among the remains of Muong Thanh village, guarded the eastern approaches to De Castries's command post. All the buildings had been swept away. The battalion of French-officered Thai tribesmen charged with its defense lived underground in bunkers. Barbed-wire entanglements and minefields encircled the hill. It would have been a good, conventional defensive position on a plain—but towering above it were the jungle-covered hills, all in the uncontested hands of the Viet Minh.

I lunched here one day with the battalion officers just a few weeks before the Viet Minh attack. The officers' mess was a strip of tarpaulin stretched over the top of a dust-covered and fly-infested table. Half a mile away, close to the eastern hills, one of the companies had run into a Viet Minh patrol. Lunch was an odd mixture of distant rifle fire, the virtues and beauty of the Thai girls who had once lived where we were eating, and bitter complaints about the inadequacy of the air support. The artillery opened fire to harass the Viet Minh, and shells of white phosphorous rustled their way overhead, bursting in the jungle—with what effect no one could say.

While we were finishing lunch a young lieutenant came in dripping with sweat and carrying two canvas-covered, rice-straw Viet Minh helmets, souvenirs of the patrol, and the disturbing news that the general enemy positions had advanced much closer.

"Go back to Saigon and tell them we want planes," said a young major when we had finished lunch. "The artillery is good, but we will need much more than that if we are to stop them here," and his hand encompassed the hills rising behind us.

At Isabelle there was even less enthusiasm about the situation. "Take these and have a look at those hills," said a captain, hand-

ing me his field glasses. "What you'll see up there are all Viet
Minh." Like spectators crowding into the seats of a stadium, the
Viet Minh were taking up their positions for the battle to come.

"After having analyzed the situation and weighing the pros
and cons, we decided to attack Dien Bien Phu without taking
risks," Giap said. His preparations took three months and were
not completed until the first week in March, 1954. The 308th
Division, the 312th, the 316th, the 351st, with new heavy weapons
and several independent regiments, including one from the 304th
Division, had all assembled. Through the winter nights the Molo-
tova trucks came in from China, unloading their cases of ammunition. The antiaircraft gunners camouflaged themselves and dug
in on the hills. The French planes flew in and out unmolested.

All the requirements of Maoist warfare were met, the overwhelming strength, the certainty of victory, the guns, the ammunition, the never-to-be-forgotten lesson of a strategically inferior foe
acquiring tactical superiority to win not just a battle but a war.

On March 12th Giap sprinkled the airfield with his first practice
rounds of artillery. A Flying Boxcar, down with engine trouble,
went up in flames. The garrison stood by for battle. The day of
the 13th passed in relative calm. The Viet Minh gunners were
merely ranging in. General Navarre diverted his air forces to cover
the second phase of his coastal amphibious operation in Central
Vietnam. A few wounded took off in Dakotas for Hanoi.

For some minutes in the early evening chill the Viet Minh guns
were silent, for a minute or two, or perhaps for ten or twenty: no
one seemed to remember very clearly. Then all the guns fired. No
one who was under it had ever known such a barrage in Indo-
China before. These contemptible peasants in the hills, the hit-
and-run bandits, were pitted against the élite of the French Expeditionary Corps in a conventional set-piece battle, and before
morning there were few who couldn't pick the winner.

In Hanoi General Cogny privately told newspapermen that the
battle was a crime against humanity. As it dragged on toward its
inevitable and disastrous end, I asked him how he would describe
it now. "I called it a crime against humanity before. Now all I
can say is it is a continuing crime against humanity," he answered.

The French dugouts and bunkers had been built to withstand
harassing mortar and 75-millimeter mortars. They were of little use
without concrete. Bunkers collapsed under the weight of fire,

smothering troops in debris. Casualties from artillery fire were fearful. The French artillery commander committed suicide.

General Cogny wanted a diversionary attack into the Viet Minh main supply route or a breakout by the garrison before it was too late. Navarre did not agree.

Giap used his human-wave tactic in the first phase. For the second he switched to trench warfare. To bring the main eastern positions under attack, his forces dug their way from the hills across half a mile of open plain. It took them sixteen days to make the journey. They inched their way forward. All day and all night there was the sound of pick and shovel. Giap was not content merely with taking his men by trench to the outskirts of the French positions. He insisted that they should dig their way right across the plain, cutting off the main sector in the center from Isabelle in the south.

The French pressed Dakotas and Flying Boxcars into service as napalm carriers, and transport crews kicked out thousands of canisters of the stuff. But the dropping level was too high, and the French Air Force, up against concentrated antiaircraft fire for the first time in its history, failed to knock out the guns. Day by day, and yard by yard, the Viet Minh tightened their grip.

In desperation the French turned to the United States for help. Navarre believed that massive air intervention by the 7th Fleet and United States Air Force planes could still save Dien Bien Phu. Plans had been worked out between the Americans and the French General Staff for this sort of intervention. Admiral Radford favored it and so did John Foster Dulles. There was uncertainty elsewhere in Washington, however, and firm opposition from America's allies.

So the garrison fought alone. A relief column marching north through Laos was a relief column in name only. Night after night Dakotas passed over the dust bowl and dropped to pinpoint lights in the ever-decreasing circles of resistance by heroic paratroopers and volunteers whose first jump was into the barbed wire and minefields and death of Dien Bien Phu.

The French colonize, it has been said, with boulevards and brothels. If you added bars to these, you had Hanoi in the spring of 1954. One by one they emptied. You drank a toast with a man one night, and the next he was hanging by parachute on his way down to Dien Bien Phu. Men went in by battalions, when there were battalions to send, and then by dozens and half-dozens and ones and twos until the boulevards and the bars and the brothels were all empty and there was no one left to go. Many men fell in the enemy lines; many more were shot before their feet touched the earth.

The end came at 5:30 P.M. on the afternoon of May 7, 1954, fifty-five days after the first attack. The Viet Minh captured or killed 16,200 French Union troops, including a general, sixteen colonels, and 1,749 warrant officers and officers. The following morning the Indo-China phase of the Geneva Conference began. In all the history of diplomacy no "great military success" has ever been better timed to win a "great political victory."

CHAPTER 5

The
Last
Confucian

AGAINST THIS BACKGROUND of shattering defeat another expatriate leader emerged from retirement to take his place in the Vietnamese scene. "We must continue the search for the Kingdom of God and Justice," Ngo Dinh Diem once wrote to his family from the Maryknoll Seminary, then at Lakewood, New Jersey. "All else will come of itself." The letter did not surprise the Ngos, Vietnam's premier Catholic family. This deeply religious expression of faith was characteristic of brother Diem.

While his family were working by more direct methods to steer him into the presidency, Diem continued to live as a recluse, though never doubting that in the hour of need he would be wanted. When the call finally came, however, his legendary qualities of integrity and honesty were of less importance in deciding it than his availability. Since the French were scuttling the ship, they no longer cared who stood on the bridge as it went down.

The decision to invite Diem to take over the premiership of

South Vietnam was, in the first instance, that of Bao Dai. It was not, as some writers have suggested, the idea of the late John Foster Dulles. The State Department was much less enthusiastic about him than Justice William O. Douglas, who, in a book published a year or two earlier, had described him as "revered" by the Vietnamese people.

Influence was not necessary. Bao Dai's francophile friends and relations who had "parachuted" into Saigon from Paris to line their pockets while preserving the fiction of Vietnam's independence had discredited themselves. The alternatives were to reshuffle this shop-soiled pack, or to call on Diem. Despite the advice of his own friends, Bao Dai chose Diem. In fact, he really had little choice. As Diem admits candidly, there was no competition.

It was logical, however, only because Diem, and no one else, wanted the job. Twenty-one years before he had been a man of great stature in Vietnam. But twenty-one years was almost a working lifetime in this revolutionary period. The Viet Minh had taken over the running while Diem stood on the sidelines. His greatest hour had been his resignation from his post of Minister of the Interior (in effect, Chief Minister) in Annam in 1933 because the French would not agree to give the Vietnamese people a bigger say in the administration of their affairs. But public figures cannot rest on gestures, however noble. Diem now was no longer a public figure. Between 1933 and the outbreak of the Second World War he thought in revolutionary terms but never acted. Instead, he read and prayed, took photographs, became a daily communicant, and pruned roses. He had hopes of the Japanese but soon abandoned them, though they protected him in 1944 from the French, who were busy filling the jails with Vietnamese nationalists, and even invited him to become Prime Minister of an "independent" government under Bao Dai in 1945. A year or two earlier he might have accepted. Now he knew the Japanese had lost the war. At this stage he had no wish to identify himself with the "co-prosperity sphere."

In the immediate postwar struggle for power, Diem was still living in a monastery when the Viet Minh marched into Hanoi. By moving from place to place, he kept out of their clutches for some weeks, though they had issued orders for his arrest. His eldest brother, Ngo Dinh Khoi, who had been dismissed by the

French from his position as governor of Quang Ngai Province in 1942, was less fortunate. Not long before the end of the war, the Japanese, through Ngo Dinh Khoi, approached Bao Dai to get his approval of a plan to murder all the Viet Minh leaders they could capture. Bao Dai vacillated, and the Viet Minh got wind of the plan. They arrested Khoi and his son and buried them both alive.

Viet Minh troops then broke into Diem's sister's house. Living with her at the time was a twenty-one-year-old girl, Tran Le Xuan, daughter of Tran Van Chuong, who had taken office as Foreign Minister in the "independent" government set up by the Japanese, and is now ambassador in Washington. As the two women backed away from the soldiers with their machetes and guns, a wolfhound named Quito, which belonged to the girl's brother, snarled at the soldiers, who prepared to shoot it. The girl threw herself on the dog. "If you can shoot it, you can shoot me, too," the girl shouted. Diem's sister protested that the girl was out of her mind. But the girl continued to shout her defiance and eventually the Viet Minh, apparently not knowing what to do, went away. Today, the girl is better known as Madame Ngo Dinh Nhu.

Diem eluded the Viet Minh only briefly. A few weeks later they seized him in the town of Tuy Hoa, south of Hue, and moved him under custody to the highlands of North Vietnam, close to the Chinese border. Here he became seriously ill, and, according to his own account, would have died but for the assistance of local tribesmen.

In January, 1946, the Viet Minh took him to Hanoi and gave him medical treatment. Ho Chi Minh even invited him to join his government, but Diem accused Ho of having murdered his brother and nephew. Ho replied that he knew nothing of it. "Whether you know anything of it or not, you are still an accomplice and a criminal," Diem replied. Ho was not put off, and argued his case on patriotic grounds. Diem, whose conflict with the Communists dated from his days as chief of Binh Thuan Province in 1931, replied that he needed to be a full partner in the government and that no secrets should be kept from him. Since he wanted Diem as the country's leading lay Catholic, and not because of his administrative or political ability, Ho indicated by silence that he did not agree.

Diem believed that Ho intended to make further efforts to win

him over at this time. Since he could not be sure, however, Diem
took advantage of his *laissez-passer* and once again went into hiding, this time in a Hanoi monastery. Events justified this prudence.
The Viet Minh wrecked the house of his brother Nhu, and arrested Tran Van Chuong. This incident is still remembered with
some amusement by Diem and Nhu, who, in their occasional relaxed moments at the palace, have given impersonations of
Chuong's reaction when he heard the Viet Minh were coming
for him.

After his escape from the Viet Minh, Diem went south to
Vinh Long to live with his brother, Thuc, then a monsignor. He
disapproved of the Communists and he disapproved of the French.
"Dominion status," was his cry. Two newspapers, one in Hanoi
and the other in Saigon, supported him, but the French would
have none of this seditious talk. They closed the papers, arrested
the editors, and suppressed Diem's fledgling National Union
Front.

Invited to Hong Kong by Bao Dai to discuss the formation
under French sponsorship of a provisional central government in
opposition to the Viet Minh, Diem found the former emperor
more interested in Happy Valley dalliance than in dominion
status. Diem himself was not interested in accepting the leadership of what he regarded as a puppet government. Once again he
declined office, and went back this time to brother Can, his ailing
mother, and his prayers in Hue, never doubting that one day they
would be answered and that, though a thousand years had passed
since the Ngo dynasty had collapsed, he would be called to lead
his country into a new era of prosperity and enlightenment.

The Ngos are one of the great families of Vietnam. By tradition, by capacity, and through a Confucian sense of duty it was
proper for them to take their place among the mandarins at the
Imperial Court at Hue. This was the correct order of things. The
system called for it, and they were ready to respond.

With this ingrained sense of duty the Ngos for several centuries
had also accepted the added discipline, and cross, of Catholicism.
It was truly a cross, for at times Christianity was identified with
the French and the French with colonialism. Like many other
Catholic families, they often suffered bitterly for their faith. Less
than a century ago, during one period of violent anti-Christian
demonstrations, a hundred members of the family were burned to

death by a Buddhist mob in the Catholic church at Dai Phong, a lovely little village on the coast of Central Vietnam and the seat of the family tombs.

Among the few family survivors was Ngo Dinh Kha, who was studying for the priesthood at Penang, in Malaya. With the family all but destroyed, Kha broke off his studies and returned to Hue, where his knowledge of French helped him rapidly up the ladder in the mandarinate. Kha married twice. His first wife died childless. His second bore him nine children. Diem, the third, was born on January 3, 1901, in an atap cottage with an earthen floor, close by the Hue cathedral.

The Ngos were aristocratic but rich only in service, not materially. As father Kha rose in rank, however, he built a more imposing brick home next to the atap cottage. According to the custom of the mandarinate, the men lived in the new house, the women in the old.

Winter and summer the Angelus at 6:00 A.M. called the family to Mass. Kha in his black turban and embroidered mandarin robes led the boys in their long black smocks and white trousers. Often Diem went barefooted, but for church he had wooden clogs.

Catholicism and Confucianism went hand in hand in the Diem household. With its piety went a sense of duty and a sense of loyalty. Kha rose to be court chamberlain, with responsibilities including that of keeper of the imperial eunuchs.

One of Diem's early playmates was Duy Tan, who, at the age of ten, succeeded to the throne when the French exiled his father, Thanh Thai, to Réunion Island, near Madagascar. The emperor's eccentricities included the retention of too many concubines, the French complained. Alone among the court mandarins, father Kha stood by Thanh Thai, a decision that cost him his job and led the Ngo family to the paddy fields, where they raised buffalo and rice on a small plot and kept their dignity and their standing in the land.

The French found Duy Tan less to their liking than his father. When he was eighteen they accused him of conspiring against them. Duy Tan fled to the mountains and was later caught and exiled to Réunion.

Diem was now fifteen. He cared little for the physical work demanded of all the children in their father's paddy field. He preferred his prayers and his books. His elder brother, Thuc, was already studying for the priesthood. Diem decided to follow in his steps. It was his earliest and dearest ambition, but he quickly gave it up.

Always top of his class, Diem, having left the seminary, was now an obvious choice for the hand-picked class of potential administrators in the French school in Hanoi. He graduated at the top of his class in 1921 and began to work at Hue in the lowest ranks of the mandarinate. He was a tireless worker. Others of his age sought worldly pleasures in their leisure hours. Diem, who had made his own vows of chastity, thought only of his work. Promotion came rapidly. Within a year he was in charge of a district. With his conical straw hat tied under his chin and two coolies, one to pull and one to push his rickshaw, he worked day and night in the interests of his peasants.

Though time may have added its tints to the memories of those who knew him forty years ago, it is deserving of record that in their recollections of Diem they mention first his industry, integrity, and honesty and only then some of the character traits that have driven so many who have worked with him since to the point of distraction.

By the time he was twenty-eight, Diem had become a provincial chief indirectly involved in the bloody French massacre of Communists and non-Communist nationalists that occurred in 1930–1931. Even from these distasteful events, when the Foreign Legion raped and murdered and the innocent suffered along with the guilty, Diem escaped opprobrium, however. He ran an orderly province and a good intelligence system. He used the law and not oppression to maintain order. To the French, he was an exemplary civil servant: to the Vietnamese, he was a talented, infinitely hard-working young official who had done his job well without dirtying his hands.

His selection in 1933 as Minister of the Interior to the Emperor Bao Dai was almost automatic. Though he leaped over the heads of many more senior members of the mandarinate, Diem seemed the obvious choice. It was a choice, however, that the French soon regretted.

As a comparatively junior administrator, Diem had conscientiously obeyed, and executed, orders, though he had been deeply troubled by the injustices the rebels exploited. At first he thought the French were sincere when they talked of reform. With responsibility came the knowledge that they were not. Instead of enlarging the authority of the Imperial Court, the French were intent on reducing it.

Plagued by French agents within the Cabinet who faithfully reported back every critical comment that Diem made, and angered by what he considered the French lack of good faith when they refused to give any real authority to the partly nominated and partly elected Assembly, Diem resigned. For the next twenty-one years he did not fill any office, or even work for a living. Depending on the hospitality and subsidies of his brothers, he never lost sight in his mystical way of the leading role he was sure he was destined to play in Vietnamese affairs.

Reports that the Viet Minh had sentenced him to death (and refused protection by the French) caused Diem to leave Vietnam in 1950. After traveling in Japan, Italy, the Philippines, the United States, and Belgium, he went, in 1953, to France. As his official biography puts it, "He felt that the day was coming for him to look after his country's fate." On June 7, 1954, a month after the fall of Dien Bien Phu, his prayers were answered. Bao Dai entrusted him with all the powers that once had been shared between himself and the Prime Minister.

Few who saw Diem step from the plane at Saigon Airport on June 25, 1954, felt that a new St. Joan had come among them. He came slowly down the steps, paused to glance at the acres of barbed wire the French had rushed in to protect their aircraft from guerrilla raids, then shyly greeted some hundreds of friends and well-wishers who had assembled to meet him. The day was hot, heavy, and oppressive. The only touch of color in this otherwise dismal scene was provided by an old gentleman in a red bandana and a sky-blue tunic. The news from Tongking was bad: from Geneva it was worse.

"Tell me about Diem," I said to a Vietnamese friend, as the squat, strangely youthful looking figure who had stepped from the past, walked stiffly across the runway. My friend talked of Diem's early ambition to become a priest, of his subsequent and private pledge of celibacy, and of the hours he habitually spent in prayer each day. "He sounds too much like a priest to drag Vietnam out of this mess," I suggested.

"Not a priest," said the Vietnamese. "A priest at least learns of the world through the confessional. Diem is a monk living behind stone walls. He knows nothing."

Diem's early discovery that he had no calling for the priesthood did not mean that he felt he lacked religious fervor. On the contrary, Diem found the Church too pliant for his own unbending will. His brother Thuc, a gentle man, and spared much of the hostility that is directed at some other members of the President's family, thought Diem was too severe for the Church, too inflexible to perform the duties of a priest among his own people.

This dogged aspect of his character, his rejection of advice, reflects his Confucian, rather than his Catholic, background. He is always right. He is the father of the people. He knows what is good for the people. Only the father knows, for the people are his total concern. How, then, could he be wrong?

Later, when he had thrown out Bao Dai and assumed the office of President, Diem designed himself a standard. It consists of a square of yellow cloth, with a bamboo grove in the center. Under this are the words, "Tiet Truc Hu," which means "Integrity and Unselfishness," or, to quote the official biography, "the President was born a man of integrity and is not attached to worldly things."

"The fundamental fact about Vietnam, and which is not generally well understood, is that historically our political system has been based not on the concept of the management of the public affairs by the people or their respresentatives, but rather by an enlightened sovereign and an enlightened government," says the biography. "The system worked because the public offices were open to all, by way of competitive examination. The system also worked because there was a strict moral code. Although in the course of our history we now and then had a bad king, on the whole the government had a strong sense of public duty and responsibility to the people.

"The problem that confronts a man like President Ngo Dinh Diem, well grounded in traditional administrative principles, but also familiar with the Western political systems, is therefore one of giving Vietnam a solid moral basis on which to rebuild a strong, healthy democratic State," the biography continues. "To think of the form before the substance is certainly to run into failure. The main concern of President Ngo Dinh Diem is therefore to destroy the sources of demoralization, however powerful, before getting down to the problem of endowing Vietnam with a democratic apparatus in the Western sense of the word."

There is the Diem philosophy. Ambassadors may come and go and talk of the need for greater political liberties for non-Communists, but Diem will have none of it. "If we open the window not only sunlight but many bad things will fly in, also," says Madame Nhu, his policy-making sister-in-law. The window—and Diem's mind—remained firmly closed.

"You think you can have a meeting of the minds with Diem," a member of his family said once. "I tell you it is impossible. To a Westerner, Diem does not just come from another culture and another hemisphere. He comes from another planet."

Reared in the Confucian atmosphere of the mandarinate, Diem is dedicated and intense and has a prodigious capacity for hard work. Recalling his childhood, his brothers say that long before dawn his oil lamp would be burning in his room as he pored over his schoolbooks. Even then, he did not take kindly to correction, criticism, or advice. His father frequently beat him for insubordination. The boy vented his rage on his mother.

Today Diem goes to bed when he can no longer keep awake. Usually, he takes a pile of work with him, and if he wakes in the night he will open a folder and carry on where he left off. He works for sixteen hours to eighteen hours a day. He used to love shooting and photography and horseback riding, but has no time for such amusements now. His only relaxation, if it can be called that, comes from the periodic field trips he makes into the countryside. Ambassadors who accompany him return worn out. Diem goes on and on. Once he fell fifteen feet down the ladder of a Vietnamese naval craft. When aides and ambassadors rushed to his assistance, he brushed them aside and carried on with not so much as a limp.

Only a week after he arrived in Saigon in 1954, Diem received the shocking news that the French had abandoned 16,000 square miles of the Red River delta, including all the key garrison towns south of Hanoi and about two million of the seven to nine million people living nominally under French control. The French had no alternative. But while militarily few found fault with the evacuation, the manner in which it was executed, especially the failure to alert the civil population, earned them a new contempt among the civil population. At the Camp de Presse in Hanoi, French briefing officers who, only a month or so before, had contemptuously referred to the Viet Minh as *les jaunes*, as if their color meant cowardice, were now careful to speak of "L'Armée Popularie Vietnamien."

On-the-spot negotiations for a cease-fire began at Trung Gia, immediately beyond the northern French defense line on July 4, 1954. The Viet Minh had taken steps to insure that the French should not forget the realities of the military situation. Three jeeps and two weapons-carriers carried the painted sign "Souvenir of the victory of Dien Bien Phu—7.5.54." The walls of a teahouse adjoining the long bamboo-matting and corrugated-iron conference hut were decorated with French parachutes captured at Dien Bien Phu. Viet Minh soldiers snapped lighters taken from the defeated French forces. On the walls were typical Viet Minh slogans: "Long Live President Ho Chi Minh," "Long Live the Lao Dong Party," and "Long Live the Fight for National Independence and Democracy."

Precisely at 9:00 A.M. the two delegations entered the conference room and were introduced by liaison officers. General Van Tien Dung, for the Viet Minh, stretched out his hand to greet Colonel Marcel Lennuyeux, and there were cordial exchanges between members of both delegations. While peasants working in the paddy fields only yards from the conference room shouted at their buffalo, General Dung, speaking in Vietnamese, made the opening address. It was well spiced with propaganda references to "eight years of patriotic war" and the "enlightened leadership of President Ho." He promised that the High Command of the Popular Army of Vietnam would make every effort to bring about a rapid cease-fire and armistice, and the reestablishment of peace in Indo-China. When the general finished speaking, all members of the Viet Minh delegation rose to their feet and applauded. Colonel Lennuyeux thanked General Dung for his remarks and talked of studying a concrete plan about "how to remedy certain unhappy problems born of war."

The following day Diem announced his government. Sixteen days later the Indo-China war came to an end. "It is an anguished peace," said General Paul Ely, who had taken over from General Navarre after the battle for Dien Bien Phu. "It is finish, my friend, finish, finish, finish," said a chemist named Quang who had become chief secretary to Diem's Committee for the Defense of North Vietnam, when I told him the news.

From Geneva, Tran Van Do, the newly appointed Foreign Minister, cabled Diem: "We fought desperately against partition and for a neutral zone in the Catholic area of North Vietnam. Absolutely impossible to surmount the hostility of our enemies and perfidy of false friends. Unusual procedures paralyzed the action of our delegation. All arrangements were signed in privacy. We express deepest sorrow in this total failure of our mission. We respectfully submit our resignation."

Under instruction from Diem, the Vietnamese delegation did not sign the agreement, which divided Vietnam at the 17th parallel, leaving the North and the bulk of the population under Ho Chi Minh and the South to Diem. As an interim measure, the armed forces of both sides were to regroup and to go back to their respective areas north and south of the 17th parallel under the supervision of a Polish, Indian, and Canadian International Control Commission. After a year the two sides were to consult about elections, which, another year later, were to unify the country.

Diem brought with him to the prime ministership the conviction that the Communists could have been defeated if only the French had given Vietnam full independence, or at least dominion status. As he saw it, those who had accepted office under the French were therefore collaborators, who, though they might be anti-Communists, had forfeited the right to be considered as genuine nationalists, worthy of inclusion in his government.

By his standards, he could trust almost no one, because with few exceptions all persons of experience were tainted. Instead of working for the Vietnamese people, they had worked for the French, who had not only lost the war but had drained Vietnam of everything they could get out of it. Many doors that were not closed to him he deliberately closed himself.

Saigon was a sink, a cesspit of corruption and malfeasance. With official French connivance, a flood of piasters had poured out of Vietnam and into France at a fictitious rate of exchange. Any Frenchman with relatives at home could participate in this by sending 25,000 francs a month to France. Phony import-export dealers bought into the racket to remit their "profits." The Bank of Indo-China cut its capital holdings in Indo-China to bedrock but continued to pile up great profits, the bulk of which came from Vietnam.

Until the Geneva Agreement the presence of the French authority had given a semblance of order to the potentially anarchic situation in South Vietnam. By controlling the purse strings and by dispensing patronage, the French commanded a loose loyalty among the disparate warlords. Just as some of the Catholic groups in the North had maintained their own private armies and cared for things in their own way, the sects ran their own affairs, while paying lip service to French overlordship. The French were the essential linchpin, and, as Diem quickly found, he was not an acceptable substitute. South Vietnam began to fall to pieces.

The sects in those days were a colorful and divisive part of the scene. Often listed among them, but not at all concerned with things spiritual, were the Binh Xuyen, who for years had preyed on traffic operating on the Saigon River and had now bought the police concessions in Saigon for forty million piasters.

Swarthy, heavy-set and illiterate, Le Van Vien, or Bay Vien, as the Binh Xuyen leader was popularly known, collaborated with the Japanese during the Second World War, and his green-clad followers led the savage attacks against the French in Saigon in September, 1945. This began an alliance with the Viet Minh which lasted for two uneasy years. By refusing to assassinate Vietnamese intellectuals sentenced to death by the Viet Minh, however, Bay Vien earned a lingering affection in some parts of Saigon far removed from the slums of Cholon and the gambling houses and brothels which for so long filled his coffers: he also incurred the hostility of the Viet Minh.

Having served for a time as deputy commander of the Viet Minh forces in Cochin-China, Bay Vien broke with them in 1947, when the National United Front, a nationalist group operating out of Shanghai, sent one of their leaders to contact dissident anti-Communists in Vietnam with the object of forming an alliance that would help to overthrow both the French and the Viet Minh.

The Front's agent, a lawyer named Tran Van Tuyen, found his way to Le Van Vien's headquarters, deep in the jungle at Gocong, about thirty miles from Saigon, and, after a week's discussion with the rebel leader, got his agreement to join the United Front. The Viet Minh did not long remain in ignorance of this decision. In May, 1948, they invited Le Van Vien to their headquarters in the Plain of Rushes, for many years a secure Communist hideout of swampland seventy miles west of Saigon, for a meeting with guerrilla committees. Prudently he took with him a bodyguard of two hundred men. The meeting had just "installed" Le Van Vien as chief of Zone 7, one of the three Viet Minh areas of Cochin-China, when the Binh Xuyen learned that some of his bodyguard had been arrested. Bay Vien escaped with the rest of his men, threw in his lot with the French-sponsored government of Cochin-China, and later, when Bao Dai reappeared on the scene, became the first colonel in the Vietnamese national army.

His friendship with Bao Dai was a mutually satisfactory alliance. By 1954 Bay Vien had extended his control to include the Saigon and Cholon police, and the already considerable Binh Xuyen interests had rapidly expanded to include the city's vice. The Grande Monde, a huge gambling slum in Cholon, catered for anyone with two bits in his pocket and raked in millions which Bay Vien shared with Bao Dai. He acquired the Noveautés Catinat, the city's best department store, twenty houses, a hundred shops, a fleet of river boats, and installed sex on a barracks-square basis in Asia's biggest brothel, known because of the unusual and spectacular motif of the cubicles, as the Hall of Mirrors. A stone's throw from this headquarters, his opium factory catered for the dens his police force theoretically put out of business.

Bigger and much more powerful than the Binh Xuyen, but with their headquarters a comfortable sixty miles away from Saigon at Tay Ninh, were the Cao Dai who claimed a following of more than a million, and, even more importantly, controlled an army of some 25,000 men.

The sect's faith is a mixture of spiritualism, Buddhism, Taoism, Confucianism, and Christianity, especially Catholicism, whose hierarchy has been roughly copied in the sect's Holy See. It was founded in 1919 by a Vietnamese criminal investigator, Ngo Van Chieu, whose experiments with spiritualism and boredom with the lack of crime led him from an island off the coast of South Vietnam to Saigon. Here he influenced a group of friends, including Pham Cong Tac, the ruling pontiff in 1954, to join him in conducting seances. From these emerged Cao Dai, the Supreme Tower, or Supreme Being, which is represented by the sect's symbol, a huge, all-seeing eye. The Cao Dai enjoyed Japanese patronage and training during the Second World War. After a brief postwar flirtation with the Viet Minh, they threw in their lot with the French who maintained and supported their army.

The third significant group of warlords in the region were members of the Hoa Hao sect. The Hoa Hao, like the Cao Dai, tended to divide and subdivide: its leader with the most guns was a heavily moustached illiterate named General Tran Van Soai.

The sect was the most recent of all the groups. It was founded in 1939, when the mysteriously afflicted, long-haired son of a rich peasant living in a province near the Cambodian border was on his sickbed. Outside, a violent storm raged. Inside, the youth, Huynh Phu So, enjoyed what his devotees described as a sympathetic nervous excitement of typhoon intensity. When it subsided, he was pale and trembling but entirely cured of his malady. He went to the family altar, prostrated himself, and from that moment became a faith-healer and a religious leader of considerable renown. The sect he named after his home village.

He traveled widely through the Mekong delta, winning thousands of converts. He laid on hands and the sick arose cured. The French placed him in a mental hospital, where he converted his Vietnamese psychiatrist. Among his friends was Ngo Dinh Diem, to whom he gave shelter when he was hiding from the French.

Early in 1944, the Hoa Hao raised its own military force, its ranks swollen by the strongly anti-French converts won by Huynh Phu So among the peasants. The Japanese provided Huynh Phu So with protection against the French administration, and numerous Hoa Hao armed bands and home-guard units appeared southwest of Saigon. Among their leaders was Tran Van Soai. Discussions between the Viet Minh and the Hoa Hao, with the object of making common struggle against the French, failed to make any progress, and on September 8, 1945, the Viet Minh massacred hundreds of Hoa Hao followers in the town of Can Tho. Tran Van Soai replied vigorously, and the rice lands around Can Tho became the scene of fearful butchery. French intervention put an end to the repeated massacres, but it also had the effect of uniting the Hoa Hao and the Viet Minh in common cause. In June, 1946, under the command of Tran Van Soai, the Hoa Hao began organized operations against the French Expeditionary Corps.

Like the Viet Minh-Binh Xuyen alliance, this partnership did not endure. The Viet Minh, extremely suspicious of Huynh Phu So, arrested the prophet and executed him at the end of April, 1947. Tran Van Soai immediately rallied to the French, taking with him a force of two thousand armed men. He was accepted in the French Expeditionary Corps with the rank of general and entrusted with the "pacification" of his own areas. From that time, the Hoa Hao armies were on the French payroll.

Diem's status with the sects was not that of a national leader, but that of an irritating and, unless checked, potentially dangerous rival. Le Van Vien knew that moralist Diem was unlikely to be tempted to accept a share of the profits from the activities of the twelve hundred young ladies who offered their services at the Hall of Mirrors. General Soai and his followers and the Cao Dai also understood that the chance to dip their hands into the French cornucopia was rapidly coming to an end and that they would need to move fast to establish other claims.

Despite this growing restlessness among the sects, Diem was still under pressure to work with them. After his first short-lived Cabinet had collapsed, Diem reluctantly filled the gaps with four ministers from each of the Hoa Hao and Cao Dai sects. An American who knew the inside story perhaps better than anyone else, and who was known for his sympathy for Diem, wrote of this period: "From September Diem became so wholly dependent on American support he would have fallen in a day without it. Yet he wouldn't accept advice, wouldn't compromise. What he did was inspired by Americans, planned by Americans and carried out with close American guidance."

This did not mean that the Americans on the spot, or in Washington, were carried away by Diem's Messiah-like complex. Many thought he was next to hopeless. But when they looked at the alternatives they recoiled. Another Bao Dai experiment? Heaven forbid! Gangster, brothel-keeper, and illiterate Le Van Vien? Impossible. General Tran Van Soai, the illiterate, Hoa Hao leader? No. No. Pope Pham Cong Tac of the Cao Dai? Absurd. Diem it was and Diem it had to be.

But no one was happy about it. General Lawton Collins, who had taken over the United States Embassy, advised his abandonment at the earliest possible date. Vietnamese troops crossed sides and joined the Viet Minh, or deserted. The army under the leadership of General Nguyen Van Hinh, the chief of staff, was divided. Diem at this time could count on the loyalty of no more than two battalions.

Politically and physically the country was in wretched shape. Canals, roads, railways, telephone and telegraph services had been either destroyed or had fallen into disrepair. Road and railway bridges had been blown up. Some parts of the country had been in Viet Minh hands for nine years and were accessible now only by helicopter.

The government was government in name only. The Cao Dai controlled the country west of Saigon. The Hoa Hao were strong in the southern delta. The Binh Xuyen had Saigon. Elsewhere the Viet Minh had been in command. Diem had nothing with which to enforce his authority. With the French and the Vietnamese at daggers drawn, the civil service, such as it was, fell to bits. Vietnamese officials, even in the Sûreté, no longer even pretended to cooperate with the French. Once, for instance I was anxious to find a friend from Hanoi who had disappeared with the flood of refugees. I inquired through Nguyen Van Huong, who had been head of Sûreté in North Vietnam and now had a minor post in Saigon.

"The French have ordered his arrest," said Huong. "If I knew where he was I'd have to seize him." He hesitated for a moment, then added: "But if you go to this address in Cholon and say I sent you, I'm sure you'll be able to find him."

One of Diem's first positive acts had been to ask for American assistance in moving the refugees from the North. His appeal to Washington and to the Catholics of North Vietnam were equally successful. Suddenly a deluge of refugees descended on Saigon. Following the advice of their priests, hundreds of thousands of northern Catholics abandoned everything, their homes, their oxen, and their fields, and with no more than they could carry crowded aboard American and French ships at the port of Haiphong. The Viet Minh, who saw in this exodus a dangerous loss of face, attempted to stem the flood with legalistic bottlenecks and brutality. They succeeded only in making the Catholics more determined than ever to escape. The figures vary, but roughly eight hundred thousand refugees overflowed into the inadequate and hastily erected camps around Saigon. Inevitably, at first these became breeding grounds for disease and discontent, though the ultimate resettlement of these people must now be listed as one of Diem's major achievements, even if it did not necessarily endear him to the Southerners, who sometimes seem to regard the refugees as privileged "foreigners."

For the most competent and best organized administration, this period would have been immensely difficult. For Diem it was next to impossible. He appeared bemused by the magnitude of the problems that confronted him. His inaction played into the hands of those who wanted to portray him as just the leader of another sect. Only in prayer and in the guidance of his family did he find real strength. And even some of his brothers had their doubts. Monsignor Thuc, among others, advised him to abandon his seemingly hopeless task.

In the first hour of major decision Diem rejected the well meaning advice to resign. Instead he precipitated the first of a long series of crises by ordering General Hinh, his disloyal chief of staff, out of the country. This was Diem, the mandarin, using authority without power. Hinh was a boyish young man with the cheerful outlook on life characteristic of a French Air Force officer, which is what he had been. He had no real ambitions for political power, and was clearly confused about where he stood vis-à-vis Bao Dai if he did attempt a *coup d'état*. For a week or more, however, while the United States was making up its mind whether to throw its weight behind Diem, Hinh had his chance. Diem brought in a reinforced and loyal guard from Hue, but they would have been no match for Hinh's forces.

By the time this crisis had passed, Diem had got rid of Hinh but was almost completely isolated. Only his family and reluctant American support stood between him and disaster. Led by the Binh Xuyen, the sects were close to revolt. When it came to the point, however, there was no unity in the opposition camp, or perhaps the Cao Dai and the Hoa Hao leaders really did draw the line at serving under an illiterate brothel-keeper.

During this period the Viet Minh forces in the South had regrouped and, in part, gone North. Whereas in Tongking the Viet Minh were fully prepared and equipped with all the administrative apparatus and paraphernalia of control to take over the "liberated" areas, Diem had nothing. He had neither the time and means to organize any sort of clandestine arrangement in the North nor the capability to destroy the Viet Minh underground in the South. Everything was in favour of Ho: everything was against Diem. The Catholic groups which stayed behind in the North could have provided an ideal fifth column but only under vastly different circumstances. For in this situation Diem was in no position either to initiate or to deter, but only to survive.

Luck, the United States, and his own dogged courage were the principal factors in his survival. At times he seemed dazed but as unwilling as ever to accept guidance. Ambassadors tried to advise, and found themselves talked down. Britain's Commissioner-

General in South-East Asia, Malcolm Macdonald, who was pressing the claims of Dr. Pham Huy Quat, a member of the fascist
Dai Viet Party from North Vietnam, retired exhausted from a
session with Diem. "He's the worst prime minister I have ever
seen," he said.

The second major crisis of the Diem régime occurred early in
1955 when the French announced that they intended to discon-
tinue their subsidies to the Hoa Hao and Cao Dai sects. Le Van
Vien, smarting under the closing of his gambling concessions, was
once again their ready ally for a showdown with Diem. Even
before their alliance was formulated, however, their ranks were
split. Diem made his first real convert. General Trinh Minh The,
the non-American villain of Graham Greene's *The Quiet American*, had already rallied and with a generous bribe was persuaded
to stay loyal to Diem.

The three sect leaders demanded that Diem should form a
government of national union. There were many who believed he
ought to acquiesce. They insisted that unity was the one essential
at this time. Diem's view was that he had to demonstrate his
superiority over the sects or forever be subservient to them. He
made no attempt to treat with the sects' members of the Cabinet.
On the contrary, he was deliberately contemptuous of them while
openly maneuvering to win the support of their own dissident
groups. He used the promise of integration in the national army
as a political weapon, and with his eyes wide open provoked first
the sects' ultimatum and finally the fighting that broke out on
March 29th, and again a month later.

He also broke the efforts by the French and Bao Dai to dislodge
him. When the fighting was still going on, and the Binh Xuyen
forces, much to the surprise of many Vietnamese and others, were
falling rapidly, Diem received a cable from Bao Dai ordering him
to Cannes for consultations. He was instructed to take with him
his own appointee as chief of staff of the national army General
Le Van Ty, and to turn over the army to Bao Dai's man, General
Nguyen Van Vi, the operational commander. In Paris, the French
joined hands with Bao Dai against Diem, and the order to go to
Cannes was followed by a statement from Edgar Faure, the French
Prime Minister, that the Diem administration was no longer
equal to its task.

Diem replied by cable that it would be damaging to the nation's interest for him to leave Saigon at that time, and, despite the strongest French pressure, Randolph Kidder, then United States chargé d'affaires in the absence of General Collins, stood firmly behind him. Kidder split openly with General Ely, the French commander, who was trying both to arrange a cease-fire and to send Diem on his way to Cannes.

The situation for Diem nevertheless seemed hopeless. He was saved by his brother Ngo Dinh Nhu and his wife. Nhu, who is so much of an anti-Communist, and knows so much about Communist tactics that he often turns to the Communist method in his own political activities, rounded up an assembly of what he called the "democratic revolutionary forces of the nation." Antecedents for the moment were forgotten. Anyone who was against Bao Dai and against the French was welcome. In the absence of any constitutional authority, this brief-lived assembly under Nhu's guidance assumed the trappings of legal authority, appointed a Revolutionary Committee, which in turn asked the approval of the assembly for the measures Nhu felt Diem needed in his triangular struggles with Bao Dai, the French, and the sects.

Since two of the members of the Revolutionary Committee had been Viet Minh political commissars, it was scarcely surprising that Saigon for a moment wondered whether Ho Chi Minh was not about to take over before his time. Nhu had the matter firmly in hand, however. I called on him in the palace to ask about the more dubious members of the committee. Nhu said they were "dynamic and revolutionary," and blamed the French for spreading lies about them. "The trouble with all the embassies here is that they patronize only the administrations of the past and lack a clear picture of the present situation," he told me. "We are through with these political cadavers with their anachronistic ideas. The Americans ought to keep in view the principal objective, which is to fight the Communists."

Under the sparkling chandeliers of the Independence Palace, Diem and the two army leaders met to hear General Vi's demands that he should take over the army in compliance with Bao Dai's order. The Revolutionary Committee, heated and emotional after having tossed Bao Dai's picture out of the window of the Town Hall, waited in an anteroom while the talks went on. Vi emerged with a triumphant smile from the conference room only to be

seized by a member of the Revolutionary Committee, who pushed
a pistol into his stomach and said, "You're under arrest."

Vi turned back to the conference room, where Ty and Diem
were talking. The Revolutionary Committee pursued him. In
front of Diem they stripped Vi of his insignia, and one of the
committee members announced his intention of killing him. But
Diem, so the story went, protested that he did not want blood on
the Chinese carpet. Vi, under threat of death and his own coun-
terthreat of paratroop action against Diem if he was harmed, was
released after agreeing to denounce Bao Dai.

Next morning, safe from the committee's pistols, Vi made his
last bid for power. The French cleared the barricades for Bao Dai's
Imperial Guards, and Vi at a press conference announced that
his statement the previous evening had been made under duress
and that, in the name of Bao Dai and with the loyal support of 90
percent of the army, he had now assumed control of the government.

No sooner had he made the statement, however, than General
Ty rallied Colonel Duong Van Minh, the commander of the city
garrison, and Colonel Tran Van Don, generally regarded as South
Vietnam's best soldier, to his side. In the afternoon Vi fled to
Dalat and then to Paris. General Hinh, hastening from Cannes to
help consolidate the coup, stopped short at Phnom Penh, the
Cambodian capital.

Diem, riding now on the wave of victory, angrily called on
General Ely to take down the barricades, and the government
forces crossed the canals into Binh Xuyen territory and swept the
wounded Le Van Vien back into his swamp and jungle lairs.

A last stand by his gunboat and a company of troops killed
General Trinh Minh The. General Soai contributed a token force
of two hundred men as an expression of the sects' solidarity,
though they were not engaged, and His Holiness the Pope declined
the last rites to The's remains when the funeral cortege ended its
journey from Saigon's Town Hall to Tay Ninh.

Hundreds of acres of Cholon, Saigon's Chinese twin city, lay in
horrifying ruin. Many fires were lit by mortar shells, and, as the
Binh Xuyen fell back across the Arroyo Chinois, where Le Van
Vien had his headquarters, they set fire to the rows of densely
packed wooden houses clustering along the banks of the canal and
extending through half a mile of crowded side streets to the

Boulevard Gallieni. The whole area roared into flames. Refugees who had already fled once from the Viet Minh in Tongking and had resettled themselves here again lost everything they had saved. Saigon was tragic enough before, but now the streets were filled at night with new flocks of refugees sheltering under hotel and shop verandas. Excreta covered the square in front of the Hotel Continental, and the rank smell of filth drifted along rue Catinat.

Thousands of homes, shops, and cottage industries perished, and with them countless unknown civilians. A tentative estimate put the killed at five hundred and the wounded at a thousand. The figures may well have been many times higher. In Saigon scores of people with families in Cholon neither saw nor heard of them again. Hopes that they fled to the country when the fighting began ebbed with the passing days. In the cinders of Cholon there was much that was once flesh and blood. A colleague queried a group of digging ghouls about what they hoped to find. "Bodies —or money," they replied.

Binh Xuyen headquarters was in ruins. Le Van Vien had surrounded himself with a considerable menagerie. Crocodiles lived in the moat between his living quarters and his offices. A full-grown leopard on chain stood guard outside his bedroom door. A phython twined itself around the main supports, and a tigress occupied a nearby cage. All had died either from mortar or artillery fire. Adding an imaginative and macabre touch, Tran Van Kheim, Madame Nhu's brother, who was then acting as press officer to Diem, announced that human bones and bits of Vietnamese uniform had been found in the tigress's cage.

Diem pursued the dissident groups into the Mekong delta and west toward the Cambodian border, where General Hinh had now joined forces with General Vi and the Hoa Hao. Resistance here was short-lived. It lasted some months longer in the southern delta where a Hoa Hao leader named Ba Cut, whose quarrel with Diem was that he had been "too passive" about the Geneva Agreement, still held out. Cai Von on the Bassac River was Ba Cut's headquarters. Here he lived with his concubine, Cao Thai Nguyet. At the age of seventeen the young warlord cut off the top of one of his fingers to remind him always to fight the French. When the Geneva Agreement gave North Vietnam to the Viet Minh, he swore never to cut his hair until Vietnam was united. A year later Diem cut it for him with a guillotine.

Bao Dai lost his head in absentia. Guided and cajoled by his family, Diem was in hot pursuit of his enemies. On October 23, 1955, he asked the people of South Vietnam to decide between Bao Dai and himself. Though people went to the ballot boxes and voted, and in some electorates the votes cast greatly exceeded the number of names on the electoral roll, the referendum was not, and was not intended to be, an exercise in democratic procedures. Like the subsequent presidential election and elections for Diem's National Assembly, it was intended to be a collective demonstration of loyalty to the ruling authority. As such, it was a sweeping success. Diem proclaimed the Republic of Vietnam with himself as President. As he puts it, "The dream of my lifetime was fulfilled."

In a broadcast to the Vietnamese people on July 16, 1955, he had already rejected the idea of unifying elections with the Viet Minh. "We have not signed the Geneva Agreements," he said. "We are not bound in any way by those agreements signed against the will of the Vietnamese people. . . . We shall not miss any opportunity which would permit the unification of our homeland in freedom, but it is out of the question for us to consider any proposal from the Viet Minh if proof is not given us that they put the superior interests of the national community above those of Communism." The real test was about to begin.

Diem has been much criticized for his actions during this period. His critics, especially the British and the French, felt that the energy he spent on his battle with the Binh Xuyen would have been better devoted to winning their friendship and support in a genuine coalition of non-Communist forces. But, as Diem himself asked in May, 1955, when the Binh Xuyen had been driven from Saigon, "If in 1954 General de Gaulle had in front of him in liberated Paris an armed band similar to the Binh Xuyen, which maintained commandos with funds drawn from gambling leases and opium concessions and which would have resorted to the threat of civil war to preserve their feudal privileges, what policy would the general have adopted?"

Diem was right. The Binh Xuyen had to go.

6

The
Case
Of
Dr.
Dan

A TRAGEDY FOR South Vietnam, and for South-East Asia, is that the qualities which helped Diem to survive in 1954–1955 are also the qualities which threaten to bring about his own downfall, and that of Vietnam, also. He lacks, among other things, all capacity for compromise. Having defeated the sects, having rid himself of Bao Dai, he should have offered the olive branch. It was unnecessary, for instance, to send Ba Cut to the guillotine.

Diem and his family drove people into opposition. Bay Don, Ba Cut's former deputy, is still active with the maquis along the Cambodian border, where he and Muoi Tri, another Hoa Hao leader, have sworn not to rest until Ba Cut is avenged. The Paris exiles, including three former prime ministers under Bao Dai, are divided among themselves, but united against Diem. Saigon is filled with spurned and able men no less anxious than Diem himself to see that the country does not fall to the Communists. Diem will have none of them. He regards a few as "amateur politicians" and not to be trusted with responsible affairs of State, and the rest as traitors. For all of them, including the intellectuals, he has the greatest contempt. Many men who rallied to Diem drifted away from him over the years. With some few exceptions they continue to regard him as a good man and honest, but as a dogged, stubborn, and often ill-informed administrator whose refusal to delegate authority sometimes brings such governmental machinery as there is to a standstill. "One of our troubles is that we got self-government before we got government," is how one former member of the palace staff puts it. "There is no real government even now."

During the Bao Dai experiment the French continued to colonize down to the lowest levels of the administration. To obtain an exit visa, for instance, it was necessary to go first to the French Sûreté and then on to the Vietnamese. At the airport French doctors and customs officials handled arriving and departing passengers, though neighboring Singapore and Malaya, which theoretically were still far removed from self-government, had been accustomed to using locals in these jobs for years.

Diem inherited the wreckage caused by the war, the vacuum created by the precipitate withdrawal of the omnipresent French civil service and the hangover from the Confucian system that had worked well enough a century before but had been corrupted and destroyed by the alien influence of the French. What he has given Vietnam is a form of imperial and Confucian rule but without the checks and balances that went with the system. His Cabinet ministers are no more than heads of departments who meet in session only when half a dozen are called together to listen to one of his lectures. On almost every matter of significance the province chiefs bypass both the Cabinet and army. Their links and their loyalties are direct with Diem. Diem is not only the President but also the government.

The situation is aggravated by Diem's myopia. Too often he just does not know what is going on. He has never believed, for instance, that the riot directed against the International Control

Commission, which resulted in the wrecking of the Hotel Majestic in Saigon, in 1954, was not a spontaneous and popular public demonstration against foreigners suspected of being soft on the Communists, though the organizers themselves, including members of the family circle, made no secret of how it was instigated.

Diem is convinced that he has won the peasants to his side. When he goes on his field trips he expects to see prosperous-looking villages and cheerful peasants. He is not disappointed, even if banana palms have to be planted outside the cottages (only to wither the following day), and well drilled peasants are moved into the area to give the proper appearance of cheerfulness and fidelity.

Lacking effective means of administration, province and district chiefs often fall back on brutality to cover up their own deficiencies. After Viet Minh troops had returned to the North, the discovery of an arms dump in the vicinity of a hamlet was often the cause for widespread arrests on suspicion and also for widespread reprisals against peasants whose only crimes were ignorance and fear.

The introduction of repressive laws and ordinances did not strike Diem as likely to cause disaffection among the peasants, however. The laws were for evildoers: and he was unaware that they were used to hound the innocent and also to turn many of them more and more toward the Viet Cong, as the Viet Minh in South Vietnam were now called by the Diem administration: the name simply means Vietnamese Communists.

Summary Viet Cong justice for a village chief guilty of corruption or brutality did not offend the peasants. On the contrary, it tended to endow the Viet Cong with some of the characteristics of Robin Hood and his band of merry men. At the same time, the Communists succeeded in exaggerating the nature and extent of government repression. Law 10/59, for instance, which convened special military tribunals to try those accused of sabotage and of "infrigements of national security and attacks on the life or property of civilians," did not result in the widespread executions that the Communists claimed. During the first year that the law operated, the tribunals investigated 431 incidents and tried 25 cases involving 131 accused. Twenty-seven were sentenced to death, 50 to life imprisonment, or 20 years, 47 to 10 years, and 7 others were acquitted.

The most flagrant abuse occurred in Central Vietnam, where

"Uncle" Can, Diem's youngest brother, an eccentric, unmarried recluse who rules with an iron hand, brought order but also disrepute. Can has his own secret service and his own slush fund and operates quite independently, even to the point of sometimes arresting those in favor with Saigon.

The more he was pressed to liberalize and to broaden the base of government, however, the more Diem resisted. He felt that the Communists wanted to subvert democratic liberties to their own ends. He did not believe the villages were ready to run their own affairs, especially in southern areas which had been under direct French and/or Viet Minh control. Cochin-China as a colony lacked the sophistication in government that the Center had enjoyed as a protectorate under titular Imperial rule. People had to be educated for local self-government, he believed. "It is much easier to fill a villager's belly than it is to cram his head," he told me when I raised the question of local self-government. "The village elders had to cooperate willingly, or under duress, with the Viet Minh. We had to weed them out time and again to get rid of the fifth column. They were not ready to conduct their own affairs. How could they manage tax collections? That requires training, and few have had it. In a time of peace it could have been arranged: but we have been allowed no peace."

During 1960 Diem realized that the students' revolt in Korea, the army revolt in Turkey, and the anti-treaty demonstrations in Japan, which resulted in the cancellation of the Eisenhower visit, had all lowered the flash point in South Vietnam. He was outraged that the American press approved of events in Korea. "This was a treasure chest for the Communists," he says. "The United States press and the world press started saying that democracy was needed in the underdeveloped countries. This came just in time for the Communists. Some of the United States press even incited people to rebellion.

"That year was the worst we have ever had, worse than 1961 or 1962. We had problems on all fronts. On the one hand, we had to fight the Communists. On the other, we had to deal with the foreign press campaign to incite rebellion vis-à-vis Korea. These were sore anxieties, for some unbalanced people here thought it was time to act. Teachers in the private secondary schools began to incite the students to follow the example of the Korean students. And then there were our amateur politicians [former ministers known as the 'Caravelle Group,' who believed the time had come for reforms] who were outdated and thought only of taking revenge."

Through these anxious months of 1960, Diem withdrew himself deeper into the family circle, and further from the Vietnamese people. He had broken finally and irrevocably with the Saigon intellectuals during the 1959 elections for the National Assembly. On paper, the elections represented an overwhelming personal victory. Only one independent candidate and one opposition candidate won seats. In Diem's view, however, even this small intrusion of outsiders into the official family was not to be countenanced. As always, he did not regard the election as an example of democracy at work. Its intention, once again, was to demonstrate collective loyalty. The function of the Assembly was to be the voice of Diem, not a forum for divisive and contrary opinions.

In deference to the Western embassies and the Western press, the government allowed some independent candidates to contest the election in Saigon, while taking all precautions to ensure they did not win. They were subject to intimidation and prosecution for all sorts of fictitious offenses. A woman candidate was taken to court because someone had added a moustache to her billboard picture. Another was fined because several of his electoral poster pictures were found to have been outlined in red. Others were disqualified because they had posters that were too big or too small. In all, eight "unacceptable" candidates in the Saigon-Cholon area had their papers declared out of order.

This was all quite restrained compared with what went on in the provinces, where the provincial chiefs even threatened to arrest would-be opposition candidates and have them charged as Communists before military courts unless they withdrew their nomination papers.

The only successful opposition candidate was Dr. Phan Quang Dan. An immensely popular figure in the Saigon electorate, the doctor was detested by the administration. No one could accuse him of being a Communist. His record was that of a nationalist and an anti-Communist. Harvard-educated and widely regarded for years as one of the most sincere and able political figures in the country, Dan, like Diem, had many excellent qualities, the least of which was a capacity for leadership. Though eight thousand troops were placed in his electorate at the last moment with instruction to vote against him, Dan won easily.

Even so, Diem decided that Dr. Dan should not be allowed to take his seat in the Assembly. Despite fairly vigorous protests by the American and British embassies, Diem was adamant. He feared that Dan might command such a following in the Assembly that he would become a "demagogue" and thus hamper his own program. Detesting opposition, Diem was convinced that the country needed only unqualified acceptance of his administration.

On the morning that the new Assembly convened for the first time, Dr. Dan dressed in a white sharkskin suit. He locked the doors of the clinic and set out for the Assembly. He did not get very far. He was stopped by police outside the clinic and taken to the local station where embarrassed policemen, most of them his friends, had orders to detain him during the Assembly session.

I met him in the clinic half an hour after his release. He was understandably bitter, and tended to blame the United States as much as Diem himself. "The only message the Americans bring is anti-Communism," he said. "They criticize the Communists bitterly for the very things they countenance here. The North Vietnamese régime at least has the advantage of being true to itself. It does attempt to work for the poor masses. Here it is just the reverse. The sad result of this is that many South Vietnamese believe that the United States is just a bigger South Vietnam with more corruption, more nepotism, and bigger concentration camps. The Americans intervene when they want to. Why don't they intervene when moral issues are at stake? They accept military and economic responsibilities. They must also accept a moral responsibility."

If some of Dan's charges were more heated than valid, he had reason to be angry. He had been charged with violating electoral procedures by offering free medical treatment to patients. In his dilapidated clinic close to the Saigon market he ridiculed the charge. "If I were to offer free medical service," he said, "I would be swamped with patients. In this city, and in this country, we need a hundred times more doctors than we have now. You can understand the deluge I would get if the sick of Saigon thought that I offered free medical treatment. Sometimes it happens that if a person comes to you and is very sick and you treat him and he cannot pay, you forget about the money. That doesn't only happen in Vietnam but in every country of the world. But to have charged me with having solicited votes through my medical practice is abominable. It means that there is no justice in this country. If I can be treated in this way, how do you think the ordinary citizen manages?"

As time passed, Dan became more and more critical of the administration. At that time, he told me, his plan was to provide what he called a constructive opposition. A little more than a year later he joined at the last moment with the army rebels who had tried to seize power in Saigon by *coup d'état*. Dan identified himself with the revolt only when it was all but beaten and forces loyal to Diem were at that moment coming to his rescue. He was arrested and, but for the intervention of the Western embassies and those among Diem's own advisers who feared the adverse reaction that such action would have aroused, he would have been placed on trial and undoubtedly sentenced to death for his part in the revolt.

By Diem's reasoning it was easy to rationalize the attempted coup as the work of United States *agents provocateur*, especially the press, and to divorce it from the reality of discontent in South Vietnam. Lurking in his mind is the suspicion that the United States would have been pleased if the coup had succeeded. Many around him felt that American officials had been too willing to assume the success of the coup, and too ready to plead for the life of Dr. Dan when the coup was over.

Diem never learns by his errors. His assurances of reforms after the coup resulted in the addition of two senior posts to the Cabinet and the creation of an army command system. Instead of introducing what his critics might have regarded as reforms, however, Diem began to tighten up the system and to install only those of unquestioned loyalty to himself in positions of trust. He weeded out the provincial chiefs, replacing the civilians with hand-picked army officers. Of the three senior officers, Le Van Ty, Duong Van Minh, and Tran Van Don, who saved him at the time of the Binh Xuyen battle in 1955, only Le Van Ty, the chief of staff, and never a significant figure, remains close to Diem. He has his supporters from whom he receives devoted loyalty. Of the rest, including some of his best officers, he is suspicious and critical. General Tran Van Don, who now commands the First Corps in the vital Quang Ngai area, was detained for three weeks after the attempted coup in 1960. Don has an almost charismatic hold over his soldiers;

but he is now both feared and disliked by Diem. This is true also of General Le Van Kim, the field commander, the best educated of the South Vietnamese military leaders and a French citizen until 1956. Minh and Kim have big titles but no forces. Their appointments under American pressure were designed to put a roadblock between Diem and the military operations. It did not work. Neither general has any real authority. Diem still keeps the controls firmly in his own hands. Early in 1962 General Don launched a major military operation. It had just got under way when Diem, without offering an explanation, radioed him to stop. He stopped.

No matter is too big or too small for Diem's attention. Since 1954, when Phan Van Giao, a former governor of Central Vietnam, fled the country to escape charges of corruption, the granting of passports and exit visas to Vietnamese subjects has been a presidential prerogative, curiously used. Once, when the wife of one of the President's own aides had a "blue" baby, the United States Air Force was alerted to fly the woman and child to Clark Field in the Philippines where proper medical attention was available. Since his wife spoke no English, the husband requested permission to accompany her. This immediately aroused suspicions in the palace. It was assumed that the man was planning to stay away permanently. The passport was refused. The baby died . . . and the man still works for Diem.

Every morning an aide prepares a digest of world comment on the President for the President. Criticism from the French or the British, or from other Asians, does not excite much irritation. But every time the criticism is American Diem becomes hurt and angry. For days on end at such times he will refuse to meet Americans, including the ambassador. The result is a vicious circle in which the American Embassy in dealing with its own correspondents has become involved. Because Diem dislikes criticism so much, the embassy tries to prevent it by sometimes being considerably less than frank with American correspondents, who, in turn, when they manage, despite the difficulties, to arrive at the truth behind the régime's often far too rosy official reports, become even more critical, which makes Diem even angrier.

Two correspondents in particular repeatedly enraged the régime in 1962. They were Homer Bigart, of the *New York Times*, a

Pulitzer prize winner of immense industry, whose methods of reporting in the Second World War, in Greece, Korea, and Indo-China, were to go out and to see for himself. The other was François Sully, a French citizen working for *Newsweek*, and the most knowledgeable of all correspondents in the Indo-China scene.

Diem spoke furiously at this time of the "calumnies" of the American press. Though there was no official censorship, the Vietnamese papers printed nothing that would offend the régime. Diem and many officials felt that the Western press should also serve as vehicles for his propaganda.

Considering the dismal situation of South Vietnam, Western reporting generally was restrained. Television teams which came across examples of extreme brutality to prisoners refrained from shooting. On rare occasions when they described brutalities, correspondents eschewed the sensational and tried to put them in perspective. None of this was good enough for Diem. Bigart was saved from expulsion only by the intervention of the embassy and his own voluntary departure. Sully was expelled despite embassy intervention on his behalf. The rest were warned that they might expect similar treatment if they, too, were guilty of writing critically.

The palace is filled with functionaries ready to carry Diem good news but singularly reluctant ever to pass on the bad. Diem talks but never listens; he looks but never sees. Any ambassador who can get in five hundred words in a four-hour conversation with him feels that he is just about hitting par for the course.

Diem talks monotonously and repetitively, rambling from one subject to another and never talking a problem through. He cannot be questioned. He smokes incessantly while he talks, grinding out a half-finished cigarette and immediately lighting another. Palace servants tiptoe quietly into the room to replace the empty package or to bring a new pot of tea. Occasionally he flashes with anger, but never does he spark with humor. Twin threads of thought provide the only continuity. One is the assumption that he is right and knows best; the other that he is the victim of lies and calumnies. Diem and the State are clearly one and the same thing in his mind. He can talk with certainty about a coming Viet Cong offensive in Central Vietnam, yet it is clear that he is less worried about this than the deep personal outrage he suffered during the attempted coup in November, 1960.

He is not helped in his public relations by his family, and notably by Ngo Dinh Nhu and his wife, who have grown bitterly anti-American. Nhu, who is nine years younger than Diem, was educated in France. Before 1945 he had settled into an academic life as chief of the archives and libraries of Vietnam at Hue. Inevitably, however, he got caught up with the revolution. Two of his closest friends from his Paris days elected to go with the Viet Minh, a blow that Nhu took personally and bitterly. He lacks the intense Catholic approach of Diem, but is, and always has been, bitterly anti-Communist. He first came into prominence in 1952 when he organized a Catholic trade-union movement, which had as at least one of its objectives the furtherance of Diem's political ambitions. He is clever, but rash and impulsive.

His wife is extremely good-looking, animated, intelligent, impulsive, vain, and also anti-American. Joe Alsop once called her a tigress, and it is an apt description.

The Nhu's anti-Americanism began in the early days of the Diem régime when they were both involved in the desperate struggle to keep him in the palace at almost any cost. Like Diem, they bitterly resented press criticism of the régime early in 1960 and were ready to charge the Americans with culpability in the November coup.

After the second attempted coup in February, 1962, when two air-force pilots attacked the palace, they became sure that there were some Americans in Saigon who would stop at nothing to get them out of the way. This attack, which was carried out under heavy cloud cover, was a brilliant piece of bombing by excellent pilots. They chose the left wing of the palace, where the Nhus were known to have their quarters, marked it out with napalm, and then came in with five-hundred-pound bombs. The first bomb failed to go off, and the family escaped to long-prepared shelters below. Madame Nhu, who fell down two flights of stairs, damaged her leg, and suffered severe burns, was the only family casualty. But for the failure of the first bomb, however, the likelihood is that all would have been killed.

One pilot got away to Cambodia; the other was shot down and

captured. Though apparently he was hazy about everything, he said under torture that he believed some Americans were behind the attempt to get rid of the Nhus. They have not been in the mood since to be impressed with the argument that a man under torture, in the hope of escaping from pain, will admit to anything his captors want to hear.

In principle, Nhu's influence with the President has been greatly reduced in recent times. His personal contacts with Diem are less close than they used to be. Nevertheless, he remains the brains and dynamic force in the palace, though much of his advice is now channeled through Dr. Tran Kim Tuyen, a former priest and doctor of medicine, who runs Diem's secret service.

A tiny, inoffensive-looking man, Tuyen put a brake on Diem after the 1960 coup. He counseled against widespread reprisals. In Saigon, if not beyond, his intelligence service is regarded as extremely effective, though its energies are directed more toward the preservation of the régime from its non-Communist enemies than they are to the elimination of the Viet Cong. One of the weaknesses is that it is not coordinated with the central intelligence organization under Colonel Nguyen Van Y, or with the separate provincial services and with the agency under "Uncle" Can's direction, which also is believed to operate in Saigon. Its links, principally, are with Nhu's secret Can Lao Party, which has become the eyes and ears of the family in the government, in the army, and in the provinces.

Thuc, the archbishop, is jolly, relaxed, and the ablest and eldest of the brothers. Luyen, the ambassador to Britain, is friendly, humorous, and liberal: he would like to see a broader and more representative régime. Can is bloody but runs a tight ship, though he often acts independently and sometimes in a way that seems least likely to further Diem's interests. Diem was saved in the 1960 coup by the hesitancy of the paratroops and the loyalty of a divisional commander whom Diem regarded as an adopted son. Later, for reasons that were beyond a guess, Can seized the divisional commander's brother and for six months held him captive.

And so the lists of those opposed to Diem grow longer. Even Nhu is known to regard himself as a likely future President. Senior generals move under constant surveillance. The air force and the paratroops are especially suspect. Everywhere there is discontent and frustration. The Catholics were once solidly for Diem: now they are split. Diem draws heavily on what he regards as the more experienced and more loyal Vietnamese from Central Vietnam and those who fled from the Communists and clearly have a vested interest in keeping the Communists out of control in the South. This means that to many peasants their provincial chiefs are quasi-foreigners. When speaking to them they even have difficulty in understanding their accents. The middle ranks of the army are discontented. Confucius ranked soldiers with beggars in the social order, and in this Confucian-inspired administration the soldier is still regarded with a good deal of contempt. The chicken and pig stealing, the raping and looting, that went on in earlier years have been cut down, if not entirely eliminated, but there is no close rapport between the people and the troops. Cabinet ministers sneer at generals as French sergeants and corporals who have risen above themselves. Once, when a highly influential young man was lamenting that he was not permitted to play a more active role against the Viet Cong, I suggested that he might ask for the command of a battalion. He recoiled in horror. I said it had been good enough for Winston Churchill when he left the Cabinet in the First World War and that this seemed to establish a reasonable enough precedent. "You can't compare the British army with the Vietnamese army," was his reply.

As an example of the problems to be contended with, a senior Vietnamese official told me about an army officer of ten years' service who was given his first home leave of fifteen days. The officer went back to his native village, fell in with the Viet Cong and returned to his unit, where he acted as a Communist agent.

The officer was prudent and did not give himself away. From captured documents, however, the army discovered what he was doing. After his arrest, the officer agreed to tell all. He began to make his confession on the third floor of an army building. The atmosphere was relaxed; but when he saw his chance, the officer ran to a window and threw himself to his death on the street below.

"Now, he knew that if he really told us everything he would have got no more than a few months' imprisonment," said my informant. "There was no chance or possibility that he would be executed. How, then, could the Viet Cong have so indoctrinated him in fifteen days that he would kill himself rather than talk?"

He answered the question himself. "Of course, they couldn't. No man could change so quickly. The point is, he didn't change. He had become so bitter during all the years without leave that he was more than ready to join the Viet Cong when he went back to his village and met them there."

Then he added a question that no one could answer, "How many more share this man's feelings?"

Yet there is no unity in the non-Communist opposition and no single group, or combination of groups, that appears as an obvious alternative. "The Americans can teach us to shoot guns but they cannot teach us to love our country," said a cynical intellectual. "This régime is too old to make friends now: it has only accomplices," said another. Among some Catholics there is a feeling that the coup, if there is to be one, must come from within the Church; otherwise there will be a dangerous and bloody witch hunt in which the Catholics will be massacred.

Perhaps the healthiest sign is that there is criticism and a quest for solutions. The worst society of all is that in which man talks only to praise his government. In Saigon the criticism goes on all the time. The Movement for National Unification, for instance, had no known links with North Vietnam, but its manifesto, which was distributed in Vietnamese, French, and English at a crowded public meeting in a Saigon hall in July, 1961, openly appealed for a neutralist solution. It was Utopian and dangerous to rely on one group of imperialists to oust another, the manifesto said. In one world of cold war, the choice of a friend implied that of a foe. The proper solution, therefore, was to throw out all foreign advisers and to unite with neighbors to form a "warless" area in South-East Asia.

Fear that this type of thinking could gravely undermine the régime led to the Diem-sponsored National Assembly decision in May, 1962, to prohibit unauthorized public meetings. Between this legislation and Madame Nhu's morality laws, which were passed a month later, even weddings and funerals now require official sanction: and dancing, both public and private, is forbidden along with beauty contests, cockfighting, and wrestling.

Extra police prowl the bars and the rue Catinat to enforce the dancing ban. Madame Nhu has a point when she says that this is a time for austerity: but it is also a time when the régime, needing popular support, goes out of its way to alienate people.

Every now and then the dragnet goes out, and a few more political opponents go off to jail. The number of Viet Cong suspects held is about twenty thousand. Genuine liberals arrested not because they are Communists but because Diem, and his brothers fear them probably total no more than three hundred, however. In August, 1962, a sweep picked up Dr. Ho Van Nhut, a doctor of medicine, and leader of the "Caravelle Group" of former ministers who, in 1960, petitioned Diem to introduce reforms. Since he had not served under Diem, Nhut did not sign the petition, which probably saved him from earlier arrest. Tran Van Ly, a Catholic leader from Hue who had fallen out with brother Can; Nguyen Van Tieu, the leader of the small Duy Dan cadre party, which used to specialize in assassination; and General Nguyen Thanh Phuong, who ironically, had played a key role in the formation of Nhu's Revolutionary Committee in the days of the Binh Xuyen trouble, were among those arrested. Phuong and Nhut no doubt had notes to exchange. Nhut was the Binh Xuyen's choice for Prime Minister in 1955, Phuong one of the principals who kept him out and Diem in. Another doctor of medicine picked up at the same time was Nguyen Xuan Chu, a leading member of the Vietnamese Kuomintang Party, which tried to overthrow the French in 1930, and paid for its failure by losing its twelve leaders on the guillotine.

Though most of these men and others like them are well known, none represented a serious threat to the régime. All were articulate critics, however. And this is a point that should be noted about South Vietnam. The newspapers are restrained by threat, but private citizens often speak out openly and critically. The secret police keep careful watch over suspect military officers but they do not restrain their tongues. Even with foreigners there is often free and frank discussion. During the summer of 1962, for instance, a group of military leaders gave a dinner for a visiting Westerner. Instead of the usual platitudinous conversation the dinner became a table-thumping criticism of the lack of fundamental liberties in the strategic hamlets. "We can put ten thousand miles of barbed wire round the hamlets and arm half a million Self-Defense Corps," said one general. "But until we stop these arbitrary arrests and give a better deal to the peasants we are never going to win this war."

The visitor went home agreeably surprised. "If this is a police state," he said, "it's the most curious one I have ever heard of." By comparison with North Vietnam, of course, it is nothing like a police state.

CHAPTER 7

The
Aid
That
Failed

N0 ANALYSIS OF the early years of the Diem régime can ignore the major role of the United States. United States aid kept Diem in power and manned the barricades against his adversaries. It reconstructed roads and railways, put goods in the shop windows, caused modest improvements in agriculture, and some even more modest industrial development.

It was not enough, however, that Diem and South Vietnam survived, or that the best part of a million northern refugees had been resettled with considerable success: South Vietnam had to be held up as a model, a shining star in the free world's firmament.

By the summer of 1959 official American optimism about the situation had become unlimited and unrestrained. Experts wrote books and magazine articles which referred to the "miracle" of South Vietnam. American military advisers and diplomats threw caution out of the window. The Communist threat had been reduced to the past tense, something that could be looked back on, a nightmare now only half remembered. "The Viet Minh guerrillas though constantly reinforced by men and weapons from outside South Vietnam were gradually nibbled away until they ceased to be a major menace to the government," said Major General Samuel L. Myers, who had just completed his tour of duty as deputy chief of the American Military Assistance Advisory Group in Saigon. "In fact," he said, "estimates at the time of my departure indicated that there was a very limited number of hostile individuals under arms in the country. Two territorial regiments reinforced occasionally by one or two army regiments were able to cope with their depredations."

From the general's further statements it seems that if the Viet Minh were unwise enough to start anything they would quickly get a bloody nose, or worse. The situation was so satisfactory, he believed, that the army was now able to maintain internal security and had reached the point where that responsibility could be turned over to the civilian agencies. The general mentioned many Vietnamese who were even more optimistic than his own statement had implied, and felt they had the capability of counterattack, or of even carrying the war to North Vietnam.

Mr. Elbridge Durbrow, the American ambassador in South Vietnam, concurred. He told a Senate subcommittee inquiring into allegations about the misuse of American aid funds that because the internal security situation had improved so much he had recommended a reduction in grants of military aid. At the same hearings, Mr. Arthur Z. Gardiner, head of the United States Operations Mission in Vietnam, described the commodity imports program under which the greater part of American aid was channeled to Vietnam as being the "greatest invention since the wheel."

History was not quite repeating itself, but there was at least a touch of irony in the situation. Senator Mike Mansfield was in the chair, and his questions led to Mr. Durbrow's optimistic expressions. Seven years earlier, when the French forces in Indo-China were on the point of final defeat, Senator Mansfield had led a Senate study mission to Vietnam. His findings: "The military prospects of the non-Communist forces in Indo-China are improving." Senator Mansfield based his conclusions on the expansion of the national forces in Cambodia, Laos, and Vietnam, increased American aid and General Henri Navarre's "psychology of the offensive."

Everyone is likely to make an error in judgment. In the case of Ambassador Durbrow, Senator Mansfield, and General Myers, however, it was not a matter of judgment but of knowledge and understanding of the tactics and techniques of the enemy and of the fundamental weaknesses of the anti-Communist position. Nothing was more certain in October, 1953, that the French were desperately close to the point of defeat, while in 1959 the Vietnamese were still pleading urgently, and unsuccessfully, for the type of aid that might enable them to hold the countryside against the military activation of the Communists' political bases. General Myers had his eye on the 350,000 Viet Minh army. He couldn't see the trees in the South for the woods in the North.

General Minh insisted that both the Communist armies in the North and their cadres in the South were a danger, that to ignore one while concentrating on the other was the way to disaster. Even after Diem himself was convinced, these arguments were overruled by the Pentagon. Diem lists Admiral Radford, who, he says, was preoccupied with nuclear war; Ambassador Durbrow, and the State University of Michigan mission to Vietnam as the principal opponents of plans for countering subversion in the rural areas. Though the security forces were constantly uncovering supplies of guns and ammunition cached by the withdrawing Viet Minh, this seemed inconclusive evidence to many Americans that the Communists' chosen weapon against South Vietnam would be rural revolt.

Diem argued that the Maoist formula remained constant and that the military bases were being prepared under their very eyes. "In China, during the Indo-China war and now here," he said, "the Communists have always sheltered in open base areas of difficult access, in areas where there are no roads. They make their headquarters in the jungle. Cautiously, sometimes only one man at a time, they move into a village and establish a contact, then a cell until the village is theirs to command. Having got one village, they move to a second village and from a second to a third, until eventually they need not live in any of these villages but merely visit them periodically. When this stage is reached they are in a position to build training camps and even to start crude factories and produce homemade guns, grenades, mines, and booby traps.

"This is all part of the first phase. The second phase is to expand control and to link up with Communist groups in other bases. To begin with, they start acts of violence through their underground organizations. They kill village chiefs, headmen, and others working for the government and, by so doing, terrorize the population, not necessarily by acts of violence against the people but by demonstrating that there is no security for them in accepting leadership from those acknowledging the leadership of the government. Even with much smaller numbers of troops than the constituted authority, it is not difficult now for the Communists to seize the initiative. A government has responsibility for maintaining supply to the civil population, of keeping roads, railways, rivers and canals open for traffic, of ensuring that rural crops reach the markets and that in turn commodity goods are distributed through the country. The Communists have no such responsibility. They have no roads and bridges to guard, and no goods to distribute."

As a first step toward meeting the Communists in the remote areas, Diem accepted his own army's advice, and, at the end of 1955, created the Self-Defense Corps. By this time he had ousted Bao Dai, proclaimed the Republic of Vietnam, defeated the dissident sects, and restored some semblance of order to the countryside. During the year that had passed since the Geneva Agreement and his accession to power, Britain and France both worked on him to concede that he would at least honor the agreement to "discuss" elections with Ho Chi Minh. Diem, who knew that to discuss was also to compromise, and that to compromise in this situation was to fall, declined.

The withdrawing French Expeditionary Corps in 1956 took with it all worthwhile equipment, but left many old-fashioned long-barreled rifles. Ammunition was scarce and some of the guns were sixty years old. These were handed out to the newly formed Self-Defense Corps units on whom the burden of village defense fell now that the Vietnamese "light" battalions, which the French had created at the end of the war and had scattered on a provincial basis around the countryside, were being withdrawn for retrenchment, reequipment, retraining, and regrouping as a conventional military force, complete with hundreds of jeeps and trucks and the accoutrement of a modern, Western-style army, 150,000 men strong.

At the end of the Indo-China War the Vietnamese army had a

theoretical strength of 225,000 men. With the suppletives who manned the small posts, altogether 400,000 were under arms. Many of the recruits were taken by press-gang methods. Troops would block off a street in a town or village and capture all eligible-looking young men of military age in nets and cart them off like wild animals to recruiting depots. In Tongking alone desertions averaged about three hundred a day for some months before the end. It passed the six hundred mark after Dien Bien Phu. Scores of posts fell to the Viet Minh without fighting, or because Vietnamese troops inside the posts opened the gates and laid down their arms.

Long before Dien Bien Phu a Vietnamese officer of field rank was boasting quite openly in Hanoi that he was working on plans for the integration, under Vo Nguyen Giap, of the two Vietnamese armies. I met him for the last time just before the 1954 Geneva Agreement in the house of the Indian consular agent. He made no secret of his intention of going with the Viet Minh. There was an obvious need for the pruning knife, therefore, quite apart from the ability of the Vietnamese economy, even with large quantities of American aid, to support such an army.

Throughout this period, Diem, who had at last grasped the lesson himself, struggled to persuade the State Department and the Pentagon that Mao Tse-tung had laid down his rigid rules for instigating a peasant revolt and that in South Vietnam all the indications were that the first phase was soon to be followed by a more violent second.

Americans and other Westerners in Vietnam today tend to pin most of the responsibility on Lieutenant General Samuel T. ("Hanging Sam") Williams, and his successor, Lieutenant General Lionel C. McGarr, for the state and type of Vietnamese army that the United States produced between 1955 and 1960. For obvious reasons it is undesirable to use names. But here is what three senior officials, including two Americans and one from a friendly ally, had to say in Saigon in the summer of 1962.

An American, one of the earliest and most astute observers of Maoist war in Indo-China, said: " 'Hanging Sam' was a great conventional instructor, but he didn't know the first thing about Communist guerrilla war. The French officer handling the intelligence organization embracing all the montagnard tribes in the High Plateau and the Annamite Chain offered to turn it all over to Williams. He was not interested. He didn't even look through the files. When things got tough on the High Plateau, we didn't even know where to begin. We had to start all over again, right from the beginning. Like most Americans who came here after 1954, Williams was contemptuous of the French. You just couldn't convince some of these people that there had ever been any fighting here. 'Hanging Sam' saw the threat as purely conventional, and coming only from the Viet Minh divisions in the North. So he proceeded to equip and organize the Vietnamese army accordingly, cutting it down from its inflated size as a loose and disorganized collection of battalions and putting it together in seven divisions. He taught it everything but the will to fight and how to fight against the threat as it developed."

The second American apportioned a share of the blame, if that is the right word, to General McGarr. "He understood conventional war very well," he said, "but didn't know anything about Communist war by seepage and didn't see it as part of his business to know."

The non-American blamed Williams. "'Hanging Sam' didn't want to know about guerrillas and therefore wasn't told," he said. "He was an extremely forceful and opinionated man and a good disciplinarian, perhaps a bit too much of a disciplinarian and bit too opinionated, since his staff tended to tell him what he wanted to know. He concentrated on creating a typical conventional-type army based on the Korean experience and intended to protect the nation's frontiers. Nowhere in the French colonial system had the Civil Guard distinguished itself. Williams was well aware of this. He dismissed it somewhat contemptuously as not even a paramilitary force, since it came under Interior and not Defense and therefore got no American aid and no training."

Diem defends General Williams, who, he says, was overruled by the Pentagon. He is also inclined to claim a good deal of omniscience and generally to blame higher Washington authority than the MAAG group. He is not wholly justified in turning all criticism from himself. From the earliest days senior Vietnamese officers, including General Minh, argued for the creation of an effective grass-roots security organization in the countryside. They *knew* how the war had been fought and lost. Diem at first had no idea. While the Viet Minh tactics were changing from attrition to annihilation, Diem was abroad. He returned with the opinion that aircraft and naval craft were the essentials and that even infantry were no longer necessary. Later he developed an attachment to artillery, which he has not yet abandoned. By the time he came round to accepting the advice of his own generals, the United States had embarked on its major plans for major reorganization, and the paramilitary forces, which Diem had created in a half-hearted way, were withering on the vine.

When he got the message, however, he pressed it vigorously and repetitively. To visitors who came to discuss specific projects with him, Diem propounded his theory of the Communist tactics. Knowing that they might be in for anything from a four-hour to a nine-hour session, ambassadors learned to ask for appointments in the morning so that they could plead the excuse of lunch to hasten away. Among military men there were built-in prejudices against accepting the principle that conventionally trained, well equipped Western-type armies could not cope with often extremely badly equipped Asian irregulars. Most were fairly vague about the Indo-China war. Many had the idea that the French had not really seen much fighting, or that they were sold out by the politicians in Paris. Even when they came round to accepting the idea that there was much to be learned from Mao's mobile war, they sometimes tended to overlook the social and economic ingredients that were essential to its success.

An even more important point, but one which received little attention in Saigon or Washington, was whether South Vietnam needed anything remotely resembling a Western-type conventional army. With the South-East Asian Treaty Organization now casting Mr. Dulles's "mantle of protection" over South Vietnam, the burden of defense against overt aggression from the North did not rest solely on the Arvins. It was wholly impracticable militarily, and highly damaging economically, to attempt to build an army large enough to act as major deterrent to aggression. Moreover, it was not necessary. Here and elsewhere in East Asia the only truly significant deterrent was the nuclear capability of the United States 7th Fleet. What was needed in South Vietnam was a small, mobile élite force, capable of sustaining itself, if need be, for long periods in the jungle while paramilitary forces looked after the Communists' subversive operations.

Diem, when he began to learn something of the Viet Minh tactics, wanted to build roads into the mountains and to dig canals into the swamps, and to make the Civil Guard a mobile paramilitary force. On all counts he ran into Washington's opposition. "On the U.S. side at that time they said my road- and canal-building program in the remote areas was not spectacular enough," he told me. "The Embassy and USOM told us it would be better to build roads to the cities where people could see them. I said, 'If you don't have roads in remote areas how can you protect the population. And if you can't protect the population they will surely be lost to the Communists.'"

According to Diem, Ambassador Durbrow and the Michigan State University group, which had been commissioned to train the Civil Guard as a conventional police force, reported unfavorably on the Self-Defense Corps. They said that since the villages had been under the control of the Communists for years, the village guard would certainly be infiltrated by the Communists and therefore untrustworthy, and that military aid given to the Self-Defense Corps would eventually be used against the government.

There were heated differences over the role of the Civil Guard. Diem was contemptuous of the police-type training given by the Michigan State University. "When I complained that we lacked security, I would be told that there was security enough," he said. "When I said the North had started a war against us, I was accused of being obsessed with the security problem. Durbrow told me I should lay more stress on the economic side. But I did much for the economic side and for education and civic education in the villages. You can build factories and mills, but if you don't have security you just build for the Communists."

In 1957, having run into what he considered the blank wall of Ambassador Durbrow's opposition, Diem paid a State visit to the United States. He had three requests to make. He wanted bulldozers to build access roads. He wanted to increase the size of the army by 20,000 men, and he wanted military training and assistance for the Civil Guard. The answer on all points was, "No."

Thus, in the critical period between the end of 1955, when General Williams arrived to train the South Vietnamese Army on the South Korean model, and the beginning of the Viet Cong war, late in 1959, there was a security vacuum in the countryside of South Vietnam. The Civil Guard and the Self-Defense Corps were untrained, incompetent, and lived on a shoestring. When they were wounded or sick they got no treatment from army doctors, and, of course, they had none of their own, nor were they admitted to army hospitals.

With an extra 20,000 men in the army Diem believed that he would have had enough competent and trained troops to replace part of the Self-Defense Corps and the Civil Guard for paramilitary training. Wretchedly equipped and shamefully treated, both groups, under the circumstances, performed remarkably well when the weight of the Viet Cong attack began to fall on them. But they did not—and could not—perform well enough.

Even the shattering reverses in Laos in 1959 failed to alert the West to the dangers that were building up in South Vietnam. All was optimism and sweetness and light. After visiting Laos, Thailand, Cambodia, and South Vietnam at this time, and having contrasted the curious Western complacency with the grave anxieties of local officials, I set out some of my own fears in an article for *The New Republic,* in which I queried whether the policies being pursued in South-East Asia were adequate to meet the Communist threat as it was developing. The article was published on December 12, 1959:

"Where once there was an adventuristic Communist tendency to take risks, and revolutions were launched haphazardly from inadequately prepared political bases, the emphasis is now on careful planning. The fundamental policy has been to remain under cover and to expand the 'patriotic national united front in order to mobilize the strength of the entire people,' as one Malayan Communist Party directive put it. What happened in Laos showed the results of such a policy: it also demonstrated the total incapacity of the Royal Lao Army to meet the Communists' politico-military offensive. Its staff proved incompetent and untrained. Its communications were almost non-existent. Though half of its twenty-five theoretical infantry battalions are territorials and serve in their own provincial regions, this built-in machinery to cope with Communist subversion and the recruiting of Pathet Lao regional forces fell down in practice because of the lack of rural administration and the easily exploited grievances of the villagers.

"If the Pathet Lao activities were confined to Sam Neua and Phong Saly, where occupation for a period of several years gave the Communists the opportunity to indoctrinate and recruit, it would be reasonable to view the situation with less concern. Since

September it has become obvious, however, that the southern provinces are also seriously infected. The unpalatable fact is that the Pathet Lao's organization of peasant soldiers is now such that it can turn on the pressure at any point. It controls the countryside just as effectively as the Viet Minh once controlled it during the Indo-China War: and so far has the deterioration in security gone that even the drastic improvement in the military capabilities of the Royal Lao Army now envisaged under the current aid program is not likely to prove sufficient for the needs of the situation. The problem is not merely the creation of a better army: the first and most difficult hurdle is to win over the inhabitants of the country's ten thousand villages and to create an environment in which the army can operate in territory which is neither neutral nor hostile.

"In Thailand the government says it is satisfied that Communist penetration of the Laos type has not occurred. In a society that suffers neither from rural poverty nor food shortages, the Communists have found it the least profitable of all South-East Asian recruiting grounds. There are, nevertheless, several factors which should occasion care in assessing the internal stability of Thailand. No less than four Communist parties, the Thai, the Chinese, the Malayan, and the Vietnamese, operate within the country.

"The Malayan Communist Party has had its headquarters in southern Thailand for at least five years, and the Thai army and police have failed even to get it on the run. In the more vulnerable and much poorer northeastern provinces, where the inhabitants feel much closer to the Laos than they do to the Thais of Bangkok, the 50,000 Vietnamese refugees living along the right bank of the Mekong, and various dissidents who have associated themselves with the Pathet Lao, have clearly succeeded in establishing ideological roots. A movement of the Pathet Lao type in this area is a possibility that cannot be ignored.

"The Thai army, with American equipment and training, is very much larger and more efficiently trained than the Lao army: but a substantial portion is always required for duty around Bangkok—not to protect the capital from military attack but to preserve the régime from a *coup d'état*. The successive elimination of the navy and the police in the affairs of government has led to the concentration of power in the hands of the army. While Field Marshal Sarit's health permits him to remain in office, it will probably continue to present a homogenous façade: many of his subordinates are not looking for military promotion, however, but for short cuts to political power and material advancement. They, too, want their cut of the melon. While they are squabbling over it, Thailand's current stability could quickly be destroyed.

"Of Cambodia's 31,000-man army the best that can be said is that Sihanouk has succeeded in keeping the Communists out of it. Like the Lao army, it is maintained by the United States and trained by France. The Cambodians are basically better soldiers than the Laotians: but there is nothing to indicate that the French have made a better fist of their training here than they did in Laos. Sihanouk believes that his policy of neutrality and his efforts to be on friendly terms with Ho Chi Minh's régime in North Vietnam have prevented the subversion of the rural population. But he is also frank enough to admit that a Laotian-type situation could develop at any time if Hanoi or Peking gave the word.

"Since the important colonial element is now withdrawn, the biggest and best of all avowedly anti-Communist South-East Asian armies is in South Vietnam. Here the American Military Aid Advisory group has knocked a hotch-potch of forces left over from the Indo-China war into an effective-looking force of 150,000 men. It performed creditably in a recent operation against Communist insurgents in the Ca Mau peninsula. Its troops are smartly turned out and well trained in conventional infantry tactics: like the other regional forces, its spearhead is an élite paratroop regiment. Whether even this is a sufficient army, or the right army, is open to doubt, however. It suffers from the handicaps of a Western-type army (dependence on roads for movement and air drops for field supply) and it lacks modern equipment. This 1960 Vietnamese army would undoubtedly prove more effective than the 1954 French army in fighting the Viet Cong, the only possible enemy. But would it prove effective enough? The Viet Cong is neither road-bound nor dependent on air support: it has retained its essential guerrilla characteristic. To date, it has contented itself with scattered guerrilla actions in South Vietnam. But Vietnamese officials I talked with recently are sure that the whole Communist regional network has been maintained. If Hanoi were to arm it and activate it and to reinforce the political and military cadres known to be at work now in the South Vietnamese countryside, Diem's forces could easily find themselves overextended.

"In the five and a half years that have elapsed since the signing of the Geneva Agreement, the Communists have succeeded in creating over a wide area in South-East Asia the political base and the military machinery necessary for the application of Mao Tse-tung's theories of Communist revolutionary war. The Western response has been to strive for the internal security of the region by the creation of conventional armies. Since even in SEATO there is no study of Maoist theories and tactics, their application inevitably leads to shock and sometimes even to the total lack of comprehension that characterized the initial Laotian, and Western reaction to the events last summer in the provinces of Sam Neua and Phong Saly. We seem to have forgotten the lessons of the Indo-China War."

The unfortunate Civil Guard and Self-Defense Corps in South Vietnam paid bitterly for this forgetfulness. The Self-Defense Corps are the home guard. At least they live within the framework of the village. But the Civil Guards, on whom the burden of maintaining lines of communications fell, live with their families in a world of blockhouses and barbed-wire entanglements. Every major road or railway bridge has its adjoining Civil Guard post. With their mud walls and rows of pointed bamboo sticks, they are at once an act of defiance and a ghastly reminder of the inhumanity of this never-ending war. Attacks in the worst areas come nightly. Help often comes only after a post has fallen, and by that time, of course, it is too late to be of any assistance to the men, women, and children to whom death from condemned cells like these is probably a welcome-enough escape.

Today, thanks to the current American aid program, they are receiving decent equipment and proper training. They know when night falls that their ammunition will at least fit their guns, and that they have enough of it. They are getting the comfort of radios, so that they may communicate with the provincial headquarters. They are less lonely than they were. But this new care and attention they are receiving has been left perilously late. Everything has been left perilously late.

In its annual report for the 1960 financial year, the United States Operations Mission in Saigon briefly reviewed the problems that had confronted South Vietnam after 1954. Then it added: "To assist South Vietnam to cope with these many problems, the U.S.

launched a many-faceted aid program, which, since 1954, has totaled $1,302 million. In the early years this aid was heavily concentrated upon emergency relief programs, and as these needs were met the emphasis shifted more toward the rebuilding of the destroyed transport and communications network, and the re-establishing of the former agricultural production so as to relieve the country from its dependence on external assistance for meeting its basic needs from abroad." The reconstruction phase was said to have been largely completed. The United States had helped materially in the fields of education, land reform and land development, health and public works. Concomitant with these efforts, "and of increasing importance now that reconstruction is virtually completed," was the drive to raise the country's industrial production, a program in which United States aid had also played a major role.

Unofficial reports written by officials were no less cheerful in their tone. Mr. J. Price Gittinger, who was responsible for administering the economic and technical project in support of the Vietnamese agrarian reform program from September, 1955, to December, 1959, wrote in similar terms in the *Far Eastern Survey*. "Since the Geneva accords were signed in July, 1954, agrarian reform has been a key program of President Ngo Dinh Diem's government in the Republic of Vietnam, and one which it has shown a marked determination to carry out—especially in its land transfer and land settlement aspects," he wrote in the issue of January, 1960. Other writers were even more glowing in their praise.

The only inference that the uninformed reader could draw from such stuff was that this great volume of United States aid, running by 1960 to more than $1,300 million, had flowed into productive channels which had rehabilitated South Vietnam and even prepared it for an economic takeoff.

Nothing could have been further from the truth. A meager 1.4 percent of United States aid, or $15 million, went to agriculture between 1955 and 1960. The much-vaunted rural help program did not exist. Land reform was a flop. Industry was insignificant.

In the first five years of American assistance, 87 percent of the nonmilitary aid came in the form of commodity imports. These were sold by the Vietnamese government. The piasters thus generated went into a counterpart fund from which the government paid the army, and with what was left over financed various economic or technical projects with the approval and help of the United States Operations Mission. In 1962, for instance, payments to the troops accounted for 7.1 billion piasters out of a total counterpart generation of 8.6 billion piasters. Out of some $1,500 million from 1954 through the financial year 1962, no more than about $300 million went to economic development. This is a substantial figure, and there are some results to show for it. But the fact remains that in neither agriculture nor industry was South Vietnam making the progress so widely claimed for it.

The nature of the aid certainly produced an impression of progress. Nearly half the imports were in the form of consumer goods and their display in the shop windows, and their use by the well heeled minority distracted attention from the lack of well-being and the mounting unemployment, or underemployment, among the majority. In a propaganda sense this was important. The seeming affluence of the South contrasted with the obvious grinding poverty of the North. In other ways, also, the aid was beneficial. More than 90 percent of the Vietnamese government's revenue came from customs duties, and much of this, in turn, came from the American commodity imports program. But since more than 50 percent of this revenue also went to defense, including the payment of the Civil Guard and Self-Defense Corps, the economy, even with these hidden benefits, was not stimulated by the aid program in the way it was so often suggested. Little progress was made in the industry, and such progress as there was in agriculture held little promise in 1960 that South Vietnam was on the way toward enjoying the favorable balances of trade it was accustomed to before the Second World War.

The land reform program, which was said to have won so many friends for the government, and which claimed Diem's attention as early as 1954, also proves on investigation to have been rather more than a disappointment. It was not accompanied by the gross brutalities that characterized the land reform program in North Vietnam in 1956, of course. It was a genuine, if altogether too conservative, attempt to help the peasants by breaking up large estates for distribution.

To listen to Diem and his officials today it still sounds remarkably successful. They claim that because of it more than 170,000 farming families have become landowners and that they have been helped since by follow-up programs consisting of loans from the

Agricultural Credit, farm tools, livestock, and extension services. In fact, less than a third of eligible peasants have taken advantage of it, and in many areas it has made no impact at all, or worse, has been used by the Viet Cong against the government. Six years after the land reform ordinance was promulgated on October 22, 1956, the government still had 150,000 hectares of distributable land on its hands.

In marked contrast to the land reform program on Taiwan, where landlords were allowed to keep only three hectares (about seven acres) of medium-grade paddy field, or twice that area of dry land, or in Japan, where ten acres of land in the rice areas was a family maximum, South Vietnam's land reform has been anything but radical. A landlord in South Vietnam may retain up to a hundred hectares of rice land and another fifteen hectares for burial grounds and ancestor worship. To have been cut down to this level may have been unpleasant for the rich: but it was precious little help to the poor in a country where half a million peasant families own farms of one hectare or less.

The program lacked regulatory machinery to control tenant-landlord registration, and all sorts of side arrangements were entered into to defeat its intention. In Central Vietnam, where there are at least a hundred thousand farms of one hectare or less, each village has public lands which, in theory, it rents out at reasonable rates to the poorest peasants. The idea is that the public lands should provide both village revenue and relief. In practice, the system usually works as yet another means for squeeze and graft by appointed village chiefs and one of the worst forms of land exploitation. No security of tenure is given beyond the crop year, and there is no incentive for crop or land improvement when the poor peasants are allowed on the land. More often than not they do not get a chance at all, and the land goes to the richest and most prominent landlord.

On the government side, there has been great reluctance, or inability, to grant land titles. Settlers from the impoverished coastal areas who were resettled in the much more fertile and sparsely populated High Plateau have not yet got titles to their new settlements. They have been assigned garden plots and are able to work on communal farms: but the incentive of private ownership is still lacking. The government has never faced up to the problem.

In areas where lack of security had for many years prevented the landlords from visiting or collecting rents from their properties, the peasants regarded Diem's land reform as an added tax, or worse. While the land reform program proper was in the mill, Diem promulgated regulations governing the maximum rentals that should be paid by tenants to landlords. The rates were fixed at 15 to 25 percent of the principal crop. Though this was meant to depend on the fertility of the land, the landlords gaining access to their family estates after many years of Viet Minh control chose to interpret the 25 percent as a legal minimum, and often charged much higher rates.

The propaganda opportunities such practices presented to the Viet Cong were obvious enough. The political subtleties of the situation were beyond the peasants. All they knew was that Diem had brought the landlords back. To be sure, they had to pay taxes to the Viet Minh and were liable to compulsory service either as porters or as guerrillas, but they knew the money did not go to the profit of absentee landlords. Thus, in September, 1957, when they discovered that in addition to the payment of what they regarded as exorbitant rentals they now faced the payment of high prices (from $7 to $428 a hectare) for land they had once all but regarded as their own they did not often respond with the enthusiasm that Saigon and Washington attributed to them.

Everywhere, but especially in the rich rice-growing lands of the Mekong delta, the Viet Cong pushed their own land-to-the-tillers program. In some areas it had begun during the first Indo-China War. Their program was drastic, radical, and (provided the peasant didn't know what was coming to him in the end) appealing. Frequently the Viet Cong used terrorist tactics to keep out the landlords, even small ones.

Lots of men who had drifted into the towns and cities during the Second World War and the Indo-China War hoped to take possession of the ancestral holdings that some of them had not seen for years, if ever. Tu Phuong, a well-known Saigon journalist, went back to his native village of Can Lanh near the Cambodian border to dispose of his own small holdings. Viet Cong agents met him when he arrived in the village and told him that the fixed governmental price was not consistent with their land reform program. The price was too high, they said. They instructed him to divide his land into three and to sell it for one-third of the government price. Tu Phuong was stubborn and not afraid of the Viet

Cong. He declined to accept their terms. So the Viet Cong killed him, and Tu Phuong joined the ranks of the "wicked landlords" who had sought to defraud the people and who had been saved by the courageous Communist cadres!

Lack of skills, lack of fertilizers, constant war, uncertain markets, and interfering authorities conspired against the peasants. The Japanese peasant pays the equivalent of 600 piasters for a ton of ammonium sulphate and tricalcium phosphate; the Vietnamese peasant pays 2,300 piasters a ton—if he buys it, or can afford to buy it. The Japanese rice sells at 1,000 piasters a ton: Vietnamese rice at 600 piasters. The Japanese yield is about five tons a hectare, the Vietnamese yield only slightly more than two. The Japanese peasant is conservative and satisfied with the *status quo*. What should we expect the Vietnamese peasant to be?

8

A
Village
Goes
Wrong

A HIDEOUS RUMOR SWEPT the bars and the brothels of Hanoi in the summer of 1954. The streetwalkers in towns taken over by the Viet Minh in the southern delta had been obliged to become street cleaners! It is no reflection on the character of the great exodus from the North that the bar girls and harlots were among the first to go. A widely circulating story among Vietnamese peasant women was that the Viet Minh troops had been in some way de-sexed.

The victory won, however, Giap's iron discipline relaxed enough to permit the troops who had been too busy fighting to marry. All over the South before the Viet Minh evacuation late in 1954, hundreds, even thousands, of weddings took place. At the worst, it seemed, the separation would be for two years. In Quang Ngai, one of the poorest of all provinces in Central Vietnam, but also one with great strategic importance, more than five hundred of these weddings were celebrated, and some twenty thousand families there have close relatives in the North.

To a lesser degree this happened all over the South. Everywhere the three thousand to five thousand cadres and troops who were deliberately left behind had friends and accomplices to support them. The heaviest concentrations were in the coastal provinces of the Phu Yen, Binh Dinh, Quang Nam, and Quang Ngai, which the Viet Cong had held in their entirety, or in large part, for nine years; in the Red belt north of Saigon, now known as the Maquis D; in the Plain of Rushes near the Cambodian border, in the Mekong delta provinces of Vinh Long and Vinh Binh, and in the Ca Mau peninsula.

Everywhere there were some, however. In Kontum Province in the High Plateau sixty cadres worked among the montagnards. In Pleiku there were about a hundred, and in Darlac, forty. Their original orders were to work among the people in preparation for the 1956 elections, which, under the "Declaration of Intent," appended to the Geneva Agreement, were to unify the country once again.

Diem's survival and refusal to agree to elections caught the Communists off guard. They had banked heavily on the French, who had signed, and were expected to honor, the Geneva Agreement, and had not reckoned that Diem would have been able to get rid of them so easily, or so quickly.

Apart from those on liaison duties, few Communist cadres made their way South before 1957. Ho was preoccupied with internal problems. The land reform program under Truong Chinh had turned into a brutal and bloody mess that led even to a short-lived peasant uprising in Ho's home province in November, 1956. Ho himself seemed anxious to portray life in North Vietnam as attractive enough to induce the Southerners to welcome unification, and 1956 was scarcely the time. In addition, the Soviet Union discouraged any early reopening of the war. The Lien Viet was absorbed in an even broader Fatherland Front, which set out to appeal to Southerners on nationalistic lines. Truong Chinh went into temporary eclipse for his land reform blunders and brutalities, and Southerners such as General Le Duan, who had once commanded the Viet Minh forces in the South, and Ung Van Khiem, the newly appointed Foreign Minister, began to come to the fore.

Instead of a quick, two-year takeover, Hanoi now had to prepare for another long-drawn-out struggle. It warned cadres in South Vietnam that life would be hard and difficult. Instructions were to open as many private schools as possible, and to form front associations among professional men, tradesmen, workers, and peasants. The cadres infiltrated as teachers into Diem's anti-illiteracy classes for adults and opened night classes of their own. They even took jobs in the private transport companies, serving as drivers and conductors in buses which circulated through the country. Far from the towns, in the mountains and swamps and in remote rice fields, they began the preparation of their political bases.

The most illuminating account ever given of these tactics was written by a cadre in a report titled "Experience in Turning XB village in Kien Phong Province into a Combat Village." "XB village" is, of course, a code name, assumed for obvious security reasons by the author of the report, which was captured early in 1962. Kien Phong is in the western Mekong delta and forms part of the Plain of Rushes, most of which has for years been a Viet Cong stronghold.

Typically in the Plain of Rushes, XB village is entirely surrounded by water. It has a population of six thousand people and was founded during the late forties or early fifties during the initial stages of the Indo-China War. Though the land was originally owned by one big landlord and fifty smaller ones, the report states, they left the region during the fighting against the French, returning after the war to reclaim their land and to collect back rent.

To begin with, XB was not a Communist village, or even a village that sympathized with the Communists. On the contrary, reading between the lines of the report, it seems that the Diem administration had done good work there, bringing governmental authority in the form of an administrative office, a security section, and a post of militiamen.

What legitimate grievances could the Communists find here to exploit? The answer was land. "Before, during, and after the elimination of our enemy's influence, the Party in XB village always used the subject of land as a means of propagandizing the people and indoctrinating the masses," the report said. "In its political and armed struggle, in its administration of the rural area, and in other revolutionary tasks, the Party well knew how to make use of the farmers' interest in land. On it we built a mass movement.

And for that reason the revolutionary movement made great progress and resulted in great success.

"At first this struggle was sporadic and weak. The farmers merely wanted the land rent to be reduced and their right to farm the land maintained. Now the farmers cling to their land. The landlords remain in the cities, leaving the task of retaking the land and collection of rent to the soldiers posted in the area. But these troops can do little. The slogan "Kill the Land Robbers" was welcomed. The farmers now know they have the force to prevent the landowners from retaking their lands and can prevent the U.S.-Diem clique from oppressing the people. Farmers are now free to farm, without paying either land rent or agricultural tax. All private and public land has been distributed and ownership is now maintained except for land near enemy army posts."

The task clearly was not easy. At first Diem's mobile troops were active in the area, and especially in two neighboring villages which were on dry land. During the first years of peace, when the Lao Dong Party made several attempts to become active, Diem's men three times broke up the organization. Three Party members were killed, two secretaries arrested, and more than a hundred cadres and others taken into custody. Finally, only one cadre remained, and he commanded no local support.

In 1959 cadres from what the report described as the "higher level," a reference to Party organizers who had been living in security in Cambodia, or deeper in the Plain of Rushes, or the Maquis D, or who had come in from North Vietnam, arrived to gather scattered Party members and to instruct them in reestablishing destroyed Party bases.

"Things were so difficult then that members were forced to hide in the fields and marshes during the day, and only at night could they slip back into the villages to do propaganda work among the farmers," the report said. "Several farmers were deeply interested in the struggle to get them land and they let themselves be indoctrinated easily. A base was established at a farm. Our cadres went on helping farmers fight for ownership of certain lands and for the reduction of rent on other land. Gradually our victories convinced some of them and we were able to bring into being XB Party, consisting of seven members."

This increase from one to seven in Viet Cong membership apparently brought a vigorous reaction from Diem's forces. Government battalions, coming both by land and water, swept through the village area. One three-man defense group lost two men killed in action in one day. Like the Party organization before it, it rebuilt and became of platoon size, while the XB organization itself grew until it had 26 Party members, 30 members in the Lao Dong Youth, 274 in the Farmers' Association, 150 in the Youth Group, and 119 in the Liberation Women's Group.

"Two thousand people, or two-thirds of the villagers, take part in Party-led activities," the report said. From one outlawed man to the active control of two thousand seemingly willing recruits in the space of only two years! This was the claim, and, in the light of experience elsewhere in the Mekong delta, it does not seem altogether unwarranted, though as the report makes clear, Party officials were often guilty of errors of judgment and unwise acts.

The fanning of the fires of revolution and "agitprop" among the farmers to seek the right of landownership and a reduction in rent was merely a first step. The report notes that despite this the "struggle remained sporadic and weak and did not constitute a mass movement." The Diem forces remained strong in the village. The Party therefore began a campaign to eliminate the influence of the leading villagers and the local security agents.

The methods adopted are not discussed, but, since the closing months of 1959 and early 1960 were marked everywhere by a vast increase in discriminate terror, they are not difficult to guess. For instance, on December 5, 1959, ten Viet Cong agents, armed with rifles and small submachine guns, kidnapped a village chief in Long An Province on the outskirts of Saigon. Three days later villagers found his disemboweled body floating in a nearby village. A similar number of armed Viet Cong murdered the assistant chief of Ho Thung hamlet on December 16, 1959, and the following day opened fire on his funeral procession, killing a village guard and wounding five other persons. These were not isolated incidents. They were part of the essential pattern of Communist control.

"We explained to the villagers the evil caused by village notables and security agents," the report said. "We awoke the people to the fact that if the American-Diem clique succeeded in permanently maintaining the organization of village notables and security, soon Mister H, the cruel landlord, and others would return to the village to seize land and collect back rent. For that reason the farmers must eliminate the influence of the village notables and sweep away the security agents."

While the Party worked to persuade the people to liquidate the Diem officials, it also went to work on the families of the officials and security agents. "It was a good method," the report noted with satisfaction. "After a while certain notables refused to work for the enemy and some took the side of the people. Thus, when our enemies tried to begin projects in the village, no one would work with them. The U.S.-Diem clique tried to win back the people by distributing drugs in the village. The offer was flatly rejected. Some of the people even debated openly and strongly with the enemy agents. Finally, the Diem clique had to abandon the village since no village council could be maintained there. The Party hailed this great success and urged other villages in the area to follow the example. Since then, in surrounding villages, we have been successful in eliminating the influence of the enemy. In the area now there only remain some Diem soldiers who live in a military post."

To this stage, XB village had merely turned from being for and with the government to being for itself. Its people's interests were narrow, shallow, and not at all in keeping with the doctrinaire Communist requirements. To play its proper part in South Vietnam's war of national liberation, it clearly had to become an active participant. It had to fight, and the more it could be made to fight, and the more the government forces could be encouraged to fight against it, the more rapidly would the people become fully identified with the Communists' goals, which do not seek merely to exclude the government from rural areas but to overthrow it.

Besides encouraging the people to grab the land and to "kill the land robbers," the Party also began to attend to public health, sanitation, education, and even the marketing of farmers' produce. It opened a first-aid station which was run by a public health cadre, who also visited the sick, and trained and appointed a midwife. "In the matter of schools," the report said, "the Party called the problem to the attention of the people at a public meeting." Well aware that Diem's officials were understandably wary of starting schools in villages which they did not fully control, the Party cunningly suggested that an approach should be made to district officials for aid in building the school and supplying the teachers. This failed, as the Party had expected, and the Communists therefore took over, raised the money by collection, and built the schools and "guided" the people in their management.

From land reform to first aid, to schools, to the organization of youth, women and peasants, the Lao Dong Party in XB village demonstrated that a small hard-core group of members could quickly control large numbers of people. Altogether two thousand people, or a third of the population, took part in the Party-led activities.

By the end of 1960 the Party had made such progress that the public establishment of the National Liberation Front in the village became the occasion of a quasi-religious festival. "The walls of the houses were whitewashed, and flags were made and raised on flagpoles in front of each house," the report said. "In all, six hundred flags were flown throughout the village, expressing the people's spirit of struggle and their support of revolution. The Party cadres had indoctrinated the people and prepared them to debate with the enemies. When the soldiers came to take away the flags, the people said to them calmly: 'This is a flag of peace. It is not a Viet Cong flag. This flag means that the people, some of whom are your relatives, or even your families, have land to till.' Most soldiers agreed with this view and took away only a few flags. One old man was concerned because his flag was wet. He feared that this would lessen the solemnity of the ceremony."

Among the people to whom the flying of flags is a ritual, or at least a significant form of mass expression, the establishment of the National Liberation Front was in a sense the crossing of the watershed for XB village. The Party now set to work to get the people to make rudimentary weapons and to join in turning XB village into a combat village, ready not merely to argue with the soldiers about schools and flags but to make war on them.

Again, however, Party officials met with resistance, and at first the cadres and the Self-Defense troops carried the burden of laying metal and bamboo spikes and the construction of "naily" boards, hideous booby traps made from needle-pointed and barbed nails set in wooden blocks, which both sides sow in tracks likely to be used by enemy soldiers.

"The people thought that the laying of naily boards was illegal and would result in terror and reprisals by the soldiers," the report said. "In the light of this the Party members laid the naily boards themselves, while endeavoring to educate the people. The Party laid more naily boards than ever before. Once during a terror sweep one of the soldiers was injured by a naily board. This caused the soldiers to withdraw. Party members correctly regarded this as a success and held a mass meeting at which it was explained that the laying of naily boards had prevented the entrance of the enemy. The cadres declared that if the people did not lay naily boards the enemy would come to collect land rents, levy taxes, impose *corvée* labor and draft young men into the army. The Party then introduced the slogan "One naily board for each square of land." So the people built naily boards and more soldiers were injured. Then the Party showed the people how to lay barricades of thorny bamboo booby-trapped with grenades and to build combat fences to keep out the troops. Among some, doubts and misgivings lingered. An old farmer opposed the plan and asked for permission to leave the area. The soldiers came before the farmer got away and told him to remove the gates. He removed a few and the Party "renewed its education work" to "explain the damage done by the mopping-up operation." The cadre explained that fencing the area, laying combat gates, laying down naily boards, proselytizing the army and engaging in political struggle all contributed to the defense of a village, protected the lives of the villagers, and kept the land intact. The Party sent its best cadre to reeducate the old farmer, and in time he became "enlightened," approved the setting up of combat gates, and "confessed his fault before the people."

The Farmers' Association took over the combat gates and the laying of naily boards. Each subcell of the Farmers' Association took charge of one combat gate, closed the gate when the government forces arrived, and gave the alarm by tocsin. Thus, when the tocsin sounded each person knew which gate the enemy was entering and how best to cope.

The army, Mao Tse-tung once directed, fought not merely for the sake of fighting but to "agitate the masses, to organize them, to arm them and to help them establish revolutionary military power." Mao would be pleased by XB village and hundreds of others like it in South Vietnam.

The more the villages resist, the more the troops come to mop up, and the more they mop up, the more the people turn to the Communists. Again, the people learn war through war. At XB village now the people compete with each other in the manufacture of naily boards. The mopping-up operations grow bigger in size, and the people resist more furiously. A farmer has invented a bottle grenade. According to the report, it was tested on a dog, which it disembowled. It is now in general manufacture in the peasant cottages. Where once only the cadres made naily boards, now everyone makes and lays them.

But for the Party officials of XB village this is far from good enough. Best progress was made in the field of armed struggle. Political struggle and proselytizing operations among the troops remained weak, and even the armed struggle itself was weak. The laying of naily boards and even various counterattacks in which the people participated were designed only to check enemy operations and not to annihilate the government forces or to seize their weapons. They were defensive, not offensive. Political struggle was weak, the report found, and not closely enough bound to the armed struggle. Instead of attacking the enemy politically, the Party only led the people to the point where they passively opposed and were content to keep terrorism out of the village. The Party had also paid little attention to getting agents to infiltrate into the army. Local cadres had failed to enlighten soldiers with whom they had contact, or to turn them into infiltration agents, or to establish political bases in local military units.

To read this and the rest of the catalog of Party failings, XB village sounds anything but a howling success. "Though the Party correctly based its actions on the people's interests—especially with respect to land—and persuaded them to join the mass movement, it did not know how to profit from the opportunity to teach the people that their rights and interests must be subordinated to the national interests of independence, peace, and reunification, or that they must focus all their resentment on, and fight against, the U.S.-Diem clique." The report then adds perhaps its most significant sentence: "Consequently, once the people are satisfied about land, the movement degenerates."

In other words, the villagers were bored stiff by the ideological lectures they were compelled to attend. And this, it appears from a final section in the report, is true also of other villages. Village Ni is also a combat village. Fenced in, it has naily boards and gates and has succeeded in keeping out the government forces, but the mass movement there remains weak. The Party in Ni village failed to understand that the key motive power in a combat village came from urging the people to stand up and fight. "Thus the people being unaware of the necessity for a combat village did not participate actively in its establishment." In other villages the peasants made naily boards but did not take part in laying them.

The Communists drew their lessons from XB village. They felt they were on the right lines, but they had to exert much greater effort to prevent the people from becoming passive. They had to develop a greater spirit of offense and be determined to attack the government forces ever more fiercely.

And what lessons should we draw? Nothing in the XB village report and nothing in the evidence gathered from villages newly released from Communist control suggests that it is necessary to match ideology with ideology. The people are not interested in Communism or in anti-Communism. Above all, they are interested in land, and what that means to their livelihood. Over and over again that emerges from XB report. They are interested in schooling and in health. The Diem administration lost its following only when the landlords returned and the Communists exploited their demands. XB village had only twenty-six Party members and thirty candidate members in the Lao Dong Youth, or fewer than one in each hundred of the population. Of the rest, fewer than one in ten were members of Front organizations, though a third were participants in Party-led activities. Since these activities included entertainments such as propaganda plays and dances, the Viet Cong, despite their skill and dedication, still had a fairly loose hold over the peasants. They were not lost to the government but only held captive by the Viet Cong.

This is true everywhere, yet, like the rerun of an old horror movie, the Arvins follow the French example. They assume guilt by association in the areas beyond their control. Tragically few seem to appreciate that this sort of war is lost, not won, by killing people.

In July, 1961, I went south from Saigon to Vinh Binh Province to watch six army and newly trained Civil Guard battalions with artillery and naval support launch a major drive along a tongue of land between the Mekong and the Bassac rivers and extending to the South China Sea. This was the Arvin's biggest operation yet. It might have been much more impressive if I had not seen a precisely similar operation with identical intentions conducted by the French Expeditionary Force in Thai Binh Province in the Red River delta nine years earlier.

Five armored cars and an armored troop carrier were detailed to act as escort for me and two Vietnamese correspondents on the fifty-mile drive from the Mekong River crossing to divisional headquarters at Tra Vinh. When we moved out as far as the regiments, we went in a convoy containing tens of vehicles and almost a company of men. Once again it was an army that thought in terms of towns and roads—and an enemy that thought in terms of people and countryside.

The area selected for the operation was downriver from Vinh Long, at the tip of the tongue formed by the Mekong and the Bassac rivers. It was about thirty miles long and twenty wide. Some of it was sandy soil and used for growing vegetables. Other parts of it were under rice, which gave way at the tip of the tongue to mangrove swamps. Only one indifferent, much-mined road penetrated the area. Until the previous month a Civil Guard post had been precariously maintained. Then the Viet Cong attacked in strength, killed eight of the guards and wounded sixteen others, thus ending for the time being all links with the government, since Diem's village councils had long been disbanded by the Viet Cong.

Viet Cong strength in the area was estimated at about five hundred, of whom about two hundred to three hundred were known to be armed. They were sufficient, however, to exercise loose control over the whole area and very tight authority over the swamp zone, where they had training camps and factories for manufacturing crude land mines and primitive guns.

It was hoped in the operation to kill about a hundred armed Viet Cong and to capture many others. But the Viet Cong slipped through the lines at night and got away by river. The artillery blazed fruitlessly into the line of advance. No one saw anything wrong in this. "The villagers have asked us to use artillery because it gives them an opportunity to run away from the Viet Cong," said the divisional commander. I don't know whether he expected me to believe him.

The following month, after the army had retired, leaving thousands of unhappy peasants behind it, Buddhist bonzes petitioned the province chief in Tra Vinh against the shelling of hamlets and pagodas and to demand the release of their imprisoned fellows. Some months later their leader, Superior Bonze Son Vong, appeared on the lists of the central committee of the Viet Cong's National Liberation Front.

CHAPTER 9

War
Again

THE VIET CONG change from political penetration to subversion to Maoist warfare was a slow but sure process, helped by the shortcomings of the Diem régime and the type of assistance it received, but deliberate, premeditated and, after 1957, carefully planned.

Between 1957 and July, 1959, the Vietnamese government reported to the International Control Commission the murder by Viet Cong cadres of ten servicemen, twenty-eight civil guards, sixty-five village officials, and fifty-one civilians. During this period Diem's forces discovered more than three thousand dumps of arms and ammunition. Most of the weapons were well greased against the weather and well packaged. More than three hundred of the dumps, scattered through twenty-eight of South Vietnam's thirty-eight provinces, were main provincial sources of supply. They included more than 600 rifles, 350 mortars and bazookas, 142 machine and submachine guns, 23,500 mines, hundreds of cases of ammunition, more than 12,000 shells, and large quantities of equipment, including typewriters and electric generators.

Two weeks before the Senate subcommittee met in Washington

in July, 1959, to hear evidence from top officials that all was well in South Vietnam, Diem published the first of three White Papers charging that the Communists in North Vietnam were planning revolt in South Vietnam. The report concluded: "The increasing reinforcement of the Communist armed forces, the importation in great numbers of arms and munitions into North Vietnam, secret arms and ammunition dumps left in the territory of the Republic of Vietnam, and subversive maneuvers carried out by the Communist cadres constitute tangible and irrefutable evidence of their deliberately aggressive intentions. It would be sufficient to recall at this point the recent statement made by Ho Chi Minh during his trip to Moscow to *Unita*, the mouthpiece of the Italian Communist Party. 'We are building Socialism in Vietnam, but we are building it in only one part of the country while in the other part we still have to direct and bring to a close the middle-class democratic and anti-imperialistic revolution.'"

July, 1959, saw the beginning of large-scale movement of armed cadres from North to South Vietnam. This was not the beginning, however, of a conventional invasion. The men who now returned were, if not without exception, almost exclusively Southerners who had gone North in 1954. They came back to their home areas, where they could confidently expect a warm welcome for the next, and terrorist, phase of the revolt which was soon to begin.

They followed three main routes: by junk along the coast; directly across the 17th parallel; and along the Ho Chi Minh trail in Laos to Kontum Province. The first two were the easiest, and the most dangerous. The third was hard, and exhausting, but safe.

The Ho Chi Minh trail sounds romantic. Like the mandarin road that led from the Imperial capital at Hue along the coast and through the porte de Chîne to China, and the opium road, which ran north from Laos into Tongking, it conveys a sense of color and adventure.

To anyone unfamiliar with Indo-China, however, the suggestion of a trail is apt to be misleading. In the West, the usual image of Vietnam is that of a land of peasant farmers in cone-shaped hats made of rice straw, plodding their way across water-logged fields of rice behind their pre-Christian-era plows and mud-encrusted water buffalo. That is true enough as far as it goes: but it does not go far enough. Most Vietnamese work in conditions more or less like this, but most of Vietnam is not paddy fields but uncultivated jungle, filled with wild beasts and sparsely populated by tribesmen who hunt with crossbows and blowpipes. In such regions, there are no signposted trails, but scores of tracks, spread out over hundreds of miles of territory. Often only wide enough for a man, or a small mountain pony, and hidden from the air by dense jungle foliage, they are usually many miles from the nearest road.

In the early years of the first Indo-China War, couriers from the Viet Minh's main bases and battle areas in Tongking maintained contact with their Southern forces along the Annamite Chain. Little of this region had ever been under French control. Much of it was unexplored, with mountain peaks rising above 7,000 feet and all of it covered with dense jungle. The journey by this route was known to take several months and to be both hazardous and exhausting. It came to be known as the Ho Chi Minh trail, and was regarded as a bit of a joke.

It ceased to be a joke in January, 1954, when Viet Minh forces in considerable strength spilled out of the jungle in Kontum Province in the High Plateau, captured a string of posts north of the provincial capital, then took the capital itself and swept on to destroy a French mobile group built around the veteran battalions of the Korean War.

"Never had our army fought with such endurance for so long a time as in the winter-spring of 1953–54," wrote General Vo Nguyen Giap of this period. "There were units which marched and pursued the enemy for more than three thousand kilometers. There were others which moved secretly for more than a thousand kilometers on the Truong Son mountain range."

Since all major actions were fought north of the 17th parallel, the Ho Chi Minh trail did not play a decisive part in the defeat of the French. But, at a critical stage of the war, while the Viet Minh were building up for the final assault on Dien Bien Phu, it enabled Giap to create a diversion which was not only costly to the French in manpower and territory but necessitated the redeployment of forces which otherwise would have been used to reinforce, or to rescue, the garrison at Dien Bien Phu. Now, in this second Indo-China War, the Viet Cong could not hope to win without it.

Through Laos, it is almost all in Kha country. Kha means slave, the name the French gave to the Alak and other tribes that inhabit the region. East of the Mekong River and through the tangled mountains and scattered, sparsely populated villages, control of the

Khas and their territory is, and has been for the past twelve years, firmly in the hands of a swarthy tribal chief named Sithone, who is also one of the members of the central executive committee of the Neo Lao Hak Xat Party, the Communist political front in Laos.

Fifty years ago the French began their fruitless efforts to pacify the area. A chieftain named Kommadom rallied the tribes to his side and for more than twenty years held out against the French. The revolt ended in 1937 when French forces with three battalions of cavalry and two hundred elephants broke into Kommadom's mountain base. Kommadom and six of his sons were killed. Three, including Sithone, survived and were sentenced to life imprisonment.

Lao Issara forces, which had risen against the French after the Second World War, rescued Sithone and his one surviving brother. Later, both threw in their lot with the Pathet Lao, and in 1950 Sithone united the tribesmen against the French and "liberated" a huge area extending far to the west of the Mekong River, and including the mountains around the town of Attopeu and the Plateau of the Bolovens. It has been "liberated" ever since.

Sithone went to prison for a second time in 1960, when he was seized by the Laotian Right wing in Vientiane along with Prince Souphanouvong and most of the other principal Pathet Lao leaders. After his escape with Souphanouvong the following year, he returned to his tribal areas and extended his control over an even larger territory.

Two members of the staff of the British Embassy in Vientiane paid him an involuntary visit early in 1962 when they sought the release of Colombo Plan doctors who had been captured by the Pathet Lao, and were themselves held prisoner for a month.

Sithone proved on first acquaintance to be a terrifying figure to the trussed-up Englishmen. Mervyn Brown, first secretary at the embassy, described him riding into a village on horseback at the head of his well armed band of guerrillas and "looking like the personification of death with a peaked military cap, enormous black sun-glasses and stern features." Even a couple of English prisoners did not seem to surprise Sithone, and he rode past them, his features set, without a second glance.

When he got to know him, Brown found him stern, but with a good smile. He doubted that he was a Communist, or that the

Pathet Lao was a Communist movement in the Mekong area. Rather, he put Sithone down as a nationalist and an anticolonialist, who blamed the French and the Americans for his two arrests.

Major Leaphard, the assistant British military attaché, who accompanied Brown, paid more attention to the military possibilities of the region. Brown noted that the tribesmen, for superstitious reasons, built their houses in small circles, Leaphard that the tracks were kept in first-class order by the villagers under the instruction of the Pathet Lao. Brown regarded a scarcity of food and potential crop-growing areas as a factor which would limit, and possibly prohibit, the movement of large numbers of troops and supplies. Leaphard was impressed with the potential for large-scale, fairly rapid and quite secret movement that the numerous tracks and their dense jungle canopy facilitated.

In the long discussions that led to the second Geneva Agreement in 1962, Averell Harriman went to considerable lengths to get the Russians to spell out their commitment to put an end to the traffic along the Ho Chi Minh trail. Their assurances on this point were one of the preconditions for an American signature to the agreement. In the first six months after the agreement came into effect, however, it became apparent that the Russians were in no position to see that it was honored by others. Planes, whether or not they were Russian, continued to drop supplies at Tchepone, the first major staging base along the trail, and in December, 1962, South Vietnamese forces found a huge dump of new Chinese weapons in the High Plateau. Undoubtedly, some Viet Cong supplies come by air and others are brought in by sea. Lacking airfields and readily identifiable dropping zones, however, they find air supply hazardous and uncertain: with American and South Vietnamese craft keeping a close watch along the coast, the sea route is also hazardous and uncertain. Difficult though it is, the Ho Chi Minh trail has been, and seems certain to remain, the Viet Cong's principal line of communication.

To the layman, unfamiliar with this terrain, an obvious question is why Vietnamese paratroopers cannot move in and destroy the Ho trail. Tchepone is an obvious target: but to attack it in strength from South Vietnam would be to reopen the Laotian war on highly disadvantageous terms. Paratroopers could be dropped secretly further south in Laos. In some areas they would be highly vulnerable to counterattack from considerable Viet Cong forces:

in others they might search for months and find no trace of a trail. Even if they were blessed by improbable luck, the best they could hope for would be to put a temporary halt to the flow of supplies along the trail. Nothing short of a major campaign to wrest control of the entire area would bring a permanent halt, and this is precisely the decision that SEATO considered and rejected in 1961. As more montagnard Ranger companies are trained, they will no doubt start to infiltrate into this area of Laos: but since the trail is not one track but hundreds it would be excessively optimistic to expect their efforts to have more than a harassing effect. Bombing in this type of country, as the French discovered years ago, is pointless. Both the use of paratroopers and bombing have been tried with little or no effect along the Annamite Chain in South Vietnam, where the trail passes through much more vulnerable, and internationally less complicated, terrain.

The importance of the trail can be overstated, of course. A supply line so tenuous and slender as this clearly places great burdens on the men at the receiving end. They are forced to rely primarily on their own initiative, on their own jungle "factories," and on what they can capture from their foes. They set off the war not with what they got through Laos but with what they seized from the Arvins.

On September 26, 1959, two Arvin companies of the 23rd Infantry Division began a routine sweeping operation in the Plain of Rushes. They were acting on reports that about forty Viet Cong, including the battalion command post of the 2nd Liberation Battalion, were in the area. Two companies, it seemed, were more than adequate for the task.

The sweep began at first light, the Arvins plowing into the quagmire, cursing the conditions, and not too much concerned about the Viet Cong. At five minutes past nine Arvin Company 12 came under heavy attack. Instead of forty Viet Cong, they found themselves outnumbered by a force of about a hundred and fifty, at this time the full Viet Cong battalion strength. The Arvins ceased to resist after about fifteen minutes. Twelve of their men had been killed and fourteen wounded. The rest surrendered all their weapons. The Viet Cong buildup had begun.

Little was heard again of the 2nd Viet Cong battalion until the early morning of January 26, 1960. At 2:30 A.M. the battalion, supported by four companies of regional troops, in all about five hundred men, attacked the ammunition and arms dump of the 32nd Regiment of the 21st Infantry Division. In an hour they killed thirty-five Arvin soldiers and wounded another thirty-one.

Judging by the Viet Cong casualties, the Arvins offered little more than token resistance. Viet Cong losses were four dead and one prisoner. The net haul for the Viet Cong in a battle that lasted only an hour was 751 weapons. If they had not made good all their previous losses in the arms and ammunition dumps, they were at least well enough equipped to launch the war.

A week later Hanoi Radio, in its broadcast of February 5th, reported the attack in the following terms: "Our attack has inflicted serious losses on the enemy. On our part, thanks to the skill of our commander and the good-will of our soldiers, we completely destroyed the enemy."

Beginning on February 15th in the Cambodian border provinces, the Viet Cong launched a major terrorist campaign against village elders and other supporters of the Diem régime. Forty village chiefs died in the first week, and the tally of guns captured by the Viet Cong went up by hundreds.

This was a period of deliberate and premeditated terror directed at all officials in the countryside who were either unjust administrators or who, by their good example, served the government well.

The province chief was the source of all power in his region. He appointed the district chiefs and, on their recommendation, the village chiefs. The qualities both the provincial and district chiefs looked for too often were personal loyalties to themselves. The welfare of the villagers was often a secondary, or a tertiary, consideration. Thus, a bad or corrupt district chief often meant that village administration in his area was also bad and corrupt, and the villagers suffered accordingly.

For the Viet Cong, this was a readily exploitable situation. They killed bad officials and good officials: the mediocre, those who saw and heard no evil (in the Viet Cong), survived. It was an effective tactic.

Every hamlet had its undercover Viet Cong agents who acted as the eyes and the ears of the regular full-time forces and regional troops. Only in their more secure areas did the Viet Cong attempt to hold a village in force for more than a few hours, and then only for specific purposes such as tax collections, propaganda, and summary executions, in which, wherever possible, the people were required to participate.

Many village and district officials were extremely bad. The Viet Cong's list of their crimes against the villagers ran from rape to cannibalism, and included murder, extortion, corruption, theft, and brutality. The execution of such people won friends. On the reverse side, the execution of hard-working and honest officials was calculated to strike terror into the hearts of those who opposed the Viet Cong. In the next year or so hundreds of village headmen and others suspected of cooperating with the government or guilty of genuine "crimes against the people" were disemboweled and decapitated, and their families with them.

Viet Cong treatment of a hamlet chief and his friends at the village of My-Chanh-Hoa near Ben Tre on April 22, 1960, was typical. During the night about twenty Viet Cong surrounded the village to block the escape of their victims. The Can Bo (political commissars) then went in and seized Nguyen Van Cat, the hamlet chief, Nguyen Van Tran, a member of the Republican Youth, and three others. All were beheaded.

Schoolteachers who taught the curriculum laid down by the government and encouraged their pupils to take part in flag-raising ceremonies and to sing the national anthem were another primary target. Several hundred were kidnapped, tortured, starved, and indoctrinated. Those who responded favorably were released. More than a hundred are still missing, and thirty are known to have been executed. Between 1959 and the end of 1961, 636 rural schools closed their doors either because of the intimidation of teachers or because the Communists were using schools to spread propaganda.

The outbreak of the revolt caught South Vietnam almost entirely unprepared. The army, as we have seen, had not been trained to cope with this sort of war, and in fact was given little opportunity in the early months. The intellectuals of Saigon, already bitter with the Diem régime, became more critical, more defeatist, and more frustrated. The peasants were heavily infiltrated. From all quarters Diem got contradictory advice. Viet Cong attacks against Civil Guard posts and Self-Defense Corps were launched in great weight and with considerable effect. Lacking any means of communication with higher headquarters, except by bicycle or by foot, many posts fell. Diem was urgently advised to pull the Civil

Guards and the Self-Defense Corps out of the villages and to concentrate, like the French, on trying to hold the main towns and
the lines of communication. He declined. "It will not help us if
we save our men and weapons and lose the country," he said.

Casualties admitted by the government soared from 138 killed
and 200 wounded in 1959 to more than two thousand killed in
1960 and more than four thousand in 1961. The Viet Cong accum-
ulated enough government weapons to equip twenty or more
battalions. Government losses totaled 12,820 individual weapons
and more than six hundred group weapons, mostly machine guns,
mortars, and bazookas.

As early as the end of 1960 Hanoi abandoned any pretense that
it was not behind the rising tide of violence. Le Duan, now first
secretary of the Lao Dong party, told the third Party congress in
September, 1960: "There does not exist any other way outside
that which consists in overthrowing the dictatorial and fascist
regime of the American-Diemist clique in completely liberating
South Vietnam with a view to achieving national unity."

The congress called for an upsurge in the revolution. "Our com-
patriots of the South have no alternative but to stand up and fight
with whatever weapons they can lay their hands on," congress
agreed. "The overthrowing of the U.S.-Diem clique and the liberation of the South constitute a task consistent with history's law of
development and with the Geneva Agreement."

The first step was the creation of a National Liberation Front.
The name itself was of historical significance. This was what Ho
Chi Minh had called the movement in 1945 when he needed an
organization to take over as a provisional government after the
Japanese surrender. The army became the Liberation Army, and
there were quickly set up all the usual front organizations, including the Liberation Press Agency and the Association of Students
for the Liberation of South Vietnam. A month or so later, the
National Liberation Front and the National Liberation Army
established their headquarters in Laos, close to the borders of
Cambodia and South Vietnam.

By the end of 1961 the Viet Cong had not only a rival military
force but a rival administrative apparatus covering all of South
Vietnam. Directed through the central committee of the Lao
Dong Party in Hanoi, its principal leaders were all Southerners.
There were zone, interprovince, and district committees and town

and village cells. There were specialized agencies for liaison, propaganda, and training, for subversive activities among the Arvins, for the creation of bases, for espionage, for military affairs, for popular fronts, and for finance.

North of Saigon the Viet Cong disputed the control of the narrow coastal strip with the government; from thirty miles inland only the main roads and isolated pockets around the main towns were not theirs. No one could say with authority how much they controlled south of Saigon. Control was hard to define. In many areas the Arvins had control when they were in an area; when they left it reverted to the Viet Cong.

Suggestions at the time that 80 percent of the delta were in the hands of the Viet Cong gave a false impression, though even more of the area was readily accessible to the Viet Cong provided they did not fall into the error of directing too much attention to themselves. Even "loyal" hamlets and villages had their Viet Cong cells. Usually these were not large, sometimes no more than four or five men to a hamlet of perhaps a couple of thousand people. One missionary told me he had been working in an area which was generally regarded as almost completely under Viet Cong control. The province chief could not enter it, and the district chief lived on the fringe in a heavily defended little fortress, rarely venturing out and never into the more dubious hamlets. Yet the missionary continued to visit his local pastors and to preach himself. "I know the Viet Cong are everywhere, but I can honestly say I'm not conscious of having seen one in two years," he said.

The Christians, the Buddhists, and others go about their business and the Communists about theirs; what village and district chiefs do not know of local Viet Cong activities cannot hurt them.

When provincial Viet Cong troops and cadres enter a hamlet to recruit, all must cooperate. Lectures must be listened to and taxes paid. Until a village is firmly under Viet Cong control, however, the local guerrillas do not show their hand. They pursue an ordinary village life, concealing their activities until such time as there are sufficient converts for them publicly to proclaim their allegiance to the cause.

By the middle of 1962 the regular Viet Cong strength had grown to an estimated 20,000 to 25,000 men. In addition, there were many thousands of regional troops and village guerrillas. Even if government claims to have killed some 20,000 since 1959 were anything like accurate, the Viet Cong had not been seriously enough hurt to discourage them from the pursuit of their politico-military goal— the overthrow of the Diem régime and the establishment of a "neutralist" coalition government on Laotian lines as a prelude to reunification with the Communist North.

Twenty thousand killed in such a war is nothing. French and French Union forces lost 94,000 men killed and missing in Indo-China between 1945 and the first Geneva Agreement in 1954. Viet Minh losses, including those killed in error or on suspicion during that period, have been reckoned as high as half a million.

Two technical developments, the use of the M113 armored personnel carrier in the rice fields and swamps of the Mekong delta and the introduction of helicopters for the surprise movement of large bodies of troops, added greatly to the Viet Cong's difficulties in open delta areas. True, the helicopter is extremely vulnerable: a man armed only with a carbine can shoot it down if he hits it in the right place. Even so, heliborne troops are much more effective than paratroopers. Troops need little training to jump from helicopters, which have not only the capability of surprise, but of repeated surprise. Reserve helicopters can fill the eagle's role, for instance, and descend when they see the Viet Cong moving. They can be used on the flanks, from the rear, or to go to the defense of a village under Viet Cong attack. Because of them the Viet Cong have no hope of converting from guerrilla warfare into mobile warfare in the Mekong delta. But this, it is useful to remember, was also true of the Viet Minh in the Red River delta.

In conjunction with their main bases in the jungle and rubber and swamp lands north and east of Saigon, however, the Mekong delta is, and seems likely to remain, an important source of Viet Cong supply. The rice, the money, the manpower and the weapons they need to continue their operations are available here to resolute men who are prepared to fight.

Nowhere have the Viet Cong suffered the sort of casualties that the French inflicted on the Viet Minh at Yen Bay, or even at Ninh Binh. In a series of four actions late in March and early in April, 1961, on the eve of the South Vietnamese presidential elections, however, the Viet Cong incautiously grouped large forces while lacking heavy support and antiaircraft weapons. In the first action of March 27th, near the Plain of Rushes, the Arvins killed about a hundred Viet Cong and lost only twenty-seven killed themselves.

In a second action north of Saigon at Ben Cat, another large force of Viet Cong was scattered with heavy casualties. Another hundred Viet Cong died in an attack near the 5th Arvin Division's headquarters east of Saigon. Finally an attempt to seize Ben Tre, the capital of Khien Hoa Province, south of Saigon, was also broken up with heavy losses to the attackers.

That the presidential elections were conducted on April 7, 1961, with negligible casualties was undoubtedly due in large part to the Arvins' March and early April successes. The following month Viet-Cong-initiated incidents dropped sharply. During the wet-season months that followed, both the Arvins and the Viet Cong reorganized.

By this time, however, the complacency of 1959 had turned into something like panic. The pessimists were predicting the early collapse of all resistance to the Viet Cong. To combat this defeatism, Vice-President Lyndon Johnson arrived to nail the United States colors to Diem's masthead. He was followed by the Staley Mission, which finally gave approval to Diem's request for military training and equipment for the expanding Self-Defense Corps and the Civil Guard, and to increase the size of the army.

The general situation showed no sign of improvement, however. When 1961 began, South Vietnam confidently expected to export 350,000 tons of rice. Though floods caused considerable damage to the delta paddy fields, the Viet Cong, and not the weather, made South Vietnam a rice importer before the year was out. By September the Viet Cong were ready to move from small-scale actions into much larger operations. An immense area stretching from north of Saigon to the Cambodian border was now effectively under their control. Phuoc Vinh, the capital of Phuoc Thanh Province, fell under heavy attack, which netted another big supply of arms. There were other big losses on the High Plateau.

In October the situation deteriorated still further. Viet Cong attacks on military targets leaped from 50 in September to 120, and major gunfights from 8 to 29. Against this background, the Taylor Mission arrived in Saigon at the end of 1961 to draw up a plan for winning the war. Official American opinions on the situation were disparate. A section of the State Department still supported the view that the place to draw the line was in Laos and that any attempt to restore the situation in South Vietnam would be futile while the Viet Cong had free access along the Ho Chi Minh trail.

There was the Arthur Schlesinger school of thought which doubted whether we could win in Vietnam with or without Diem, the Rostow camp which had come up with the theory, presumably based on the Malayan experience, that the ratio of regulars to fight guerrillas had to be at least twelve to one, and the Galbraith cynics who said that if this were the case then the United States ought to be careful not to let any guns fall into the hands of the Sioux. Others, such as Senator Mike Mansfield, Walter Lippmann, and James Reston, seemed to think that there was something to Sihanouk's (and Mao Tse-tung's) idea of a neutral belt through South-East Asia. There were those who said that Vietnam could not be held without American troops, and others who argued that American troops would be disastrous.

Before 1962 was very far advanced, however, it was apparent that, from a military point of view, the Taylor report made a lot of sense. The aircraft carrier *Core* shuttled in and out of Saigon bringing helicopters. Hundreds, then thousands, of American officers and noncommissioned officers arrived to help knock the Vietnamese military and paramilitary forces into shape. They were best received—and most useful—in training roles, especially with the Civil Guard and the Self-Defense Corps, both of which were grateful that their long period of neglect was about to end at last.

In answer to the Taylor Mission, however, a military delegation from Communist China led by Marshal Yeh Chien-ying, President and Political Commissar of the Academy of Political Science, Vice-Chairman of the National Defense Council, and Chief of the Armed Forces Supervision Department, arrived in Hanoi from Peking on December 15, 1961. The delegation included the commander of the Chinese Air Force, General Liu Ya-lou, another veteran of the Long March, and General Hsia Hua, one of Mao Tse-tung's earliest followers.

At a formal banquet one evening in Hanoi, Yeh said that the United States was using Diem to wage a real war against the people in South Vietnam and that the Chinese people could not remain indifferent to these activities. Recalling that General Giap's visit to China in 1949 had "made valuable contributions in enhancing the fraternal friendship between the peoples and armies of our two countries," he predicted that the visit of the Chinese mission would "add a new page to this friendship which flows on eternally like the Yangtze and the Red River."

Whether coincidentally or otherwise, the Chinese visit to Hanoi coincided with a top-secret instruction from the Lao Dong Party to its cadres in South Vietnam to establish there the People's Revolutionary Party. The instructions, which were captured in South Vietnam early in 1962, said that the new organization should appear to be a new party and look independent, though in fact it was to be nothing else than a unified North-South Vietnam Lao Dong Party under the orders of the Party's politburo, which consists of Ho Chi Minh, Truong Chinh, Pham Van Dong, Vo Nguyen Giap, Le Duan, Le Duc Tho, who succeeded Le Duan as commander of the Viet Minh forces in South Vietnam in 1951; Nguyen Duy Trinh, Le Thanh Nghi, the régime's specialist in economics; and Hoang Van Hoan, another of Ho's early protégés from the Revolutionary Youth Movement.

For the figurehead in the National Liberation Front, Hanoi chose Nguyen Huu Tho, a popular Saigon lawyer, known to be a fellow traveler but not generally regarded by his contemporaries and associates as a dedicated Communist. Diem arrested him in 1954 when he was vice-chairman of the Saigon-Cholon Peace Committee. He was sent first to Haiphong and later to Phu Yen Province in Central Vietnam, where he was freed by a Viet Cong attack in 1960. The vice-chairmen of the Front included two doctors, Dr. Phung Van Cung and Dr. Vo Chi Con, and an architect, Huynh Tan Phat, none of them nationally known but about as prominent in Vietnamese society as the average member of Diem's National Assembly. The tribesmen from the High Plateau had their representatives, the Buddhists and the Catholics theirs.

As in the days when the Lao Dong Party took control of the Lien Viet Front, however, the People's Revolutionary Party was in the "vanguard" and its principal representative, Nguyen Van Hieu, became secretary-general of the Front. A Saigon journalist in his early forties, and a former professor of history, Hieu is regarded by his contemporaries as a talented newspaperman, an amusing companion and a dedicated Communist, who for several years, and with great skill, managed to keep out of the hands of Diem's security police. When his wife, a chemist, was arrested some years ago, Hieu fled to the country and joined the maquis. Subsequently, his wife escaped from South Vietnam through Cambodia and rejoined Hieu in Hanoi.

Between February 16 and March 3, 1962, the National Front for the Liberation of South Vietnam met somewhere in, or near, South Vietnam. The most popular guess in Saigon was that the meeting for prestige purposes was held in South Vietnam and not across the border in either Laos or Cambodia. The congress rates a position in the struggle for Vietnam along with the historic congresses that at intervals during the preceding thirty-two years had directed the course of the Communist movement in the Indo-China States.

Ever since 1946, and notwithstanding their victory at Dien Bien Phu and the bitter disappointment that followed the Geneva Agreement, the Viet Minh have been conscious of the limitations of a "war of national liberation." They feel that in small colonial or semicolonial countries it should not be fought to the bitter end in the field, but only to the point where the enemy can be brought to the conference table and there defeated. Politics, in effect, is the logical extension of war. This was the policy that linked the "great military success" at Dien Bien Phu with the "great political victory at Geneva." This was the policy in Laos. It now became policy in South Vietnam. On February 15th, on the eve of the congress which began the following day, Peking came out in favor of a Geneva conference to settle the South Vietnam war. On February 28th, while the congress was still in session, Hanoi supported this proposal. Two weeks later Ung Van Khiem, the Southern-born Foreign Minister of North Vietnam and founder-chairman of the Liberation Front in 1960, issued a statement calling for the consultation of all Powers concerned at Geneva. *Nhan Dan*, the Lao Dong Party newspaper, spoke even more bluntly two days later. "We demand a conference," it said.

News of the congress was withheld for a month. When, on April 15th, Peking and Hanoi announced that it had been held, the thirty-six-page communiqué was couched in predictable terms. "The South Vietnam National Liberation Front has called on the South Vietnamese people to unite broadly to defeat the war of aggression waged by the United States and its lackeys, so as to achieve independence, democracy, peace, and neutrality. . . . The general task of the South Vietnam National Liberation Front is to unite the entire people in South Vietnam, resolutely struggle against the U.S. aggressors and war provocateurs, overthrow the

Ngo Dinh Diem ruling clique, U.S. imperialism's lackeys, form a broad national democratic coalition government in South Vietnam, defend peace, carry out a policy of neutrality, and advance toward the peaceful reunification of the fatherland." Diplomatic relations were to be established with all countries. Military alliances were eschewed. In the final paragraph, the co-chairmen of the Geneva conference, Britain and the Soviet Union, were called on to end the war.

As always when they try to masquerade in the lamb's clothing of neutrality, the Communists had difficulty in hiding their teeth. The pleas for peace were heavily interwoven with the usual Peking-style clichés about the "imperialist and colonialist countries headed by the U.S. having unmasked themselves as warmongers and aggressors, oppressors and exploiters of the peoples." The "imperialists and their agents" were said to pay lip service to the policy of peace and neutrality, "whereas they actually consider peace and neutrality as a good signboard to cover up their dark colonialist intentions, to mislead the people, to break their unity and divide their patriotic movement with the aim of carrying out their policy of neo-colonialism." On the other hand, "the socialist camp, including thirteen countries and 1,000 million people with the Soviet Union as its center, is the principal opponent of the aggressive bellicose colonialist forces."

Soon after the congress, Nguyen Van Hieu returned to Hanoi and led a Front delegation to Peking, Moscow, and eastern Europe and then on to Switzerland, Egypt, Cuba, Burma, and Indonesia. Deliberately the congress had named only thirty-one members of the fifty-two-man provisional central committee. Some of the remaining places were not disclosed in order to protect those working in government areas in the South; others were left open for recruits.

Hieu's mission had three main tasks: to seek aid and international support for the Front's struggle in South Vietnam, to gain international acceptance for the central committee of the Front as a provisional government, and to make contact with leading Vietnamese exiles in Europe, with a view to filling some of the Front's gaps with nationally known names.

For many months discussions had been taking place in Geneva and Paris between North Vietnamese representatives and the Paris "exiles." Most of the exiles are as suspicious of the Viet Minh as they are antagonistic to Diem; they also lack unity. Their one common denominator is their belief that they could do better than Diem if they got the chance.

The Front's guess was that expediency would cause some at least to swallow their anti-Communism and to make common cause. In Saigon the name of Tran Van Huu, Prime Minister of Vietnam in 1950–1951, was frequently mentioned. Huu is vain and ambitious, apparently acceptable to the Viet Minh, and now popular with the French. His leadership in the Front in pursuit of a Laotian-type settlement in Vietnam could be a sore embarrassment to the West. There are many others, however. They include Dr. Nguyen Ngoc Bich, who regards the Viet Cong's war as legitimate because, in his view, it is being fought in quest of rice. Nguyen Van Tam, another former Prime Minister, and his son, General Nguyen Van Hinh, the former chief of staff, are others. The name of Nguyen Manh Ha, who served as Minister of National Economy in Ho Chi Minh's first coalition government and who used to be active in Catholic youth movements in Tongking, is also mentioned.

An odd figure in all these maneuverings is Ba Cut's old concubine, Cao Thai Nguyet, who was forced into marriage with a former member of the Viet Minh and now acts as go-between with the various groups. Suave Prince Buu Loc, Bao Dai's cousin, who preceded Diem as Prime Minister in 1954, is listed as a catalyst.

As part of Hieu's complementary mission to pave the way for the international recognition of the provisional government as soon as it is announced, Cuba was an obvious stop. He was received there by Castro and arranged for a National Liberation Front mission to be stationed in Havana. President Sukarno received him in Indonesia. A Front delegate will be attached to the Afro-Asian Solidarity Committee in Cairo, while other representatives will be stationed in bloc countries in eastern Europe.

Back in Peking late in September, 1962, Hieu and his delegation met with a delegation from North Vietnam led by Ung Van Khiem and Chinese politburo member, Peng Chen, who was just about to leave at the head of a Chinese delegation to North Vietnam. At a banquet in Hieu's honor on September 24th, Peng Chen said that every struggle waged in South Vietnam gave great encouragement and support to China. "Their struggles are ours," he said. "The people of China and South Vietnam are the closest of brothers, friends, and comrades-in-arms. They have a common aim and a common enemy in their struggle and will always fight shoulder to shoulder until final victory is won."

However unwillingly, both North Vietnam and its South Vietnamese offshoot were now being drawn closer to the Chinese side in the ideological dispute with Moscow. The aged poet Kuo Mo-jo, who, as chairman of the China Peace Committee, is often used as a keynote speaker when dealing with foreign delegations, took occasion at the banquet to denounce President Kennedy as "more cunning, more treacherous and more vicious than Eisenhower." "U.S. imperialism is U.S. imperialism and Kennedy is Kennedy," he said. "Cholera germs are cholera germs, and whoever says that imperialism can change its nature, or that it has already changed, whoever wants to say that Kennedy is a warm or peace-loving man, is really saying that cholera germs can change their nature and that the germs now want people to be healthy and have long life."

Once again events beyond Vietnam helped to bring the Chinese and North Vietnamese régimes closer together. This time India was the unwitting cause of the trouble. For years the Indian members of the International Control Commission in Vietnam had trod warily. Neither side cooperated with the Commission. Though both North and South reported their catalog of charges, the Poles consistently vetoed collective reports, and the Indians were unwilling to join with the Canadians in reporting back to the Russian and British co-chairmen of the Geneva Agreement without absolute proof, which, under the circumstances, was hard to get. By the middle of 1962 there was no longer any doubt, however, that the Viet Minh were up to their necks in stirring up a "war of national liberation" in South Vietnam. Though they acted covertly, there was nothing secret about their intention. In a majority report to the co-chairmen, the Indians and Canadians came to the conclusion that in specific instances there was evidence to show that armed and unarmed men, arms, munitions, and other supplies had been sent from North Vietnam to the Viet Cong in the South with the object of organizing, supporting, and carrying out hostile activities, including armed attacks, against Diem's armed forces and administration.

Long before the report was made public by the British Government as a White Paper in June, 1962, Hanoi, which had been tipped off by the Poles, launched a bitter attack on the Canadians and the Indians, who were even accused of accepting bribes from South Vietnam. The Indians were even more bitterly attacked than the Canadians. Suddenly they were "tools of the imperialists" and of the "fascist Ngo Dinh Diem gang." In particular, Hanoi objected to the charge of engaging in "subversive activities," pointing out accurately enough that the Geneva Agreement made no mention of subversion and did not empower the International Control Commission to investigate it.

Nothing could have suited Peking better. At a time when it was moving toward a showdown with India in the Himalayas, and engaged in its continuing and bitter dispute with Moscow over Russian aid for India, it found itself with a warm supporter in the Democratic Republic of Vietnam. Any doubts now about where North Vietnam stood in the ideological dispute were quickly dispelled. "Relations between Vietnam and China and between the Lao Dong Party and the Chinese Communist Party are characterised by unity, unity and unity forever," said Ho Chi Minh. Even between Russia and China protestations of friendship were still commonplace; but no longer was there ever a reference to Party unity. Ho had chosen his side in a way that left no room for misunderstanding.

The week following Ho's statement the National Liberation Front announced that it had decided to extend economic aid to "the fraternal Algerian people to help them overcome their difficulties in the early stages of their economic construction." The act was economic: the intent was political. This was clearly the forerunner of the announcement that a provisional government of reunification exists in South Vietnam. But first there is a need to "liberate" a more worthy home for it than the jungles of southeastern Laos. With no village in the Mekong delta safe from surprise attack by land or water or air, or even a combination of all three, the Viet Cong cannot expect to "liberate" an area here and regard it as secure. Comparatively little of South Vietnam is rice land, however.

North of the delta, and extending all the way to the 17th parallel, is the rugged Annamite Chain, sparsely populated, only partly explored, and already largely in Viet Cong hands. Here in these mountain fastnesses, the Viet Cong are preparing to move from guerrilla warfare into mobile warfare, just as twelve years ago Giap moved into the offensive from similar mountains and jungles in North Vietnam. Here, also, they are preparing to establish their government.

Listen to Diem as he explains it: "Ho and Giap started in Thai Nguyen and Tuyen Quang, rocky areas, difficult of access and covered with dense forest," he says. "No one worried about these forest areas very much. The French in the early days didn't expect trouble from China, so they held the line with posts covering the north and west of these Viet Minh bases. Viet Minh harassed the posts and the roads from their secure base area, and soon they became isolated. The French posts elsewhere in the north were even more isolated. At the same time, the Viet Minh engaged in other activities in the Red River delta, in the richest provinces. The French did not have enough troops, so they withdrew some of their forces from the outposts, which now became very vulnerable. The Viet Minh attacked and the whole line was lost except for a few isolated posts. The Viet Minh then controlled a very large area and began to open up new bases which enabled them to wrest control of the roads from the French.

"We are now in a similar situation in the Annamite Chain. It is the same story over again. The difference is that the Annamite Chain is much larger than the two provinces which Ho Chi Minh started from: it extends all the way down Vietnam to the fringe of the Maquis D, outside Saigon."

From his mountain headquarters in Quang Ngai Province Major General Nguyen Don, the Viet Cong commander in the northern Annamite Chain, is building up his forces. Diem believes he will strike for the sea and thus attempt to secure the manpower and the rice of the coastland lowlands, while cutting South Vietnam in two. Others predict that he will hit back across the High Plateau, cutting the lines of communication between Diem's isolated garrisons, seize all of Kontum Province, and clear the way both for the "liberation government" and the supply line that runs through Laos and North Vietnam to Communist China.

Badly overextended already, with almost all their regular forces tied down in static defense, the Arvins are hard pressed here to maintain the *status quo*. One division alone is responsible for no less than 17,000 square miles of territory, 150 miles of seacoast, and 125 miles of Cambodian and Laotian border through which

Viet Cong technicians from North Vietnam have begun to pour like water through a sieve. Here, somewhere, the offensive will come. Marshal Peng Teh-huai once advised Giap to strike through the mountain resort of Dalat to the coast at Phan Rang if the French refused to sign the Geneva Agreement in 1954. The attack could come along this line, or against Ban Me Thuot, or down to the coast at Phu Yen. When and where it will come is a matter for speculation. That it will come is certain.

10
War
On
The
High
Plateau

In the first hour of daylight, at a time when men are busy with their breakfast rice pots, and the air is still and clear before the midmorning winds, the telltale smoke of a campfire hangs in the treetops along the frontier of Laos and South Vietnam like the dye from a marker in a calm sea. Early in March, 1962, Vietnamese and American aircraft on dawn patrol noted a significant increase in the number of these campfires across the rugged, sparsely populated border. An American reconnaissance plane that ventured high above Tchepone, the Communist staging base in Laos, returned with a hole the size of a football in its fuselage from heavy antiaircraft fire. Day by day the fires moved southward and spread out across the wilderness of mountains and narrow jungle tracks east of the Mekong River and into Sithone's domains.

About the same time, Vietnamese troops landed by helicopter in a surprise assault on a Viet Cong headquarters in the Annamite Chain. The raiders captured documents warning the local Viet Cong commander to plant more vegetables in readiness for a bigger flow of cadres from North Vietnam.

To the Vietnamese officers and many of their American advisers the Laotian smoke signals and the Viet Cong order fitted together like the pieces of a simple jigsaw puzzle. The regular Viet Cong soldier is a master of concealment and camouflage. With green leaves and twigs thrust into the net that covers his basketwork helmet and the pack on his back, he becomes a chameleon at the sound of an aircraft, blending himself into the roadside foliage. A haystack, the thatched roof of a peasant's cottage, a tunnel or a cave under a village, all provide him with cover. He can stay for hours with a bamboo breathing tube in a pond, or under the murky water of a rice field. But he has yet to find a way of concealing the smoke when he cooks the rice that he carries slung over his shoulder, or around his waist, in a cotton bandolier.

As the camp fires crept closer to the first spill-out zone on the Ho Chi Minh trail, American-trained montagnard scouts moved into the jungle along the Laotian border. Through the winter and early spring of 1962 a monthly average of about two hundred to three hundred cadres and hard-core soldiers had come this way to swell the ranks of the Communist insurgents in South Vietnam. One Viet Cong lieutenant who surrendered to the Arvins confessed that he was part of a regiment which had entered South Vietnam by the Ho Chi Minh trail, that he and his troops had been trained in special warfare and guerrilla techniques, and that they had taken three months to make the journey. Another lieutenant, captured to the east of the High Plateau in Quang Ngai Province, admitted that he was on his seventeenth trip by sea to South Vietnam.

In May and June, after two months of hard slogging through the jungle from Tchepone, the overland flow into South Vietnam increased sharply. The rate doubled, then trebled. All through the Annamite Chain the Viet Cong bases began to fill up. Where

once there were only platoons there were now companies and even
battalions.

Even so, some Americans in Vietnam were skeptical. They said
that the tribesmen scouts who wear G-strings and carry crossbows
could not count above ten. But the scouts not only had numbers
but descriptive accounts of equipment. They had seen pack
elephants carrying mortars and what seemed to be antiaircraft
guns, or artillery, strapped to their backs. They spoke of large
dogs held on leashes and other details that were patently beyond
their powers of invention. Soon there was no longer any argument.
At the end of June, west of the High Plateau town of Kontum
and about ten miles from the Laotian border, a full Viet Cong
battalion clashed with Vietnamese forces. After contact it withdrew into what was subsequently found to be a large Viet Cong
base. Heavily defended and widely dispersed, it straddled the
border, one-third in Vietnam and two-thirds in Laos. It had
accommodation for a thousand men and was complete with
vegetable plots and rice fields.

Three weeks later, a helicopter carrying Lieutenant Colonel
Anthony J. Tenczza, of Fairfax, Virginia, a highly decorated
veteran of the Pacific and Korean wars and chief military adviser
to the 22nd Division at Kontum, was shot down by .50-caliber
antiaircraft fire close to the Viet Cong encampment. Colonel
Tenczza and two other Americans were killed. Two Vietnamese
officers and a third American were reported missing. One American escaped unhurt.

Powerful American-type antitank mines appeared on the road
running north from Kontum. The American advisers argued
whether they were made in China or captured in Korea: they did
not question their lethal qualities or how they had come to South
Vietnam. Sixty miles from the southern High Plateau town of
Ban Me Thuot an attack on a Viet Cong position produced
hundreds of packages of plastic high explosives. Their markings
were all in Chinese. For the first time, Civil Guard posts came
under fire from 57-millimeter recoilless rifles. Artillery had not yet
been reported in use, but the capture of a fire plan suggested that
its appearance would not be long delayed.

Many in the South argued that all of this constituted a direct
act of aggression by North Vietnam. It was, in fact, a form of

aggression by proxy, a tactic that the Communists have mastered in Indo-China. Viet Minh guerrillas went to China in 1950 and came back as regular forces to smash the French Tongking border posts at the porte de Chîne. Pathet Lao troops from Laos regularly trained in North Vietnamese bases, and this invasion of South Vietnam was by South Vietnamese who left parents, brides, and children and went north with the Viet Minh in 1954.

With Laos abandoned to a neutrality that does not preclude a Communist takeover and certain, whatever the intentions and the political coloration of the Vientiane government, to remain the major supply route for the Viet Cong, the key to the war now lay in the High Plateau. Basically, the struggle here is less a matter of real estate than a competition for the loyalties of the primitive, neglected mountain people, numbering anything from about 600,000 to 1,000,000. The French called them the montagnards, the mountain people. To the Vietnamese, they are mois, or savages. They are not one people, however, but many. Among them are at least twenty tribes, some of whom speak as many as ten dialects. Missionaries have devised a written language for one tribe, the Rhade or Ede, and are working on an alphabet for another, the Sedang. The rest communicate among themselves only by spoken word. Most live in thatched longhouses like the Dayaks of Borneo, and the Polynesians of Tahiti. Others crowd into primitive huts of atap and bamboo. Those of Malay-Polynesian stock are creamy brown in color, with fine features. The Mon-Khmers are heavier and darker. Even among the most advanced tribes, a belief in the sorcerer's magic persists, while the savage Katus, in Quang Nam Province, have not yet abandoned human sacrifice as a means of appeasing animist spirits.

In French days the High Plateau was a Domaine de la Curonne, under the titular authority of the former emperor and then Head of State, Bao Dai. In effect, this meant "Vietnamese keep out." Only in the small town of Kontum, where coastal Christians fled after a Buddhist massacre in 1855, were the Vietnamese present in any number. The French, who established some fine rubber plantations in the rich red soil of the High Plateau, tended to regard the montagnards as living museum pieces; troublesome, certainly, and often in need of a punitive expedition, but far too precious to be exposed to Vietnamese exploitation.

Vietnamese settlement began after 1954, and would have been

much more extensive if President Ngo Dinh Diem had succeeded in convincing the United States that the development of strategic-economic roads through the High Plateau should have high priority in the economic aid program. Diem failed to persuade the United States Operations Mission to do more than reconstruct about a hundred miles of road linking the two Plateau towns of Ban Me Thuot and Pleiku and to rehabilitate an existing road from Pleiku to Qui Nhon on the coast. Nevertheless, about 150,000 Vietnamese migrated to the Plateau. They came as fugitives from the Communists in North Vietnam and the poverty-stricken coastal areas of Central Vietnam. They also came with little understanding of, or sympathy for, the montagnards. Many became merchants in the Plateau towns and were soon involved in bitter disputes with montagnard farmers, who accused them of cheating. They mobilized the montagnards to work on the roads and often forgot to pay for their labor. Montagnard schools and hospitals built by the French fell into disrepair. The montagnards became bitter and angry.

They looked on the Vietnamese settlers as colonizers and land-grabbers and they reacted as the Indians reacted in the westward movement of American settlers across the United States in the nineteenth century. They either fled or fought. Later, with the arrival of Vietnamese troops, relations between the two peoples became worse. In few cases, however, did the settlers leave the valleys, the towns, and the main roads. Beyond, in the foothills and the mountains, the montagnards and the Viet Cong made common cause.

Here on the High Plateau, perhaps more than anywhere else in South Vietnam, one is struck by the twilight character of the war, an atmosphere almost of unreality, or at least of ambivalance, that permits the Viet Cong to commit the most ghastly brutalities one day, while lining up the next to cheer a Catholic bishop on the way to one of the more remote and Communist-dominated areas of his diocese.

This happened to Bishop Nhu of Long Xuyen Province in the Mekong delta, it is true, but the Plateau has a fund of such stories. There is the case, for instance, of the French priest who, with the full knowledge of the Viet Cong, acts as a government agent in paying the Civil Guard troops for their vigil on an isolated bridge because ambushes prevent the district chief from getting to the post. The Catholic Relief Service, which keeps trucks constantly on the road and drives to most parts of the country, proclaims its identity in large painted signs, which its drivers regard as the best form of insurance. Once the Viet Cong stopped a driver and asked him where he was going. He replied that he was carrying supplies for a priest who lived nearby.

"If you're not, we'll shoot you," said the Viet Cong, climbing aboard the truck. Since the priest was new in the area, the driver drove his captors with considerable anxiety to the rectory. But the priest's ready acknowledgment that he was indeed working for the Catholic Relief Service resulted in the release of both the man and his supplies!

Such stories are in contrast with the murder of Father Theo Bonnet outside the montagnard village of Ngo Ro Nge on December 13, 1961. Five days earlier Father Bonnet had been in the provincial capital of Kontum to assist the Sisters of the Miraculous Medal in the ceremony of renewing their vows. He told the sisters he knew he was in danger but had decided to return to work among his montagnard villagers "as if the Viet Cong did not exist."

He left Kontum on the afternoon of December 8th, and arrived at his rectory in the village of Kon Kola on Saturday, December 9th, a few hours before a group of Viet Cong, who warned the villagers that the father would no longer be allowed to move about.

The Viet Cong were joined early next morning by three Can Bo who entered the priest's house to "indoctrinate" him. The village Christians thought the Can Bo planned to murder Father Bonnet and gathered round the rectory. When they had gone the priest came out and talked to his parishioners.

"What did they say to you, Father?" they asked.

"They said that I was not to go to other villages," he said. "When I asked what I would do with my time, they replied, 'Rest.' "

The priest said that he could not rest, but must teach religion. The Can Bo then asked who built the church.

"The Christians of this village," replied Father Bonnet.

"Who gave the order?"

"God."

"God! He doesn't exist."

"Who made heaven and earth?" the priest asked.

"No one," replied a Can Bo. "They made themselves."

"Then in that case the church of Kon Kola also made itself," said Father Bonnet.

To ease the mind of his parishioners, Father Bonnet, a shy but much loved man who had lived among the montagnards for nine years, spoke two of their dialects and Vietnamese, and who could sing and walk barefooted over the mountains with the best of them, said that finally the Viet Cong had agreed he could continue with his duties in the rest of the parish.

The next day he announced that he was going to the village of Ngo Ro Nge. The villagers tried to dissuade him. "As God wills, then, I'll go alone," he said.

Fifteen Christian montagnards decided to leave with him. They set off unarmed for the village of Wang Klen, where Father Bonnet celebrated Mass. Late in the afternoon he reached the village of Kon Jrau, where he celebrated a second Mass.

It was nightfall when the priest and his followers approached the village of Ngo Ro Nge. Outside the village Christian montagnards appeared to warn the priest not to enter. The Viet Cong were there. But he disregarded their advice and passed through the ring of about twenty armed montagnard Viet Cong who guarded the approaches. Inside the village three Can Bo Kinh (Vietnamese, as distinct from montagnard, commissars) were addressing the villagers. They ignored the priest as he passed on the way to the thatched chapel.

Early in the morning the priest heard confession and said Mass. Afterward he hurried. Having arranged his things, he said: "Let's leave quickly. The Viet Cong want to kill me." He ate at most half a bowl of rice, then went swiftly from the house and out of the village.

Two young montagnards caught up with him and preceded him by a few steps. The other thirteen took their leave in a more leisurely manner and were some distance behind when Father Bonnet jumped a small stream, and, almost at a run, began to climb the hill on the other side.

The montagnards heard a burst of fire. Hit three times, Father Bonnet fell, his right hand clenched around his rosary. He died in two or three minutes.

The montagnards threw themselves down around the priest. "Shoot us too!" they shouted into the jungle.

When the montagnards got back to the village, the Viet Cong

were mocking the dead priest. They left, firing their guns in the air in celebration of his death. The whole village came to pray and grieve as the body of the priest was carried in. He was buried at Kontum, which has a population of perhaps ten thousand. Ten thousand came to his funeral. And the montagnards tracked down the Viet Cong who had "indoctrinated" him and shot them dead as they ate their lunch by the side of a mountain stream.

Six months later the Viet Cong kidnapped an American doctor and two missionaries from the leprosarium at Ban Me Thuot, and carted them off into the jungle to train their own medical orderlies. Generally speaking, however, abduction and accidental death in an ambush, or in the case of mistaken identity, are the gravest dangers still being run by priests, doctors, and other foreign missionaries today. All of them are against the Viet Cong. But this the Viet Cong expect and allow for. Catholics, they say, cannot be "educated" in a generation, and cadres are warned not to expect a "high degree of political consciousness" among them. A Viet Cong organization, the Friends of the Workers in Christ, hopes to take the matter in hand; but so far it has not made much headway.

This is not to denigrate the work the missionaries have done in the High Plateau, nor to serve as an apologist for the Viet Cong. For years the missionaries were about the montagnards' only friendly link with the non-Communist world, and they have been undeterred by the possibility of captivity or violent death. As for the Viet Cong, they are capable of infinite brutalities, but to regard them as a simple terrorist organization is to misunderstand the nature and the gravity of their threat. To deal with terrorism is easy. It is much more difficult to cope with an organization that seeks mass support by promises, however specious, of pie in the sky.

Two access roads lead to the High Plateau from the coast of Central Vietnam, one from the port of Nha Trang and the other from Qui Nhon. A third and much longer road links Ban Me Thuot with Saigon. Civilian supplies continue to move freely by road. On these roads, and on most roads elsewhere in the country, the Viet Cong have mobile checkpoints. Armed guards check the destination of goods and hold Vietnamese travelers who do not appear on their "wanted" lists for an hour's political indoctrination. "Wanted" persons disappear and are usually never heard of again. French planters and French businessmen, who are obliged to pay for "protection," usually are allowed to pass, though their casualty rate is growing. Other Westerners are liable to indefinite detention, or to be held pending the payment of substantial sums of ransom. In fact, several Western embassies, profiting from the experience of two Australian officials who were detained by the Viet Cong for several days in September, 1961, carry "capture" kits, including spare toothbrushes, insect repellent, and other materials designed to make life in a Viet Cong camp more bearable.

Lacking the protection of an army convoy, therefore, it is easier to travel to the High Plateau these days by air. Within minutes of taking off from Saigon the plane is over one of three main Viet Cong bases immediately north of the capital, the Duong Minh Chau, which runs north of the Cao Dai town of Tay Ninh in the western delta and links up through a small corridor area known as Long Nguyen, with the Maquis D, the biggest and potentially most dangerous of all these bases with its three thousand hard-core Viet Cong who operate there as a constant threat to all ground communications north from Saigon.

Together the three zones occupy an area about the size of Rhode Island. Since 1946 the Viet Cong's jungle camps here have not been seriously disturbed. Beset with other problems in its early years in office, the Ngo Dinh Diem government failed to extend its writ to the Maquis D and have been ruing the consequences ever since. For the Viet Cong have set up permanent installations and even run their own trucks and jeeps, all within a couple of hours' drive of Saigon.

When the Australian government looked around for a convenient place to give South Vietnam a pure-bred Jersey dairy farm under Colombo Plan aid, it found what appeared to be ideal pastureland near the town of Ben Cat, about forty miles north of Saigon. It did not know that Ben Cat was on the edge of Long Nguyen. For a year or two the cows grazed unmolested. Now both cows and their armed guards come under repeated attack.

In one attack eight cows and a bull disappeared, leading to facetious suggestions in Saigon that the Viet Cong planned to start their own stud farm in the Maquis D. On another occasion the initial reports suggested that not only a gallant guard but also his wife had lost their lives in the defense of the cows. Embarrassed Australian officials wondered whether they should not confer some posthumous honor on the couple, but changed their minds when they discovered that the man had been lured from duty by a local village maiden and that they had died in *flagrante delicto* under the watchtower.

On the outskirts of the Maquis D the green yellows of the partly flooded rice paddies quickly give way to broccoli-like jungle. Here and there are razed clearings, where villages have been pulled down and the inhabitants moved to defended hamlets, which differ from the strategic hamlets in that they are more heavily protected. Lacking the mellowing influence of time, they stand out stark and brown against the surrounding green of the countryside. Beyond are isolated hutments which are too deep in Viet Cong areas for early resettlement, and deeper still the villages which defiantly fly the Viet Cong flag.

The rivers are deep and dark beneath the trees. The plane bumps along a couple of thousand feet above the jungle roof, and for many miles there is no sign of life. In the foothills of the Annamite Chain the jungle changes. The greens are lighter and the trees bigger but fewer, towering above the dense secondary undergrowth. There are occasional patches of grass of an even more vivid green, like the fairways of a well cared for golf course, and some small, bright blue lakes. This is the beginning of the montagnard country. The tribesmen show their presence by a bared hillside, where they have slashed and burned the undergrowth to sow their corn in the ashes. When this poorly fertilized soil is exhausted, they move on.

Ban Me Thuot, capital of Darlac Province, is sleepy French-tropical, with scarlet and green flamboyant trees shading the streets and its clip-clopping mountain ponies from the sun. It is a frankly encouraging place. The shops are primitive but well stocked with all manner of consumer goods, including such things as Swiss watches, jewelry, and utilitarian hoeheads, crosscut saws, chains, plastic hoses, and galvanized iron. Tailors' shops, with their windows fitted with dummies, appear to do a thriving business. The market bustles with activity and brims with food—chickens, ducks, and pigs in wicker baskets, potatoes, onions, cuttlefish, sacks of rice. Despite the difficulties of supply, this is a town of abundance. I sat on a stool near the market one day and had a three-course meal of soup, rice, and noodles mixed with chicken, for about eight cents.

If the way to a man's heart is through his child's smile—and it probably is—then the American Military Advisory and Assistance Group here have performed notably. Children run into the street at the sight of an American, or what they assume to be an American, to clutch him by the hand or shirt or trousers and to exchange laughs and jokes and a word or two of English and Vietnamese.

MAAG operates from one of the hunting lodges of the former Emperor Bao Dai, a magnificent rough-hewn wooden building roofed with shingles half an inch thick. Its task is to advise the 23rd Arvin Division, which has its headquarters at Ban Me Thuot. A Special Forces detachment outside the town has the additional task of training Rhade Ranger companies.

As usual in South Vietnam these days, the picture here is mixed. Lieutenant Colonel Billado, a veteran of the Solomons, New Guinea, and Korea, and now principal American adviser to the Arvin division, thought that enough of the 50,000 Rhade tribesmen in Darlac Province might be attracted by military training to defend one village. But while the first group was being trained, several thousand tribesmen camped outside waiting their turn. By July, 1962, in addition to having trained enough tribesmen to defend sixty villages, the training of seven Ranger companies was under way.

Though the risk of giving guns to people who accepted them with such childish delight was patent, there was no evidence that the montagnards had any intention of using them for purposes that were not intended.

Many Vietnamese remained doubtful, however. In 1958 Saigon caused bitter resentment by ordering the destruction of all crossbows, the montagnards' silent but effective weapon. This was a heinous crime in the eyes of the montagnards, who generally found the Vietnamese more demanding than the French in their taxes and in other ways (a tax on elephants was the sole French source of revenue from the montagnards).

Once when the Viet Cong attacked a market village and went off with supplies of rice and food loaded into the trucks belonging to a Canadian Catholic mission, the Arvins arrived, pushed into the surrounding countryside, and ordered four thousand montagnards to regroup at the town of Koya. They made no provision for feeding them, however, and before the Catholic Relief Organization could bring pressure on Saigon—at least to make rice available—

the inhabitants of one of the villages had fled deeper into the mountains. There was no expectation that they would ever return.

The Viet Cong attacked and held another market town for only two hours. The Arvins replied by bombing the surrounding villages, though there was no evidence that the Viet Cong were anywhere in the area, and the montagnards themselves walked forty kilometers to assure the Vietnamese district officer of their loyalty and innocence.

Around the more securely held Vietnamese towns such unfortunate incidents are less likely to happen. The montagnards are obliged to swear allegiance to the Vietnamese government, to promise to arrest and to turn in all Viet Cong sympathizers, and to defend their villages against Viet Cong attack before they get guns and military training. Since prevarication among many tribes is a serious offense, punishable by exile or slavery, Vietnamese officials are hopeful enough that the guns will not be turned against them.

Some of the Vietnamese working with the montagnards are dedicated men, who speak the dialects and, having studied the tribal customs and habits, are scrupulously careful not to give offense. One of these is Captain Nguyen Van Nghiem, psychological warfare officer of the 23rd Arvin Division.

"It was difficult for the Vietnamese people to understand the montagnards when we first came to the High Plateau," he told me one afternoon as we went by jeep to the montagnard village of Kmrang Prong on the outskirts of Ban Me Thuot. "The Ede are very superstitious, and, until we got to know them, we thought they were also very vindictive. When they are sick they call in a medicine man. They use their buffalo for blood sacrifices. They even believe that tigers can change into men. The men have the power in the village. The wisest man becomes the chief—if the elders approve of him. But the women have the money. They own the family house and the family buffalo. When an Ede marries he not only gets a mother-in-law but has to live in the same house with her."

Anything from three or four to sixty longhouses make up a Rhade village. Kmrang Prong has about twenty such houses, and a population of 375. The houses are lofty, the thatch thick and waterproof, and the bamboo floors airy and cool. Entry is by means of two ladders to a platform at one end, where the women thresh the rice, or grind it in pestles and mortars. The women's ladder consists of a pole with carved steps, surmounted by two breasts. The men's ladder wears a pair of horns.

Kmrang Prong was by no means an average village. It had an infirmary with a Red Cross sign and a montagnard who had had two weeks' training in the administration of some basic drugs, and also a school. Only one man wore the usual G-string, but since he had just returned from hunting with his bamboo arrow container slung across the shoulder, it seemed likely that the others in tattered shirts and shorts, and one in a threadbare British service jacket, were dressed for the occasion. To these people the organization of the village against the possibility of Viet Cong attack appeared to be more of a game than it is in many other parts of South Vietnam, where the digging of moats and the preparation of bamboo palisades has been a time-consuming, irritating, and unprofitable chore. A lookout sat perched sixty feet above the ground in the fork of a banyan tree. An underground passage ran from the center of the village compound under the perimeter fence so that in the event of attack a runner could slip out to call for help.

Captain Nghiem clearly had established the best of relationships with the villagers. He drank rice wine through the communal straw, pointed out the great value of the green earthenware urns in the chief's house, and commended him on his brass gongs and enormous musicians' platform, which, in one single piece of teak, stretched for sixty feet along the inside wall of the longhouse. "It is unfortunate," he said on the way back to Ban Me Thuot, "that these people have a great fear of sudden death. It is thought to be very unlucky."

"You mean that they don't like to fight?"

He shrugged his shoulders and made what one learns to recognize as a typical Vietnamese reply, "Who knows?"

With his own people, the problem at Ban Me Thuot is not that they don't want to fight, but that after years of French and conventional American training they simply don't know what to do against the politico-military tactics of the Viet Cong. The divisional commander, who graduated from a French staff college, has the reputation of being a good staff officer, but an abysmally poor divisional commander. "We just can't get it out of his head that safety doesn't depend on numbers," said one American adviser. "This and the blockhouse mentality left over by the French are almost impossible to break up."

All through the Indo-China War the French believed that the proper way to move was in strength—and by day. If they had enough troops and could make a big enough show of strength, they thought, the Viet Minh would refrain from attacking. It was a hopeless tactic. Where every road turning in the Annamite Chain, or the High Plateau, is ready-made for an ambush position, they merely presented themselves as even bigger and more profitable targets. By the end of their war in 1945 they were not losing mere platoons, but once an entire *groupe mobile*.

The effect of a large column moving in Viet Minh, or Viet Cong, territory is either to invite a massive and disastrous ambush, or to frighten the enemy away. In either case, the result is bad. For no military commander in his senses would voluntarily concede both surprise and the choice of terrain to his adversary: military operations are equally pointless if they do not result in the enemy's embarrassment. Yet nothing will convince the 23rd Division's staff that they should become night fighters, and even in the daytime they are reluctant to use small units. They argue, also, that troops cannot be left for more than ten days to two weeks in the jungle and that protracted, small-scale commando-type operations are therefore impracticable. To the question, "How do the Viet Cong manage?" they usually reply vaguely, "That's different."

The difference is that the Viet Cong have learned to be self-sufficient and self-reliant. The jungle is theirs by default.

Here, as elsewhere, the Arvins are desperately short of trained sergeants and corporals, the essential for small-unit operations. And since the 23rd's area includes no less than seven provinces, stretching from the Cambodian border to the sea and embracing an area of mountains and jungle almost as large as New Hampshire and Massachusetts put together, there are no troops to spare for really major operations. Medium-sized operations have been quite unfruitful.

Once a battalion acted on information against a concentration of Viet Cong occupying high ground at the junction of two ridges. Instead of taking the long way round, the Arvins went up the valley between the two ridges. They came under immediate observation and fire from both machine guns and mortars. They lost ten killed and many wounded in the first attack. The Arvins then called for air support, but instead of using this to recover the initiative they retreated and, inevitably, got hit badly on the way.

The Arvins put the strength of the regular Viet Cong troops in the divisional area at about five thousand. All the cadres and about 20 percent of the troops are from North Vietnam. They are not North Vietnamese, but are selected from the roughly five thousand Rhade tribesmen who went north with the Viet Minh in 1954, with a stiffening of Vietnamese. The rest are locally recruited and trained, and are in turn used to recruit and train their fellow montagnards, of whom substantially more than 150,000 of possibly 200,000 in this area alone are with the Viet Cong.

11
Tam
Cung,
Or
The
Three
Withs

IN KONTUM PROVINCE, at the northern end of the High Plateau, the Viet Minh left only sixty cadres in 1954 to cover an area about the size of Pennsylvania, among a mixed population of about 70,000 montagnards and 25,000 Vietnamese. The cadres were all unarmed, or armed only with knives, and their task was not to fight but to win over the montagnards. They practiced what the Viet Cong call *tam cung,* or the three withs, eating with, sleeping with, and working with the people. They discarded their Vietnamese dress and wore the G-string of the montagnards. They learned to use the crossbow and the blowpipe with its deadly poisoned arrow. They married montagnard girls and had families. In some villages, they even introduced a rudimentary form of schooling, and supplemented the sorcerer's healing magic with some fairly primitive medical help of their own.

As time went by and they talked of the evils of the "My-Diems" they found many ready listeners. They worked on simple themes best calculated to appeal to the sensitivities of the montagnards. Hanoi Radio broadcast special sessions in Rhade and other tribal tongues. It promised an autonomous State for the tribes when they had thrown out the "My-Diems." Not every village has a communal radio set, of course, but many have one or two transistor sets, or small dry-cell battery-type radios. Everywhere in this region, and extending across the border through Laos and northeastern Thailand, the clearest signals come from Communist radio stations —Peking, Hanoi, or the Pathet Lao Radio at Xieng Khouang in Laos.

Having identified the montagnards' own grievances against Vietnamese settlement and land appropriation in the High Plateau, the Viet Cong moved into a more militant phase of persuasion. It was all done very simply. The Viet Cong worked on both the young and the old. They encouraged the village elders to sponsor Viet Cong sympathizers as village chiefs. And they urged them to fight against the Vietnamese intruders who came to "steal" their land. As they progressed, they taught the montagnards to build barricades around the villages and to make primitive weapons out of bamboo spikes with which they booby-trapped the trails when scouts reported the approach of Vietnamese forces.

Thus, quietly and almost unobserved, the Communist processes in the High Plateau began to change from subversion to military action. Where once the Viet Cong had only political agents, they now had military bases, deep and inaccessible in the mountains but no less dangerous for that. The next move was to activate the bases, to arm the montagnards, and to send back Southerners, including montagnards, who had gone north in 1954.

Had it been shut off from all physical means of communication with the North, the South would certainly have been plagued with much less of war than it has on its hands now. But the essential point is this: without the long and careful political and social preparation that went on in the remote mountains and forests among the susceptible and neglected montagnards and peasants, the Viet Cong would have had no bases from which to launch their war of national liberation.

The more than 800,000 Northerners who came South in 1954 are a ready-made fifth column to send back into North Vietnam. Ten times more numerous than the Viet Minh Southerners who went north, they have the potential to create real trouble. But despite a peasant uprising in Ho Chi Minh's home province of Nghe An, following the hideous brutalities of the Communists' land reform program in 1956, Diem has had no means of taking advantage of the unrest and no political bases from which to work. This does not mean that he has not tried, of course. Many agents have gone north and are still operating there. But the difficulties are formidable. In 1960 hand-picked Northerners were sent to a training camp near Saigon to prepare themselves for their return home. Within weeks the Viet Cong had a complete list of the names and villages of origin of all trainees. Since Viet Cong agents have been discovered everywhere, including the General Staff, this was no cause for surprise: but it effectively scuppered this attempt to carry the war into Ho's own territory.

By training Vietnamese recruits secretly outside Vietnam, and moving them into the North without contact again with the South, it may be possible to take advantage of the counterrevolutionary potential in Ho's zone. This sort of thing is going on now, but not, I fear, with any marked success.

True, anyone can learn to be a guerrilla. The theories of quick concentration and dispersal and the tactic of hit-and-run ambushes are elementary. There is much more to it than the way the Viet Cong fight, however. While all the people are certainly not in favor of the Viet Cong, their cadres have succeeded, to an extent that is now significant, in making this a people's war. Sometimes willingly, sometimes against their will, sometimes without really knowing what is happening, the people of a hamlet become involved in the struggle—on the Viet Cong side. Self-preservation requires involvement, and involvement must eventually require loyalties to the cause. Thus, while the instigation of a revolt in North Vietnam has so far proved beyond the capabilities of the Diem régime, it was a natural and relatively easy step in South Vietnam. Once the foundations were laid and the political bases prepared, the revolt moved on its way.

When it began in that fateful year of wishful thinking in 1959, there were no more than five thousand armed Viet Cong in South Vietnam. Within a year, on the High Plateau alone, the Viet Cong marshaled more than a thousand men for a single operation.

The first attack came simultaneously from two directions as a pincer movement which took in the axis of Kontum, Pleiku, and An-Khe. The official Saigon view was that it was intended to isolate the High Plateau and that it failed because of an effective Arvin counterattack. At first it was said that the attacking forces were part of the 325th Viet Minh division, which had been reported near Tchepone in Laos. Later, only the officers were said to have come from the 325th, but the Arvins insisted that orders were given in Vietnamese, a montagnard dialect, and Chinese, which "proved," according to the official complaint to the International Control Commission, "the presence of Chinese soldiers among the attackers."

This charge was far from proved. What was established proved alarming enough, however. Where only a year or so earlier there had been only a handful of Viet Cong political agents, there were now organized Viet Cong battalions and companies. The Viet Cong unit which hit the outpost of Dak Dru, for instance, was positively identified as Company 3 of Battalion 20 by a young montagnard, Y Lon, a native of Kontum Province, who had gone to North Vietnam in 1954 and studied at the Viet Minh nationalities school before returning in mid-1959 with twenty-nine others to help start the war in the High Plateau.

Looking back at the action now, some Vietnamese officials believe that if their counterattacks appeared to be successful it was largely because the Viet Cong had achieved their objective— the capture of large numbers of weapons to distribute among the montagnard recruits. Such was the shock and disorder at the time that the Viet Cong troops, who went to the outskirts of Kontum, the provincial capital, would have had little difficulty in taking the town. However, as a Vietnamese proverb says, "One does not attack a tiger before catching the deer." It was much too early to risk the capture of large towns. This is a final, not an initial, step in Maoist warfare.

During the following year the Viet Cong consolidated their hold over the montagnards. They multiplied the number of "combat villages" and raised new forces. Lieutenant Colonel Nang, a montagnard of the Sedang tribe, who had once served as an officer in the French Army, established his headquarters in the mountains to the east of Kontum. From the parade ground at 22nd Division headquarters in Kontum officers can point out the mountains where he lives. On the map they can almost pinpoint his village. Why, then, can't he be taken and the base destroyed?

The chief of staff explains: "A big Viet Cong base such as Nang's consists of a scattering of Viet Cong houses through a wide number of villages. We've penetrated many times and captured weapons and documents, but even with paratroopers and helicopters we can't really hope for the split-second surprise we need. Always the Viet Cong vanish. They never stop to fight on our terms. Of course, we destroy the camp. But to destroy the camp is not to destroy the Viet Cong. They grow their own rice and food supplies, but often the rice and vegetable fields are scattered over many miles. If we destroy the montagnards' supplies, we only help to turn them against us." A flight by helicopter over this wild country confirms the difficulties. Sometimes an isolated thatched cottage hidden in dense jungle foliage provides a clue. But even a helicopter traveling just above the trees must give at least a few seconds' warning of its approach. A few seconds are all the vigilant Viet Cong appear to need.

They have concentrated and attacked in significant force on the High Plateau only once since the attack in October, 1960. Their object again was to secure more arms and ammunition. Working in conjunction with their agents inside the posts of Poko and Dakha north of Kontum, in September, 1961, they attacked and captured both. For the first time they wore the uniforms of regular Viet Cong soldiers and used the system of bugle calls that terrified so many men in so many other similiar posts during the Indo-China War.

Government forces recovered one post in a few hours, the other in several days, and again claimed to have inflicted heavy casualties on the Viet Cong. Early reports said a hundred Viet Cong had been killed, and this figure was subsequently increased to a hundred and fifty, but no mention was made in the official communiqué of the Viet Cong agents who opened the gates and let the attackers in, or why, subsequently, so many Viet Cong escaped.

Within hours of the attack Colonel Tri, the divisional commander, had launched a counterattack in battalion strength.

Though the battalion was ambushed by the Viet Cong, it held its ground. The divisional commander then called on the corps commander for paratroop support. Since the corps commander was in Dalat with his mistress, his chief of staff held the request (which had to be approved by Saigon, where paratroopers are regarded as coup troopers) for two days. By the time it got to Saigon and the paratroopers were sent in, the Viet Cong had begun to run out of ammunition and were disappearing into the jungle. The paratroopers killed a few Viet Cong, captured some others, and again "identified" the attackers as members of a regular unit of the 325th Viet Minh Division. From the Viet Cong point of view the operation was a major success. Though they encountered heavier resistance than they had expected, they gathered in much ammunition and many guns.

Ten armed men are all the Viet Cong need to attack a strategic hamlet, and ten or twelve guns from a raid seem to be a sufficient reward for any casualties they may suffer in the initial resistance by Self-Defense Corps. They move through the jungle in small roving bands similiar in size and makeup to that which killed Father Bonnet. Their six main bases here are all deep in the jungle—and all secure. One straddles the Laotian border, two are on the Cambodian border, and three are deep in the Annamite Chain.

At least one Arvin military leader in the area is determined to play the Viet Cong at their own game. He is Major Quy, himself a tribesman from North Vietnam, who commands the 40th Regiment at the post of Dak To, twenty miles north of Kontum along a much mined and ambushed road.

Major Quy has a reputation among the American advisers in Vietnam as the most aggressive of all the Arvin commanders. He is small, with a broad face and a pugnacious approach. "You will find us different here," was his introduction when I met him. "We work in fives and tens and go out into the jungle for three weeks or more. That's the only way to fight the Viet Cong." To Quy the jungle is neither hostile nor neutral, but an ally to be used.

To test out a Ranger company which American Special Forces officers were training nearby, Quy drove his jeep into the camp at midnight and let loose a burst of machine-gun fire. The following day he replaced the Ranger commander.

Major Quy's headquarters sit on a bare knoll above the village of Dak To. The entrance is past a huge image of the Virgin Mary and Child inside a crypt fashioned from immense rocks. Perched on top of the crypt these days with a carbine across his knee is an Arvin soldier. Blockhouses and barbed-wire entanglements guard the approaches. A notice in English says, "Please, no pictures." When one looks out the window in Major Quy's office at the mountains crowding around the headquarters and back to the war map with its four red squares marking the presence of the four constantly expanding Viet Cong bases, the reason is readily apparent.

Major Quy sits astride the exit area on the Ho Chi Minh trail northeast of the Cambodian border. He is becoming something much more than an irritant to the Viet Cong. "They want to pinch me off," he says. "And they think they're bringing in the stuff to do the job." The "stuff" includes 81-millimeter mortars, 57-millimeter recoiless rifles, and heavy antitank mines.

Major Quy keeps a couple of samples of the mines in his office. They are about the diameter of a soup plate and three inches deep with a pressure plate on top. "They would knock out a tank," said Major Quy, "or blow a jeep to pieces." Only a day or two before I saw him, an American jeep on the road from Kontum to Dak To had had the narrowest escape from one of these mines. The better to pick their ambush targets, the Viet Cong had discarded the pressure plate and detonated the mine with a long piece of string. However, the Viet Cong soldier in the ambush miscalculated the Americans' speed, and they had passed before the mine went off, blowing a sizable hole in the road and much smaller ones in the back of the jeep.

"Where do the mines come from?"

"From China—over the Ho Chi Minh trail."

I asked why the mark and the markings were painted in English, and suggested they might have been old American mines captured in Korea.

"They look American," said Quy. "But I'm sure they are made in China. Explosives, weapons, all sorts of materials are coming in now from China."

Then he added, "They can bring in all they want, but we can still beat them if we win the Sedangs."

The Sedangs, with a tribal membership of about 40,000, were the last montagnards in Vietnam seriously to resist the French.

Their final revolt, the Uprising of the Sacred Waters, began in 1931 with the report that the daughter of a man believed to be the incarnation of Set, the bearded son of the thunder god, had given birth to a python child. The montagnards took this as a sign that the French would soon be thrown out. Pilgrims flocked to the village where the child was said to have been born to buy sacred waters from the father of the child. The waters were supposed to bestow miraculous powers, including immunity from violent death. In anticipation of the golden age, tribesmen stopped working their hillside plots and started fighting the French.

Though there is no promise now of a golden age, the Sedangs were the first montagnards to resist the Viet Cong and the first to get American guns and military training. This began early in 1962. By the middle of the year two battalions of montagnard Self-Defense Corps had been formed and 658 guns distributed in fifty-seven armed villages. The battalions were organized into platoons, with a maximum of two villages to each platoon, or a minimum of ten armed men in each village.

Having failed to win these people by pursuasion, the Viet Cong then reverted to terror. Late in June, 1962, they entered a Sedang village on the remote eastern border of Kontum Province. The villagers drove them off with crossbows, and two days later resisted a much larger force for more than an hour. Using automatic weapons, the Viet Cong forced their way into the village, killing twelve of the defenders and marching off with the rest of the young men. In such circumstancs, it is not surprising that the Viet Cong are beginning to lose the goodwill they built up in earlier years, while the able and the fit among the tribesmen are responding enthusiastically to American military training.

Their American instructors give the Sedangs the highest praise. "Every man, woman, and child among the montagnards is an effective soldier," said Captain Robert López, a Special Forces officer, who took his first two companies of montagnard scouts on a two-day forced march through the jungle to present them as fully trained units to Colonel Nguyen Bao Tri, commander of the 22nd Division. "You don't have to worry about supply with the montagnards; if you've got five hundred of these people with you, you've got five hundred fighters."

López had practiced his own version of *tam cung* with his scouts, eating with them, traveling with them, and sleeping with them in the jungle. When he first went out on long patrol, he found it almost impossible to keep up with these wiry mountain men. Often they offered to carry his rifle or his pack. Gritting his teeth, López always refused. By the time he had finished training his first two companies, he was ready to take his turn carrying the mortar.

Without a word of the montagnards' language and with no interpreter, he taught them everything from the use of basic weapons to the more complex techniques of scouting. He had no official funds to provide recreation equipment, so he went to Kontum and with his own money bought a volley ball and net. In no time the montagnards, who loved the game were expert. "I gave them the net and the ball as a graduation present," said López. "From the way they reacted, you'd have thought I was giving them the world."

He couldn't get rope to make a bridge over a river on the way to the training area. Instead he used rattan, just two strands of it twisted together. The montagnards went across hand over hand, with their guns over their shoulders. "It took us two hours to run the company through when we began," said López. "By the time we were through our training, we could do it fully loaded in eight minutes."

Out in the mountains with the montagnards López lived on his nerves. Even in camp he slept with a loaded pistol under his pillow, two grenades next to him on the floor, and a carbine under his coat on an adjacent table. He awoke at the slightest noise, and, since he reacted and armed himself in a similar fashion even in the security of the MAAG headquarters at Kontum, where I shared a room with him for a couple of nights, he tended to be a somewhat disturbing companion.

He didn't care to sleep. He preferred to talk about the montagnards. "People told me they couldn't be taught to observe, or to count above ten," he said. "I used to send them out with pencil and paper to watch a road, and they would come back with pictures of everything they saw. They were accurate down to the most minute detail. And as for their sense of direction . . . I think I know how to find my way in the jungle. But one day when I was sure we were ninety degrees off course I left it to the montagnards. They brought us out bang on. If I'd insisted on having my way we'd have been cutting trail for another week."

I was about to write that López is that rare mixture of tough soldier and kindly humanitarian who appreciates that the war in Vietnam will be won by human understanding rather than by bullets, but the combination is not really so rare among the American officers and men in the field. Some are disdainful of civic action, to give it its bureaucratic designation, but there are many who have seen very quickly, certainly much more quickly than the legions of diplomats and officials in Saigon ever saw, that the people are all-important.

López prowled like a panther up and down our room at the MAAG compound dressed only in a pair of undershorts while he fascinated a USOM official named Bob Utzinger and myself with his tales of the montagnards. Children and dogs, it seemed, were the only creatures that López had had much use for. Now he added montagnards. His was not a job but a love affair with a whole tribe. He told of the montagnards' jungle lore, how a bird flying in a certain way from a bush meant fresh eggs to eat, and how he had learned to tell the edible from the inedible jungle plants.

He had a way of telling a story that created its own atmosphere. Utzinger and I exchanged notes later and agreed that we both felt the tension as López described the approach on a new montagnard village of unknown loyalties.

The moment of real fear as the patrol moved closer, expecting at any moment to hear the hiss of an arrow from a crossbow, and the relief when a villager appeared instead with a cross around his neck. "I'm not religious, but, boy, do I pray every time I see a cross out there," López said.

López talked until late in the night and he began again early in the morning. His account of the misery and sickness in the villages sent Utzinger scurrying off to get him some of the USOM medical instruction sheets, with their simple colored diagrams showing such things as the need for hygiene and elementary medical care. "This is wonderful, wonderful," said López. "Only, now I want medical kits. You must get them for me."

Later, in Saigon, I had a note from Utzinger to let me know that López was getting the kits. They contained thirteen basic medical supplies for treating diseases such as dysentery, malaria, worms, skin infections, tracoma (which is very prevalent and causes much juvenile blindness), lice powder, aspirin, sponge gauze, and adhesive plaster. Some doctors shudder at the thought of almost totally untutored montagnards getting their hands on drugs such as aureomycin and sulfadiazine. Even official village health workers get only two weeks' training and are then paid ten dollars a month. No doubt there will be countless cases of incorrectly diagnosed complaints. Doctors' fears that inadequate doses may cause some diseases to become drug-resistant are also justified. But the alternative, unfortunately, is not better medical care but none at all.

The need is acute and urgent. The health of villagers close to the provincial capitals of Ban Me Thuot, Pleiku, and Kontum is reasonably good. A mile or two beyond, it is appalling. Pat Smith, an American doctor of medicine in her mid-thirties who came from working among copper miners and their families in Kentucky to become the most beloved woman of the High Plateau, says that in some villages she visits, 80 to 90 percent of the people are sick. The leprosy rate here, which varies from 5 percent to 7 percent, is the highest in the world. The largest tribe of all, the Gerai, with perhaps 200,000 members, usually does not isolate its lepers, but allows them to live among the villagers, with the result that its leprosy rate is far higher even than 7 percent.

Leprosy is only one of the many deadly diseases in the High Plateau. Dysentery, malaria, and pneumonia are endemic. Another disease with some of the characteristics of cholera strikes down its victim in as little as two hours.

One of the myths of the High Plateau is that the French provided good medical services for the montagnards. Dr. Smith, who has tramped through the jungles for more than three years, scoffs at the idea. The montagnards were most reluctant to use the government hospital, she says. In Kontum only one doctor was available outside the provincial capital. Though the situation has improved slightly now, ninety-nine out of a hundred villagers still get no medical attention.

Dr. Smith claims no credit for it herself, but certainly one of the reasons why some thousands of montagnards have left the Viet Cong areas and accepted government resettlement is because of people like herself on the High Plateau and the Australian, Dr. Stuart Harverson, who works on the other side of the Annamite Chain, deep in the heart of Viet Cong country, at the village of Ba To in Quang Ngai, the most heavily threatened of all provinces.

Dr. Smith, a Roman Catholic, works for Grail International. Dr. Harverson, who fled from the Communists in China, is with the Worldwide Evangelization Crusade, an interdenominational Protestant mission. Dr. Smith says the montagnards are coming out because they know the need for medical treatment, while Dr. Harverson feels that in his area, at least, the Viet Cong having lost the battle for the hearts and minds of the montagnards, have fruitlessly fallen back on force and terror. In one case montagnard villagers who had accepted resettlement in a strategic hamlet were burned out three times by the Viet Cong and threatened with death if they built again. Everywhere, Dr. Harverson reported, the Viet Cong plundered and killed, and though living conditions for the montagnards were not good in their relocated areas, they were at least better than they were with the Viet Cong. The opportunity clearly existed here to seize the concept of a people's war from the Viet Cong.

CHAPTER 12

War
On
The
Coast

THE PROVINCE OF Phu Yen runs from the watershed of the Annamite Chain to the Central Vietnam coast. It has a population of 356,000, including some 25,000 montagnards, and a hard core of about a thousand Viet Cong who, until May, 1962, had almost undisputed control over most of the province.

Phu Yen is Buddhist, and everywhere along the roadsides there are small Buddhist shrines; but there are also some 30,000 Catholics, who live mostly in the coastal towns and villages, of which Tuy Hoa, the provincial capital, with a population of about 20,000, is the largest.

A valley south of Tuy Hoa is rich and well irrigated rice land. Other parts of the province are dry and desperately poor, and even the more sophisticated Vietnamese practice the slash-and-burn type agriculture on the hill slopes that one associates elsewhere with the more primitive montagnards.

178

The province chief is an engaging army officer, Major Duong Thai Dong, who gets on well with Americans. Until they came, the major's writ scarcely extended beyond Tuy Hoa itself. He had a beachhead between Tuy Hoa and the sea, where he lived behind sandbags and barbed wire. The Viet Cong tolerated his district and village chiefs as long as they did not interfere. They had arrived at a *modus vivendi* with the Civil Guard, whose idea of daring at one post was to run across the bridge they were supposed to protect, put a foot into Viet Cong territory, and then to run back again as if all the fiends in hell were at their heels.

Even so, Phu Yen from a security point of view was no worse than its neighboring provinces and a good deal better than Quang Ngai, which stretches almost all the way across the country, and Quang Nam, which is bordered by the South China Sea in the east and Laos in the west. Quang Ngai has a million inhabitants, almost all of them desperately poor. Sand patches in the middle of agricultural areas stand out like salt pans, or snowdrifts. This is the largest and most miserable of all provinces in South Vietnam, and also the most dangerous. With its built-in fifth column of some twenty thousand families with relations in North Vietnam, and with every advantage of terrain on their side, it is here that the Viet Cong, under Major General Nguyen Don, are most formidably installed. This is the Viet Cong equivalent of the Viet Minh's mountain bases north of the Red River delta, which served them so well between 1946 and 1954. It is from this region that they will eventually move into mobile war.

The Thompson plan was not to seek an immediate showdown with the Viet Cong on such ground of their own choice, but to move in an orderly way through the more or less neutral areas, or areas under only partial Viet Cong control and so on into Viet Cong territory. Thompson saw no shortcuts. Clearly something had to be done about the coast, however. The Viet Cong were now running their rule over the coastal road and railway. They had advised civilians not to travel on troop trains and not, in any event, to sit near soldiers in the trains. Unchecked, the situation would soon have deteriorated to the point where only traffic that met with Viet Cong approval would have gone through. The answer was Operation Sea Swallow.

In May, 1962, not long after Operation Sunrise had begun near Saigon, this basically similar but, in practice, vastly different type of operation began at Tuy Hoa. It embraced the Thompson idea of defended villages, but it also set out to give the villagers what he also regarded as vitally important—a sense of security and interest in their own well-being and in the conduct of their own affairs.

Large sums of United States aid were made available for resettlement, for medical aid, and for security. Whereas Operation Sunrise had begun with great brutality, and villagers were moved at bayonet point, and few, if any, facilities were available for resettlement, the officers responsible for field control in Sea Swallow were insistent that people should not be moved until houses were ready for them, and, moreover, that compensation should be paid for destroyed homes.

This was to be the pilot scheme for a series of "clear and hold" operations in the central coastal areas. The idea was to move from the narrow coastal plain by a series of three bounds along the valleys and high into the foothills of the Annamite Chain. In the first phase of 89 days, 156 strategic hamlets were to be built. The next step was to push out into the more heavily dominated Viet Cong areas and there to establish defended villages, where the population would be given direct army and Civil Guard protection. The third was to take on the Viet Cong in their own areas, pushing deeper and deeper into the mountains and threatening even the Ho Chi Minh trail. Villagers in the strategic hamlets were to have the right to elect their own village councils, a radical step which the government agreed to only with the greatest reluctance, and would not agree to farther south. In the Center, however, Diem was of the opinion that the mandarinate had left a residue of sophistication and responsibility among the people that perhaps warranted the experiment, whereas in the South, which had been administered as a French colony, with all that implied, the experiment was not warranted.

Sea Swallow began well. Dong fell in with the American plans for making the operation a genuine battle for the hearts and minds of the people of Phu Yen. Major Cronia, his American adviser, was determined to see that the blunders of Operation Sunrise were not repeated. The MAAG team of advisers and instructors was first-class, and there was more material for the job in hand than anyone had seen before in Vietnam.

When the American advance guard arrived at Tuy Hoa in

February, they slept with their guns beside them in a compound near Major Dong's home on the beach and under the protection of his bodyguard. The Viet Cong were actually in the town of Tuy Hoa, which meant that they had, in effect, already cut the country in two. No one appeared on the streets at night and very few people by day. The Viet Cong were not especially aggressive, however. They contented themselves with raising taxes in the town. Shopkeepers were required to pay up to 5,000 piasters, or more than $60, a year, the peasants a tenth of that sum. In surrounding villages the Viet Cong rounded up the young men in batches of about twenty at a time and took them into the hills for about ten days' basic training. They were so well organized, in fact, that they even mounted loudspeakers in the villages for their indoctrination sessions.

Then came Operation Sea Swallow. Well within the first 89 days Tuy Hoa was a transformed town. Business had picked up. The shops were doing the best trade they had known in years. People were cheerful and friendly. I sat one day on the steps of Major Dong's guest house to catch up with some notes. In a few minutes a swarm of ragged gamins had gathered around the gate to shout their two words of English—"hello" and "goodbye." They had been gathering empty beer cans, a much prized commodity for the manufacture of household utensils, from the MAAG camp, and were full of impish jokes and laughter. Quite obviously, to these children a few minutes' chatter with, and inspection of, a long-nosed foreigner was as good as a visit to the movies.

Candy, smiles, and correct behavior won the children and the adults, also. Tuy Hoa was a happy town, though everyone was sure that the Viet Cong were still about underground, watching and reporting. A Protestant missionary, who may not have been as objective as he should have been, said he had seen a picture of the Virgin Mary hanging over a Viet Cong flag when he visited a house in the mistaken belief that its occupants were members of his flock. He said the Viet Cong everywhere were posing as Catholics to get guns. True or false, Tuy Hoa was a tonic for the cynical. Here, at least, the battle for the hearts and minds of many people was being won.

Beyond the town there were some even happier developments. About an hour and a half's drive by jeep from Tuy Hoa, and about twenty miles from the coast, is the village of Hoa Phong. By the middle of July, 1962, this marked the limit of the Arvins' advance. A concrete canal built by the French before the Second World War and brimming with clear, sweet water irrigated miles of fertile land from Hoa Phong to the coast. The rice was lush and green by the side of the road, which had long fallen into disuse. There were banana palms laden with huge bunches growing on the higher ground, and also fields planted with tobacco, a cash crop.

The French got back to Hoa Phong only once in all the years after the Second World War and then only long enough to build a concrete blockhouse which soon fell into the hands of the Viet Minh. Under Diem the village was technically under the control of the provincial chief. Though neither he nor the district chief could get to it, and no buses or other transport went to the provincial capital, the village chief was still an official appointee, as was the schoolteacher. But the village chief took orders from the Viet Cong, and the village school was also used to teach Viet Cong propaganda. Yet all the time a missionary living in Tuy Hoa made frequent visits to his church in Hoa Phong and was never aware that he had seen even one member of the Viet Cong.

Though the Viet Cong gathered their taxes, they did not distribute the hundreds of acres belonging to absentee landlords in Saigon. It was a curious and unwise omission. Perhaps they were too confident. But in any case it was their undoing. When Hoa Phong was reclaimed, some of the best rice-growing land in Vietnam was available for the resettlement of other villagers living far beyond in the Viet Cong areas. They gave Major Dong and Major Cronia something tangible to offer in the way of inducement.

First the two majors went to work in Hoa Phong itself. The village with its fine and well irrigated valley had suffered badly because it could not get its cash crops out and consumer goods in. The live-and-let-live policy of the Viet Cong did not run to the free exchange of goods with the Tuy Hoa market.

This was quickly changed. Trishaws loaded with supplies came down the road to Hoa Phong and stocked the empty shops. Instead of the appointed village chief, the villagers voted for a five-man council. The elected members did not grow rich on the pay since they had to split up the fifteen hundred piasters that had gone originally to the village chief; but, as one pointed out, the job was not so demanding that it did not leave time for other work. Medical help came in, and building materials. Hoa Phong had never had it so good.

The word of the changes spread deep down the valley. One day late in July, villagers twenty miles away in Viet Cong territory decided to try their luck under the new administration. They came in batches of about a hundred, driving their buffalo but not bringing much else with them. They didn't have much to bring. Within a week or two, 1,300 villagers had left the Viet Cong, and the flow was continuing. This meant that a new village had to be built. The funds were available immediately, and not only funds but such things as corrugated iron sheets and barbed wire to erect proper defenses against the Viet Cong.

In villages such as Hoa Phong small groups of Americans risked their lives night and day to make the operation a success. Farther out, two Special Forces captains and a handful of sergeants settled in a village in the heart of Viet Cong territory and set to work to train hand-picked Vietnamese commandos. With every conceivable type of weapon to defend themselves, they issued an open invitation to the Viet Cong to come out and fight.

I dropped in one day with Lieutenant Colonel Lou Conein, a former officer in the OSS, who led a daring commando raid on a Japanese divisional headquarters at Lang Son on the China border in 1944. We had met in 1954 the day the Viet Minh took over Hanoi. Dressed in a full colonel's uniform, complete with ribbons, but wearing a slouch hat, Conein went down the lines of the Viet Minh troops as they came into Hanoi, taking pictures of their uniforms, equipment, and guns. He missed nothing, not even the pictures of doves of peace with olive branches that decorated the mugs which hung from the straps on the troops' packs. Conein got away with it because the Viet Minh had no idea what to expect in Hanoi, where the International Commission with its Poles, Canadians, and Indians, had arrived to supervise the takeover.

Now he was back in business, and we came in by Helio-Courier to land on the small dirt strip that served as the Special Forces' link with the outer world. Though this was a quite heavily populated area, not a man, woman, or child had come near the village since the Special Forces had arrived. The Viet Cong watched from the hills, and clearly did not like what they saw.

Less spectacular, but no less courageous, was the task of training home guards closer to the coast. A veteran in this task was Captain Herman Lieberman, of New York, who had worked through his third village in a couple of months. In the village of

Dong Tre, beyond the Arvins' lines, he trained 130 men in three weeks. At the end of that time the Vietnamese asked him if he couldn't spare the time in the same village to give at least some basic instruction to another eighty-three. Instead of taking a couple of days' leave, Lieberman ran the men through—and left a very happy village behind him.

At first it was an anxious village. No one ever showed a light. When Lieberman and his team arrived, the Civil Guard lieutenant locked himself in his room each night, and once, when the Americans had been there only a couple of days and there was a rumor that the Viet Cong were about to attack, he rushed to the church and bolted the doors behind himself and his family.

The villagers were reserved at first: but soon the Americans were welcome in the people's homes. "The people had nothing," said Lieberman, "absolutely nothing. Their most prized possession would be a right nice banana tree or a handsome papaya."

Four thousand turned out to say goodbye at the end of the training period. "Real pretty the girls were when they dressed up," said Lieberman. "Sure, they had only rough clothes, but they made themselves tidy. It was a real feast."

There were some disturbing aspects to Dong Tre, nevertheless. Along with several other adjoining villages it was more Catholic than Buddhist. So many people went to Mass on Sunday when Lieberman was there that they couldn't all fit into the church but overflowed into the street. The driving force behind the home-guard training scheme was the local priest, a Vietnamese, and a man with great energy and enthusiasm. The village chief was a man of straw. The result was that all the guns went to the Catholics and none to the Buddhists.

The day the guns were given out was a big occasion to Dong Tre. The home guards spruced themselves up and went to the churchyard for the distribution. The Buddhists clustered round the yard, pressing their noses against the iron grille to watch the ceremony. It worried Lieberman at the time, and it worried him more when his squad leaders used to lead their men through the gardens of the Buddhist temple. "Every time the Catholic church bells started to ring, the Buddhists would open up in competition and beat their gongs," he said. "It made a terrible din."

In another village, where the guns also went to the Catholics and not to the Buddhists, he found both the trainees and the

Catholics generally very restrained. Though there was a Catholic church, it had no cross, nor was there a cross to be seen elsewhere in the village. "In fact, the only cross I saw at all was in a glass window of the church, and it was small, obscure, and hard to see," he said. "I didn't have to guess why."

In Saigon, officials have the obvious answer to the suggestion that it may be dangerous for both the Catholics and the cause to arm only the Catholics in primarily Buddhist provinces and districts: at first only the Catholics are willing to fight. It is as simple as that. From Ca Mau at the southeastern tip of Vietnam to the 17th parallel, Catholic priests now lead their own private armies against the Viet Cong. The most famous of all is Father Nguyen Lac Hoa, a former battalion commander in the Chinese Nationalist Army, whose Sea Swallows killed more than a hundred Viet Cong guerrillas and lost twenty-eight of their own men when they intercepted an attack on the hamlet of Kinh Quoc Gia in May, 1962. Father Nguyen's Sea Swallows have 1,200 men under arms. They are the largest of the private Catholic armies: but there are many others, and many more will be created under the present plans to train 50,000 members of the Republican Youth each year.

It is a difficult problem. Since Catholics are ready and willing to fight, and others often are not, there is no alternative but to use them. This, in turn, tends to confirm the quite widespread Buddhist idea that Diem is in fact only the leader of another sect and that the war is a private quarrel between opposing sects and ideologies, the Communists and the Catholic Personalists.

Many articulate Catholics are themselves concerned with the problem. They have not forgotten the repeated Buddhist massacres of Catholics along the coast of Central Vienam, and they are intensely concerned that the war against the Viet Cong should not lead to renewed Catholic-Buddhist animosities. They fear, as one put it, the tribalization of the Catholics.

There were other problems in Operation Sea Swallow, some of them even more urgent than this. The American advisers had been at Tuy Hoa for a month before they were accepted as battalion level by the Arvins. They were not permitted by the Arvins to go out with the troops on offensive patrols, and it was made quite clear that their advice was not wanted at company level—

where it was most needed. An adviser in intelligence kicked his heels for two months before he was accepted.

In all its aspects, the purely military side of Operation Sea Swallow fell far short of the high level of the civil operations. The troops themselves were reluctant to fight, and their officers, even senior officers, unwilling to take the risk that the troops might have casualties. One military operation which was planned to last for only a day went on for five because an Arvin soldier was killed on the first day and thereafter the troops dug in and refused to move.

About twenty-five miles along the main north-south railway line from Tuy Hoa and about eight to ten miles from the mandarin road is the town of La Hai. The district chief lives in the town behind a mass of concrete and barbed wire. On the flat in front of the town and a mile or so from it the second battalion of the 47th Arvin Regiment established its headquarters in May, 1962. One company of infantry and a battery of artillery, with its guns pointing north, south, east, and west were deployed in defense of battalion headquarters.

It was a sticky area with a sticky road leading to it. The night before I traveled there with a group of MAAG advisers, fifteen Viet Cong had opened fire on two military trucks, wounding two Arvins. The road is narrow and winding, through dreary and obviously poor countryside, with here and there a defile tailor-made for an ambush. The peasants' plots of ground are small and unproductive and their houses tiny, with thatched roofs, dirt floors, and mud walls. About the only sign that anyone has any money to spend is an occasional Mitsubishi sewing machine, sitting up in the entrance of a hut like the lamp in a picture window, or a washing machine on the veranda of a hillbilly's house in the Appalachians. Everyone wears black homespun, which is not the most cheerful-looking dress at the best of times. Nowhere is there the friendliness that the Americans have grown accustomed to in Tuy Hoa.

On the way to La Hai we passed the battalion commander going to Tuy Hoa for supplies. His escort consisted of three armored cars and two platoons of truck-borne infantry. This is not an uncommon escort: but it is at least worthy of note that MAAG officers customarily made the same journey with only two jeeps.

In the absence of the battalion commander, the executive officer, a lieutenant, briefed us on the situation. He had no idea how many Viet Cong were in the area, he said, but there were plenty to be seen, and he pointed to the hillsides where Vietnamese peasant women were working their crops in the slash-and-burn fields. Five or six miles along another valley and close to the Song Can River he indicated the battalion's second company. The third, he said, was some miles farther along the same valley. The Viet Cong were extremely active on the north bank of the Song Can River. Every night they moved down the hill to Dong Tre village.

Dong Tre! The name was familiar. This was the village where Captain Lieberman had trained the Self-Defense Corps, wasn't it?

That was true, the lieutenant said, but Captain Lieberman didn't know that as soon as the Americans had gone the Self-Defense Corps had packed up and gone to live in the town of La Hai, leaving their families behind them. They were too frightened of the Viet Cong to remain in Dong Tre. (The lieutenant's statement proved, on investigation, to be quite untrue.)

It was at this point that one of the Americans suggested that we should go to the battalion's second company about a mile from Dong Tre and investigate for ourselves. The lieutenant demurred. It was unsafe to use the road; besides, he had had no lunch.

"You don't have to come," said the American. "We are quite happy to go by ourselves."

We started off with a former paratroop battalion commander who had lost his job because one of his relations was involved in the attempted coup in 1960 and was now working as an interpreter. With much ill-grace the lieutenant and a large escort also came.

It is difficult to do justice to what we discovered when we got to the company. It was dug in on a steep, bare ridge overlooking the slow and shallow Song Can River and had been there for two months. The position was not a bad one. It would have been vulnerable to mortar fire, or to an attack by machine-gun fire from other and higher ridges to its rear. For its purpose, however, it was adequate.

For the rest, it was appalling. One of the Americans asked the questions in the course of his job. Mostly, I just listened.

Where was the ammunition dump?

Back along the ridge.

Could we see it?

Of course—but when we got to the edge of the ridge there was no dump.

Where was the platoon dump, then?

There was no platoon dump.

How long since the heavy machine gun had been tested?

Two months.

Two months? And this is a bad Viet Cong area?

No reply.

The troops were in threadbare clothing with worn-out boots. Why?

No reply.

Where were the Viet Cong?

Across the river.

Had the company ever patrolled there?

Yes, twice.

When was the last occasion?

Two nights before.

And the previous occasion?

Two months before.

Where did patrols go then?

To the fence of Dong Tre village.

But surely Dong Tre village was where the Americans had trained the Self-Defense troops?

Yes. But now the Viet Cong went there.

What did the company do when the Viet Cong were there?

Call for artillery.

Incredulously—*On* the village?

Well, around it.

We said we would go to the village.

It was too far.

It was not too far.

Well, it was too late.

It was not too late.

In any event, it was too dangerous, and there were no troops to be spared for escort.

The American did not persist. It was the Arvins' area, he said and their command. We would not intervene.

As we turned to leave, the interpreter said the company commander would like him to know that things would be better the next time the American came.

On the way back to Tuy Hoa, the American speculated about it. "That's why we're here," he said. "To make them better."

It is also fair to speculate whether they can and will, though it may be unfair to generalize, and to damn an army because of the disheartening evidence uncovered by the few spot checks I have recorded in this book. On the evidence of trustworthy witnesses, some units and some commanders are excellent. Almost everywhere, however, there is a lack of junior leadership. The men who make armies are the noncommissioned officers and second lieutenants. The Arvins have some good ones, but they are spread very, very thin. The Americans prod and urge the Arvins into action, and they inevitably resent and resist it. No one had taught them about this sort of war and how to fight it, and tragically few regular units show any desire to learn. Lack of leave, lack of promotion and favoritism have caused many officers to become disgruntled. Loyalty to Diem and to those who are loyal to him are the ways to promotion. Ngo Dinh Nhu's Can Lao Party's secret cadres watch and report. Every officer is dossiered. Morale, understandably, is poor.

How the army will fight when it feels the weight of the heavy Viet Cong ambush of the type that the Viet Minh used with such effect against the French is a cause for real concern. In the opinion of many MAAG officers, it is too much to hope that the success they have had with the training of the Civil Guard and the Self-Defense Corps will be repeated here. The army needs to be dismantled and put together all over again. In principle, as more and more Republican Youth, Self-Defense Corps, and Civil Guard forces are trained, it will be released for active, aggressive operations of its own: but this, it is wise to remember, was also the Salan and the Navarre theory against the Viet Minh a decade ago.

Nothing suggests that even if larger mobile forces are available they will be used effectively. Six thousand troops participated in the Morning Star Operation west of Saigon in October, 1962, against what was believed to be an extremely heavy concentration of troops. But even helicopters failed to surprise the Viet Cong, who broke up into small groups and went into hiding.

In this war there is no substitute for sweat and blood. Until the Arvins are prepared to go out into the swamps and jungles for long periods, to live and to fight under the conditions in which the Viet Cong live and fight, their successes will be few. A Viet Cong battalion or company has the initiative in a stretch of jungle only as long as it has the jungle to itself. Surprise by paratroops or helicopters is almost impossible to achieve in such conditions: but put an Arvin battalion or company in the same stretch of jungle, and the Viet Cong immediately lose their freedom of choice. This is elementary: but it is not yet understood in South Vietnam. Paratroopers, helicopters, M113's, the Air Force, and even artillery are all used as substitutes for infantry. Hearsay reports about Viet Cong concentrations are everywhere the signal for the use of artillery against unobserved targets. Night and day the big guns are used: just like firecrackers to scare off devils. It would be better for the Arvins, and their relations with the population, if they threw every fieldpiece into the South China Sea.

Sea Swallow was a success, however, despite the Arvins, and despite Saigon's almost open hostility to the operation. Nothing was too trivial to promote mischief. An American officer, seeking to confuse the Viet Cong, used the code name Sea Swallow for the operation. The Palace regarded the use of the name as plagiarism and designed to steal some of the glory from Father Hao's Sea Swallows at Ca Mau. Because the Americans were so closely identified with the operation and so intent on providing the materials that would help to make it successful, officials close to Diem chose to regard it as a personal slight, especially when its humane and clearly successful resettlement program was contrasted with the brutal failures of Operation Sunrise. Major Dong found himself in disfavor for identifying himself too closely with the Americans, who in turn were accused of squandering material that was more urgently needed, according to Brother Can, for other areas.

And so the war drags on. On both the American and Vietnamese sides there are constant frustrations and constant difficulties. The economic aid program, for instance, which Mr. Gardiner, the former USOM chief, described as "the greatest invention since the wheel," cannot now turn fast enough to cope with the needs of the situation, or even to sop up the additional aid that the United States is prepared to grant. South Vietnam just cannot absorb enough imported goods to generate the piasters it needs for all the projects it has in mind. The administration wants either lump sums of American dollars to spend where it thinks fit or, alternatively, American approval for the use of American aid to buy non-American goods.

Faced with a balance-of-payments problem of its own, the United States finds these proposals unattractive, and suggests, instead, that some measure of inflation in South Vietnam under such conditions is inevitable and certainly to be regarded as a lesser evil than the loss of the war.

One angry dispute occurred over the importation of spindles for textile mills. In their efforts to become self-sufficient in textiles, the Vietnamese wanted to buy Japanese spindles, which were less than a third of the price of American spindles. They buttressed their argument by pledging not to increase the number above 120,000, the figure required to supply the country's needs, and agreed that the cost should not exceed $1.5 million. Three companies were concerned in the deal, one owned by American and Chinese capital and two smaller companies which were Vietnamese owned. Initially, USOM blocked the entire deal, but finally agreed that the Japanese spindles could be bought—but only by the American- and Chinese-owned company.

American officials in Saigon declined to discuss their side of the case. Vietnamese officials had no inhibitions. "There are even worse cases of dollar imperialism than this," said one official. "A couple of years ago when we were building the Cogido paper mill, we negotiated with all sorts of firms and finally decided to accept an Italian quote. We weren't planning to use American aid, but some triangular francs. We had just signed the contract at the National Bank when two Americans from USOM arrived and tried to snatch it away. Quite literally, there was almost a fist-fight over it—much more than just a scuffle."

Such incidents are unimportant in themselves. In the context of the main issue, however, which is, after all, to beat the Viet Cong, they assume a significance out of all proportion to their true importance. They add to the frustrations. Little goes smoothly or happily. There are frustrations on all sides, and they are as deep among the Vietnamese themselves as they are between Diem and the Americans and the administration generally and the Americans.

One talented young Vietnamese official put the frustrations of his own group in these words: "What we suffer from more than anything is the bottleneck at the top. It's impossible for a hard-working and capable young man to get through it. It's easier to be a do-nothing, inefficient, even corrupt Cabinet Minister than to risk your neck by opposing the President." He attributed the bottleneck to a variety of reasons, to Confucianism, to Diem's isolation, to the power and influence of the President's family, and to the French educational system. "This is the most hopeless situation of all," he said. "The Viet Cong threat is small in comparison."

Some recent suggestions that the situation in South Vietnam now corresponds to that which existed in Indo-China about 1952 are obviously overstated. The situation corresponds to a much earlier period, perhaps about the beginning of 1950, when Chinese technical assistance first began to make itself felt and the Viet Minh guerrillas, assembling in larger and regular formations, moved from purely harassing tactics to mobile war.

Both the big picture and the small are unpleasantly familiar, however. Vietnamese nationalists used to say it was more important to get rid of the French first and that then the Viet Cong could be taken care of. They regarded the removal of the French as a precondition for victory. Sometimes even the same people express similar views about the Diem régime. But one looks in vain for the alternative. A military coup either at the general-officer level, or in the Laotian pattern, at the captain or major level, might be worse.

On their side, however, the Viet Cong lack the spark that lit the Viet Minh. Stories of the land reform campaign in 1956 and of continuing peasant unrest in North Vietnam continue to seep through to the South. The Communist image is no longer that of pristine purity. To many, if not the majority, the virgin Viet Minh has become a Communist whore, and try as they may, with the paint and powder of neutrality, the Viet Cong fail to conceal their true identity.

The United States is deeply and irrevocably committed. The appointment of General Paul D. Harkins to lead the Military Assistance Command cut off Washington's own lines of retreat. General Harkins is responsible directly to CINCPAC and to the Joint Chiefs of Staff in Washington. If the Viet Cong win, it will be more than just another victory for the Communists. It will also be a major defeat for the United States, with repercussions that will be felt not only in South-East Asia but throughout the world.

One way or another France had to get out of Vietnam and all of Indo-China. For the United States any sort of withdrawal before its objectives have been achieved will be extremely difficult, though it will be under increasing pressure to agree to a Laotian-type settlement in the interests of "peace" and "neutrality" in South Vietnam. The longer the war drags on, the greater will the pressure be for political agreement.

Despite the use of Malayan tactics, Vietnam is no Malaya. The insurgents there were alien Chinese who lacked the support of the indigenous Malays. They had no Mekong delta to tap for their rice supplies. They could be starved out. In South Vietnam they may often go short of food, but it will be much more difficult to starve them out. And when, and if, the going gets too tough, the hard-core Viet Cong will have their sanctuaries in Cambodia and Laos into which they may retreat. Long before that happens the South Vietnamese may just grow tired of the war. There is real danger that there may come a day when they will no longer want to be "saved."

In this, Laos is the final key. The day the United States signed the second Geneva Agreement and accepted the "neutrality" of Laos, it also signed away any hope of winning a quick war against the Viet Cong.

13

Why
We
Lost
In
Laos

Laos is slightly larger than England, Scotland, and Wales put together. It has an estimated population of from one million to three million: no one knows for a certainty, and even the best informed guess may be quite wrong. Its people are divided into four general groups. The ethnic Laos, who are Buddhists of the Hinayana, or the Lesser Vehicle, gentle, gracious, good-looking, courteous, indolent, and noted for their interest in the art of making love. They live in the lowlands, especially in the Mekong Valley, and account for perhaps half the population. They are closely related to, and outnumbered by, the ethnic Lao who live across the Mekong in the northeastern provinces of Thailand.

Next in the social order are the Thais, the Black, the White, and the Red, who are distinguishable, so the experts insist, by the color of the clothing, and live in the valleys of the north. They are closely related to, and also outnumbered by, the Thais of the Thai Country of North Vietnam, and of southern China. They are just as good looking, somewhat fairer and harder working than the Lao, whom they are inclined to treat with some contempt—and to suffer for it when administrative priorities come to be decided. The heavy underlay of animism, which is present everywhere in Laos, tends to push Buddhism aside among the Lao Thais.

The influence of animism persists mostly as a form of ancestor worship among the third group, the opium-growing Meos, who are scattered through the mountaintops of northern Laos. Their agriculture is of the slash-and-burn type.

At the bottom of the social scale are the Khas, or slaves, who, as their name suggests, are the poorest and most backward of all. They also live in the mountains and use the slash-and-burn type of cultivation. They are the principal ethnic group in Attopeu Province in the south and Nam Tha in the north, and are very numerous in another five of the twelve provinces.

Divided into some sixty tribal groups, they are primitive and neglected. In many areas they grow enough produce only for their own needs. Money is a curiosity. Even barter trade is confined to a few. Many have no wheeled transport, and no potter's wheel, though nearly every family has its own spinning wheel.

Surrounded by Communist China, Burma, Thailand, Cambodia, and the two Vietnams, and with no navigable outlet to the sea, Laos is unenviably placed geographically. It is also one of the least-developed countries in the world. Only a thousand children in the entire country were receiving elementary education in 1945, and secondary education was provided, in French, for just two hundred. Even now, there are fewer than three thousand students in secondary schools. There is only one Western-trained Lao doctor. Roads are few, and awful. Some houses in the towns have telephones, but there is no link between towns, and the total number of telephones is less than a thousand. The French once built a railway station as part of a quickly abandoned long-range plan to link Laos with Vietnam by train. The station remains, but no lines have ever been laid. Communist China, in what it likes to regard as a neighborly gesture, is building a road into the northern province of Phong Saly, and another into Nam Tha. Several roads and tracks also connect the north with North Vietnam, but the Mekong has no bridge to link it with Thailand, and the only route into South Vietnam is the Ho Chi Minh trail.

Vientiane, the administrative capital and its 15,000 inhabitants, lay dormant on the banks of the Mekong when I first saw it in the early fifties. An eccentric American was found one day practicing his golf shots along the main street: as he pointed out, the shops were shuttered and there was no one about for him to hurt. By 1962, however, Vientiane's population had grown to 70,000 and its shops were filled with everything from Scotch whiskey to French perfumes, its streets with Mercedes-Benz cars, and its nightclubs (newly opened) with taxi dancers. Luang Prabang, the Royal capital, which is farther up the Mekong, and Savannakhet, which is farther down, have populations of about 10,000. For the rest, Laos is a land of more or less self-sufficient but small and isolated towns and villages. Distance is reckoned not in miles or kilometers, but by the number of days or weeks or even months that it will take to travel from one point to another along narrow jungle tracks infested with tigers and poisonous snakes. Laos may have many natural resources hidden under its jungles. No one has yet found out. The French, who ruled it from the late nineties to the early fifties, were concerned to preserve it, unexplored and totally undeveloped, as a buffer against Thailand and the British in Burma.

If the French did little to develop Laos, however, they did not interfere beyond their own needs with its traditional form of rule through the King and a handful of leading families associated with the Court. Among these families was a deep sense of duty, conveyed here not by Confucianism but by Hinayana Buddhism, which places great store on good deeds, and the tradition of service inherited by the élite. Just as every male Lao at some time or other shaved his head and his eyebrows, discarded his clothes for the yellow robes of a monk, and depended for a period of three months on food placed in his alms bowl, while he attended to the needs of his temple and village, the leading families customarily devoted their lives to service. Ostentation and the accumulation of wealth was the shortcut to exile by the Court at Luang Prabang.

Laos was backward, feudal, paternalistic and, to Westerners

going there for the first time, all very complicated. Nothing was usual about Laos. It was one country but also three. This was brought about by the amalgamation of the Kingdom of Luang . Prabang, the seat of the French *resident supérieur* at Vientiane, and the Principality of Champassac. The King exercised titular control over the entire country from Luang Prabang, but in effect the administration was based on Vientiane, with Luang Prabang and Champassac concerning themselves with matters that did not directly involve the French, and then, of course, with their official sanction.

Even this placid backwater, where little more exciting ever happened than the *boun*, or festival, of Bang Fay, which on the fifteenth day of the waxing of the May full moon commemorates the birth, enlightenment, and death of Buddha with rockets, religious processions, love courts, fertility rites, and fun, did not escape the revolutionary and nationalistic unrest that spread through South-East Asia at the end of the Second World War. The King and his immediate family, and Prince Boun Oum of Champassac, remained loyal to the French. They were prepared to accept the return of the protectorate which had been established in 1895. Other leading families rose in revolt. At their head were three princes, all of them sons by different mothers of Prince Boun Khong of Vientiane, a member of the younger branch of the royal house of Luang Prabang. They were Prince Petsarath, the eldest son; Prince Souvanna Phouma, who came somewhere in the middle; and Prince Souphanouvong, the twentieth and last son, who had been working as an engineer in Vietnam when the Second World War broke out, and, under the influence of his Vietnamese wife, had thrown in his lot with the Viet Minh. Petsarath was born in 1890, Souvanna Phouma in 1901, and Souphanouvong in 1912.

Their efforts to rally the Laotian people to resist the return of the French were short-lived. The Lao Issara (Free Laos) forces were no match for the French. On March 21, 1946, effective resistance came to an end when the French smashed their tiny army in the Mekong River town of Thakhek. With Thakhek in flames, Souphanouvong and thirty-three companions fled across the Mekong to Thailand in a small boat. A French fighter plane swept down the river and raked the boat with machine-gun fire. Thirty of Souphanouvong's companions in the boat were killed. With a bullet through his lungs, he was dragged from the sinking boat with three other survivors by friendly Thais who put him into a hospital and nursed him back to health.

Defeated in battle and with the Mekong River towns now in the hands of the French, the Lao nationalists withdrew to Bangkok, where they set up a government-in-exile under Prince Petsarath. A month or two later the French, in conciliatory mood, set out to remove the causes of Lao dissidence. They agreed to elections for a constituent assembly and that Laos should become a constitutional monarchy under the sovereignty of Luang Prabang.

In Bangkok these moves split the Lao Issara down the center. Oxford-educated Prince Petsarath had an eye to the monarchy, and no time for the French. Souvanna Phouma, who is a French aristocrat at heart, and was married to an extremely attractive French woman, wanted more independence but was willing to fight for it by peaceful means. Souphanouvong, whose wife had once worked as Ho Chi Minh's secretary, wanted war. Only the aging Petsarath was disappointed. Souvanna Phouma went back to Vientiane and was soon Prime Minister. Souphanouvong and two other exiles took off for the Laotian jungle and rallied a few representatives of the major Lao families, a handful of long-dissident tribesmen, and some dedicated Communists from Ho Chi Minh's Lao Dong Party to continue the fight.

The rebels were a colorful, and mixed, lot. Souphanouvong, who took a degree in civil engineering at the École des Ponts and Chaussées in France, is an articulate scholar. Strong, thick-set, and with a dominating, extroverted personality, he is the opposite of Souvanna Phouma, who is mild and gentle. Souvanna Phouma is fair. Souphanouvong is dark: he occasionally sports a Ho Chi Minh beard, consisting of a few straggling black hairs, and his thin black moustache is always neatly clipped. With a knotted scarf around his neck and his favorite leather-encased pipe in hand, Souvanna Phouma looks like a comfortably placed country squire. Souphanouvong, though he likes to be addressed as Altesse, looks the part of the revolutionary.

His two earliest and closest associates in the rebel movement were not Communists, initially at least. One was Phoumi Vongivichit, whose father had once been governor of Vientiane and who himself accepted office under the French as governor of Xieng Khouang. His ability is as sharp as his humor. A year or two older than Souphanouvong, he is now rated by South Vietnamese intelligence as the top man in the Pathet Lao Communist hierarchy.

Another who came to Communism late, and perhaps not at all, is Singkapo, a member of Thakhek's leading family, who commanded the Lao Issara and later the Pathet Lao.

These days, however, Western intelligence rate two of the ten young officers who accompanied Souphanouvong to Laos from Hanoi in August, 1945, as holding the real power in the Pathet Lao movement. They are Kaysone, who was born at Savannakhet in 1920, and Nou Hak, who was born in the same town ten years earlier. Kaysone's father was Vietnamese and his mother Lao. Just before the Second World War he went to Hanoi to study medicine, and became a close friend of General Vo Nguyen Giap. Instead of following Souphanouvong to Bangkok in 1946, he returned to North Vietnam for military studies. In 1949 he was sent back to Laos to establish guerrilla bases and to link up again with Souphanouvong. He replaced Singkapo for a time as commander of the Pathet Lao forces but has since acted as chief Viet Minh representative with the Pathet Lao. He is a member of Ho Chi Minh's Lao Dong Party.

Nou Hak is the son of simple Lao peasant folk. He was first of all a truck driver and then an opium smuggler. In March, 1945, at the time of the Japanese *coup d'état* he was on a business trip to Vietnam. Cut off from Laos, he joined the Viet Minh and for several years fought with them against the French in Tongking, before returning with Kaysone to set up the first bases in eastern Laos in 1948–1949. He is also a member of the Lao Dong Party.

Around this hard core of Souphanouvong's Pathet Lao were the rugged Sithone, the Kha leader, who inherited his war against the French from his father, and Phaydang, a leader of the opium-growing Meos in Xieng Khouang Province. Tough and resolute, and far removed in outlook from the Laos of the lowlands, Phaydang wore his hair in a chignon at the back of the head and fought the French with a crossbow and poisoned arrows.

These were the men, with their handfull of followers, who met in August, 1950, to set up the Pathet Lao armed forces, and the Neo Lao Issara, or Laotian Liberation Front, and a "government" under the premiership of Souphanouvong, with Prince Petsarath as nominal Head of State. Phoumi Vongivichit, Kaysone, Nou Hak, Sithone, Phaydang and Tiao Soukvongsak, a cousin of the present King, were members of his Cabinet.

The aims of the new "government" were to drive out the French, to "unite with the brotherly people of Vietnam and Cambodia," that is, the Viet Minh, and "to stand in the world camp of peace and democracy and oppose aggressive plots of the imperalists," that is, the Communist bloc.

Once again, the French were amused. Apart from Sithone's tribesmen, who had "liberated" all of Laos east of the Mekong River but which, after all, had never been truly in French hands at any time, the "government" was government in name only. It represented little more than itself. A British intelligence agent called it "a preposterous falsehood designed to mislead the outside world, where information about the internal affairs of this inaccessible kingdom was not readily available."* But he was also misled. The "government" mattered more than anyone in the West could guess. Some months later the Viet Minh organized the National United Front of Vietnam, Laos, and Cambodia. This new Front, which meant that henceforth the Viet Minh would control the Pathet Lao operations, was set up under the chairmanship of Ton Duc Thang, chairman of the Lien Viet Front of North Vietnam, and an old-line Communist. Souphanouvong represented his Laotian "government."

Two years later two full divisions of Viet Minh "volunteers," carrying Souphanouvong and his "ministers" and a few hundred members of the Pathet Lao "army" along with them, fought their way into Laos and "liberated" the provinces of Sam Neua and Phong Saly. Here, in the village of Sam Neua, on April 19, 1953, Prince Souphanouvong declared his "resistance government" to be the only lawful government in Laos. His announcement spurred the French into granting a greater measure of autonomy to the Royal Lao government. In October of that year, the French and Laotian governments signed an agreement which recognized Laos as a fully sovereign State within the French Union. Prince Souvanna Phouma became Prime Minister.

Thus, when the Geneva Agreement of 1954 brought the Indo-China War to a halt, the two half-brothers headed rival governments, one in the village of Sam Neua, the other in Vientiane.

* Donald Lancester, *The Emancipation of French Indo-China* (London: Oxford University Press, 1961).

Under the terms of the agreement, the Pathet Lao were to concentrate in Phong Saly and Sam Neua, pending reunification of the two armed forces and a political settlement, while Souvanna Phouma's Royal Lao government administered the entire country. In principle, but not in fact, this settlement avoided even temporary partition: the Pathet Lao had no intention of surrendering their autonomy at this time and under these conditions.

Negotiations between the two governments began early in 1955 but made no progress. Skirmishes between the two forces occurred repeatedly in Sam Neua Province, and it was not until February, 1958, nearly four years after the Geneva Agreement had been signed, that the Royal Lao forces were permitted by the Pathet Lao to enter the town of Sam Neua.

During these intervening years the United States and the South-East Asian Treaty Organization had come strongly into the Laotian scene. Geneva had permitted the French to maintain two military bases in Laos and to station instructors there to train the Royal Lao Army, which at the close of the war had had a theoretical strength of 15,000 men. The real strength was probably no more than 10,000, and its standards of training and efficiency were extremely low.

In April, 1954, when John Foster Dulles, responding to the urgent pleas of assistance from General Navarre and fearful of the effect that the loss of Dien Bien Phu would have not only in Indo-China but also in France, had proposed allied intervention to save the entrenched camp, he had also suggested that a regional treaty organization should be formed. A SEATO study group met in Washington for the first time on April 20, 1954, when the battle for Dien Bien Phu was still at its height. By July, Britain as a somewhat reluctant foster mother, was trying to gain acceptance for the treaty organization among its own former colonial territories in South and South-East Asia. It found India bitterly opposed, the more so when Pakistan became interested. Burma, having had a visit from Chou En-lai, was more disposed to ride the tiger than to fight it. The government of Ceylon, then under the leadership of vehemently anti-Communist Sir John Kotelawala, was tempted but elected to stay firm with the majority of the Colombo Powers (India, Burma, Ceylon, Indonesia, and Pakistan), which, under India's de facto leadership, concluded that the alliance would increase, rather than reduce, tensions in the area and, in any case, had their own plans for a radically different approach to the question of Asian security through the Afro-Asian conference.

Eventually, however, three Asian nations, Pakistan, the Philippines, and Thailand, joined with the United States, Britain, France, Australia, and New Zealand, and on September 8, 1960, SEATO was born. Bangkok became the capital, and the member countries pledged themselves to deter further aggression, so far as the United States was concerned, specifically Communist aggression, in the South-East Asian area, including Laos.

Although it was promptly labeled a "paper tiger" by Peking, SEATO was the framework on which the United States now hung its plans for collective security in South-East Asia. In these plans, the Royal Lao army was to have a small but highly significant part. According to Bill Lederer, co-author of *The Ugly American* and the author of *A Nation of Sheep*, who was at this time special assistant to the commander in chief of American forces in the Pacific (CINCPAC) and therefore in a position to know, the proposal that the Royal Lao army, in fulfillment of its allotted role, should be increased from 10,000 to 25,000 was opposed by the United States Department of Defense, which was overruled by the State Department.

Laos had no money to pay, or to maintain, such an army, of course. Its exports, except for the illicit sales of opium, were negligible, and, short of putting the printing presses to work without hard currency backing and causing runaway inflation, it had no way of raising the money from its indigenous sources.

The answer once again was what an American in Vietnam had called the "greatest invention since the wheel"—the commodity imports program. For every thirty-five kips run off the Laotian presses to meet the army paycheck, the United States government put a dollar to the credit of the Laotian Treasury in American banks. Under procurement authorization, importers in Laos could then obtain dollars to buy goods abroad against the payment of kips (at the rate of thirty-five to the dollar) into the counterpart fund kept by the National Bank of Vientiane. In addition, the United States also made direct cash grants of dollars to the Laotian Treasury which were then sold to importers for kips. The idea was that this would stimulate a flow of goods into Laos which would soak up the kips coming off the printing presses, thereby preventing inflation and enriching almost everyone.

Laos got $40.9 million under this scheme in 1955. Vientiane almost overnight became the happy hunting ground of crooks and entrepreneurs of half a dozen nationalities. The black market for the kip soon moved to a comfortable 120 to the dollar. This meant that an importer with 35,000 kips could buy a license to import goods worth $1,000 which he could then sell on the black for 120,000 kips, with which he could buy another license to import goods to the value of $3,400, which could be turned into the best part of half a million kips, and so on. . . . Laos's importers had found the secret of the philosopher's stone.

In a country where every village girl learns to spin and weave, among the least of Laos's requirements were imported textiles. In 1957, however, when the racket reached its peak, Laos imported (in principle, and at the prevailing rate of exchange) $8,900,000 worth of yarns, textiles, and clothing. It also imported about $4 million worth of processed foods, wines, beers, spirits, soft drinks, and tobacco; and "transport equipment and parts," a euphemism for luxury automobiles, worth $7 million. It even imported television sets, though of course it had no television station.

Some of the goods came into Laos and were then reexported to Thailand. Automobiles, for instance, often arrived in their crates and were sent back unopened across the river. Much of the trade existed only on paper, however. Many goods entered Laos only in principle and were sold directly in Thailand.

This misapplication of aid funds, scandalous though it may be, was of more concern to the United States taxpayer than it was to Laos. That the United States was being gyped until 1958 when it insisted on a more realistic exchange rate and the introduction of various—and largely effective—economic reforms, including free convertibility, did not necessarily mean that the purpose of the aid was being defeated. The government got the kips to pay the troops and collected sizable amounts of customs duties even on the goods that were imported only on paper. In fact, in the view of many vigorously anti-Communist Laotians, including King Savang Vatthana, the orderly fulfillment of the commodity aid program might have been even worse, since it would have resulted in an even larger flood of goods into the country. The King's view of the commodity imports program was that it gave to the towns an artificial standard of living which was beyond the capacity of the country to sustain, and that far from helping the villagers, it caused the abandonment of handicraft industries, and, worst of all, by promoting a desire to get rich quickly, destroyed the traditional concept of service which the Laotians expected from those in positions of trust and responsibility.

Nowhere was this more true than in the Royal Lao army. Until 1954 the officers with few exceptions had been French. Now, in the rapidly expanding force, sergeants, and very poor sergeants, not only found themselves with commissions but holding general's rank. In the normal course of events they would have occupied insignificant places in Laotian society. Exposed to the venality caused by the misuse of American aid, and in a position to take advantage of it themselves, they joined merrily in the haymaking. The French, who were preoccupied with African affairs and in no mood to take their Laotian military responsibilities seriously after the 1954 Geneva Agreement, paid little attention to army training. The 25,000-man Royal Lao army was thousands under its nominal strength. Officers drew rations and pay for non-existent troops, built bungalows, and bought women with the balance.

General Kot, who, at the time of the second Geneva Agreement, commanded the 4th Military Region and had his headquarters at Pakse, was an interesting example of the officer class. He confided in Westerners who visited him that he needed women, like food, three times a day. They were his constant companions. At his principal home, which he had made into a mansion with army funds, the girl he had taken from the local commander at Saravanne and an army corporal working in the house were both pregnant. He admitted quite cheerfully to twelve legal children, but confessed that he had not counted the others.

Kot was not content with just one house. He had a second in the hills outside Pakse. Soldiers cultivated his garden, and in those days an army tractor with a trailer was detailed for his personal use.

Against this sort of background of corruption in the Royal Lao army and in Vientiane, it is scarcely surprising that the Pathet Lao moved onward and upward. During these early years they followed the precedent set by General Vo Nguyen Giap, who in 1949 sent his guerrillas into South China to be trained and organized into regular forces. Pathet Lao troops went to Dien Bien Phu and Yen Bay in North Vietnam while the commissars set out to capture the Laotian countryside. "Their organization was both horizontal and vertical," said a long British Embassy study entitled "Viet Minh Support for the Laotian Rebels," which was given restricted circulation in 1959. "It comprised cells, family groups, and associations, and front organizations for women, youth, farmers etc. This series of interlocking organizations can be said to resemble a spider's web with the Lao Dong Party [the Communist Party of North Vietnam] at the center. It provides the Party with both an intelligence network and a means of propagating directives down to the lowest level. Intimidation is used to coerce those who show signs of resisting. In Laos, as in South Vietnam, assassinations of village headmen and others in key positions who proved uncooperative have not been infrequent."

In November, 1957, Prince Souvanna Phouma, who had become Prime Minister for the second time, reached an agreement with Souphanouvong for the demobilization of all Pathet Lao forces with the exception of two battalions which were to be integrated with the Royal Lao army, for Pathet Lao representation in the Royal Lao government and for elections. The Neo Lao Hak Xat Party emerged as the political wing of the Pathet Lao. Souphanouvong and Phoumi Vongivichit took their places in the Cabinet, and in a supplementary National Assembly election held on May 4, 1958, the Neo Lao Hak Xat Party contested thirteen of twenty-one seats and won nine, while their electoral allies, the Peace Party, won four. To Souphanouvong went the largest individual vote in the elections. Since there were fifty-nine seats in the Assembly and the Right-wing Rally of the Lao People held thirty-six, there was no question of the Pathet Lao taking over—yet.

In part, the result reflected the division among the anti-Communist forces; but in considerable part, also, it was a vote against the corruption of the Right and for the seeming probity of the Left. It shocked Vientiane and it shocked Washington.

The quest now began for alternatives and for more dedicated anti-Communists. Washington's suspension of the commodity imports program, on which the government still depended for most of its finances, helped to move neutralist Souvanna Phouma out of office and to bring to the prime ministership Phoui Sannanikone, one of the leaders of the resistance against the Japanese, and a member of one of Vientiane's leading families. It also marked the appearance of a new political force on the Right, the Committee for the Defense of the National Interest, which was formed on the simple, and unfortunately incorrect, assumption that younger members of the Right were more likely to succeed than the older.

One of its first members was General Phoumi Nosavan, who was born in Savannakhet in 1920, just a few days after the Pathet Lao's Kaysone. Phoumi had just returned from a staff course at the École Supérieur de la Guerre. By adoption and by marriage he was connected with one of the leading families in Savannakhet. Though the French once regarded him as a river pirate, he had risen rapidly in the ranks of the Royal Lao army after a brief period with the Lao Issara forces in 1945. During 1959 and 1960, with strong American support, he went up like a rocket at the Bang Fay festival. Like a rocket, also, his political ascendancy was brilliant but brief.

Reacting strongly to the measures now being taken against them, the Pathet Lao began to activate their political bases in the countryside by bringing back their trainees from North Vietnam. Vientiane cried that it had been invaded, a cry that it was to repeat on many occasions during the next three years. In a sense it was an invasion, though the soldiers entering the country were Pathet Lao who had been trained and armed by North Vietnam and were now returning home. That one of the first areas they acquired was around the town of Tchepone, later an important Russian supply drop center and the first staging post in the Ho Chi Minh trail into South Vietnam, was, as events have since indicated, even more significant for South Vietnam than it was for Laos.

Phoui appealed to the National Assembly for special powers for twelve months to deal with a situation which he described as "grave, if not critical." Phoumi Nosavan moved into the Cabinet as Minister of Defense.

That the two Pathet Lao battalions would meekly accept integration with the Royal Lao army at this stage was obviously out of the question. The crisis, after simmering for several months, broke in May. On May 15th the government placed guards around the homes of Souphanouvong and his fellow deputies in Vientiane. On the following day it brought off under threat of force the integration of a Pathet Lao battalion stationed near Luang Prabang. The second Pathet Lao battalion, which had been camped on the Plain of Jars, midway between Vientiane and Sam Neua, where it was encircled by four battalions of the Royal Lao army, packed its bags the following night and, complete with wives, children, and all its guns and domestic animals, took to the hills and headed for the North Vietnam border. Royal Lao guards, nodding at their posts, did not even see them go.

And so the war began. In the critical months that followed, it became apparent how badly the French had fallen down on the job of training the army, which at this time consisted of twelve regular infantry battalions, twelve provincial battalions, two parachute battalions, a battalion of artillery, and an armored reconnaissance battalion. Though the French were permitted under the Geneva Agreement to maintain a training mission of fifteen hundred officers and noncommissioned officers in Laos, the mission had been reduced to little more than a caretaker's guard. Neither qualitatively nor quantitatively was it equal to its task.

As the monsoons blanketed the northern mountains in July, 1959, and the first batches of Viet Cong troops began to move through Laos along the Ho Chi Minh trail into South Vietnam, the Royal Lao government seemed about to collapse under the pressure of Communist invasion. Sam Neua Province, target of the Viet Minh invasion in 1953, was again the target of this attack. The Royal Lao army had two battalions stationed in Sam Neua at this time. They were spread lightly through the countryside, in the villages, through the valleys, and high in the mountains. As few as half a dozen men held the small posts. Some teams were four days' march from company headquarters, along tracks that the rains sometimes made impassable.

Surprised by the Communist attacks, these little garrisons simply folded up and took to the jungle. Lacking any means of communication, most of them were unable to report to higher headquarters for days. Nearly two weeks had passed, for instance, before Vientiane could even confirm that things had gone wrong in Sam Neua. Even then the only intelligence came from soldiers whose positions had been overrun, and from refugees. Since the first are notoriously given to exaggeration to justify their own flight and the second usually carried away by rumor, Vientiane was easily convinced that the country had been invaded not only from, but also by, North Vietnam.

Attacks on August 30th seemed to provide the final proof. Along the unpaved main street of Sam Neua town, past the cottages of mud and thatch and the whitewashed Roman Catholic mission church grown grimy and peeling in the rain, came scattered groups of Royal Lao soldiers in soiled green uniforms and weary peasants in black—all fleeing from an enemy most had not seen, but which, they all agreed, followed close behind.

The Royal Lao air force shuttled between Vientiane and Sam Neua's dangerous and tiny airstrip, where a hundred men and women strove to tramp down the rough and broken surface with their bare feet. Though there had been almost no fighting, there was already a shortage of rice and salt and ammunition.

From the wide stone veranda of his headquarters in the French colonial governor's residence, General Soukhavong Amkha, the Royal Lao military commander in Sam Neua, watched the refugees arrive. He listened to their stories, and soon the map in his war room was ominous with red columns pointing straight at Sam Neua. There were two broad arrows in the north, each representing two enemy battalions; three other battalions were shown to be approaching from the east.

The conclusion, General Amkha believed, was obvious: the Province of Sam Neua had come under major attack by the Viet Minh. As he saw the situation, there was a total of ten enemy battalions in Laos, all of them in large part manned by the Viet Minh. This plausible deduction could be buttressed by what appeared to be substantial evidence. It was clearly established, for instance, that on August 30th there had been a successful attack against four Lao garrison posts scattered along the Nam Ma River and close to the North Vietnam border. Since the attacks had all begun at 6:00 A.M., there was also evidence of careful coordination. Each attack had been preceded by a mortar barrage, and at Muong Het, by far the largest post with a garrison of two hundred and fifty men, the Lao troops were convinced that they had also come under fire from 105-millimeter howitzers fired from across the North Vietnam border.

The following day General Ouane Rathikoune, the commander of the Lao armed forces, visited Sam Neua and carried back to Vientiane the alarming news that the provincial capital could no longer be held. On September 4th Laos appealed to the United Nations for assistance and the dispatch of an emergency force.

On September 3rd, while the government was drafting its appeal,

I went to Sam Neua. There I found that any change, in the opinion of General Amkha, had been a change for the worse. Following the fall of Muong Het, the enemy had brought up heavy equipment and rubber pontoons with which to ferry it across the Nam Ma. Villagers had been conscripted to carry the supplies over the mountains, and, as the broad arrows on his maps clearly showed, the attack on Sam Neua was about to begin.

While a Dakota circled the steep green peaks that rise above the village and banked sharply to cascade supplies to troops waiting below, a survivor from the attack on one of the border posts told his tale on the veranda, with General Amkha himself acting as interpreter.

The soldier's name was Ba Mai. A tall and seasoned campaigner, he was obviously not the sort to give way to panic easily. With eleven years of service behind him in the army, he had attained the rank of adjutant, or top sergeant.

Well before dawn on August 30th, Sergeant Ba Mai said, he had sent out a patrol of twenty-five home guards. There was some shooting in the darkness, and not a single man from the patrol returned. In the main attack the enemy forces had directed their mortar infantry assaults with red and green flares, quickly knocking out the company command post and killing the captain. Ba Mai resisted for two and a half hours and then pulled out. Three of the home guards were killed and one was wounded on the way back. His platoon had no other casualties.

It struck me as unusual that in a two-and-a-half hour fight the defenders had not suffered greater casualties, even though the attacking forces, according to the sergeant, had both mortars and recoilless rifles and were "right on top of us" when the decision to abandon the position was made.

Ba Mai's account of the attacking force and its deployment was also far from convincing. He had already explained that the four company posts, manned by seventy regular soldiers and about a hundred and twenty home guards, were between a hundred and two hundred yards apart and therefore deployed over a distance of between three hundred to six hundred yards. Yet, in estimating the size of the enemy force, he said it stretched for two kilometers and consisted of at least a thousand and perhaps as many as fifteen hundred men. Ba Mai could not explain why this unusual military formation was employed and why the enemy had not attempted to encircle the garrison instead of stringing itself out in a long line.

Like other soldiers before him in much better trained armies, Ba Mai was undoubtedly seeking to explain defeat in terms that were compatible with saving face. More sophisticated staff officers would have compensated for this in evaluating the reports that came in from Ba Mai and others like him. But General Amkha accepted as fact what the most junior Western staff officer would have rejected as fiction. This was the basis of the appreciation that the town could not be held and of the official complaint to the United Nations.

Yet from close examination of General Amkha's war map and some supplementary questions about his own activities it emerged that though four days had elapsed since the attack north of Sam Neua, he had made no attempt to send out patrols or to establish contact with the enemy. His war map was, in fact, based largely on refugees' stories and rumor, and even on defeatist tales spread deliberately by enemy agents.

For several days the defenders of Sam Neua, now several battalions strong, waited to be overwhelmed by an enemy with whom they had had almost no real contact and of whose very existence they could no longer be sure.

Then General Amkha declared abruptly that the threat to Sam Neua had ended. The enemy force of four battalions, which he had reported marching across the mountains complete with heavy equipment and coolie chains to carry it, had disappeared back across the Nam Ma, taking all of its equipment with it. It was all ludicrous and impossible but only the beginning of the almost unbelievable tale of the Royal Lao army.

The temptation now was to blame the French for failing to train the army properly. In part, as I have indicated, this was correct, but, with the notable exception of the Meo tribesmen, who are natural guerrillas, the Americans who took over fared no better.

With Souphanouvong and all but one or two of the key members of the Pathet Lao now moved from house arrest to jail, Prime Minister Phoui and the Committee for the Defense of the National Interest fell out. The "young Turks" accused Phoui of not being tough enough with the Pathet Lao and the United States threw its influence behind General Phoumi, who, though eschewing the role of Prime Minister, began to exercise more and more influence in his role as Minister of Defense.

Elections on April 24, 1960, were conducted with the specific intention of eliminating the Neo Lao Hak Xat Party and its friends from the Assembly by all and any means that were necessary, including the stuffing of ballots and the use of armed forces to coerce electors. Not surprisingly, though the result was highly gratifying on paper, and both the Neo Lao Hak Xat Party and the Peace Party were thrown out, this did not rally the country to the anti-Communist cause. On the contrary, it won further sympathizers for the Pathet Lao and precipitated the Kong Lae *coup d'état*.

In May, Prince Souphanouvong and his fourteen fellow detainees, having converted their guards, walked out of prison and rejoined the Pathet Lao forces in the jungle. Shocked by the corruption, venality, and inefficiency of the successive Royal administrations, Captain Kong Lae, then an almost unknown, and, at the time, quite apolitical commander of one of the two paratroop battalions, took advantage of the absence in Luang Prabang of most of the Cabinet, including Phoumi, to seize power. His coup had nothing to do with the Pathet Lao. It was a spontaneous act, and having pulled it off, Kong Lae was at a loss to know what to do next. In need of counsel he turned to Prince Souvanna Phouma. Four days later, under the guiding hand of Souvanna Phouma, all members of the National Assembly in Vientiane met to pass a vote of nonconfidence in the government. It was then announced that the King had asked Souvanna to form a new government, which in turn was duly approved by the National Assembly. The new government's main policies were to adopt a neutralist position in foreign affairs and to have discussions with the Pathet Lao with the aim of establishing internal peace.

There now began a sparring period between Souvanna Phouma and Kong Lae on the one hand and Phoumi on the other. Phoumi's first reaction to the new government was that it had been formed under pressure from Kong Lae and was therefore illegal. In opposition to Kong Lae's own Revolutionary Committee, which listed the former Sam Neua commander, General Amkha, as one of its members and subsequently earned him a long period in prison, Phoumi set up a counter *coup d'état* committee in Savannakhet. Since all military commands were still under his control and his committee assumed control of the civil administration outside

Vientiane Province—and the Pathet Lao areas—he seemed, at first, to be in a strong bargaining position. He threatened to march on Vientiane, and troop movements were made in its direction. He was assisted by the ambivalent attitude of the King, who changed his mind about the new government, withheld his final consent to the new Cabinet, and broke off communications with Souvanna Phouma, by strong United States support, and by his association with the inept but, in southern Laos, popular Prince Boun Oum of Champassac.

With most of the army deployed against the Pathet Lao and scattered widely over the countryside, it soon became obvious, however, that Phoumi could not march, at the height of the wet season, on Vientiane. It was also apparent that Kong Lae was something of a hero in and around Vientiane. By distributing guns to the villagers he soon had the capital and the surrounding countryside secure against the sort of small-scale attack that Phoumi might have been able to launch at this time.

Phoumi and Souvanna Phouma met on August 23rd and again during a full meeting of the National Assembly at Luang Prabang the following week. Phoumi agreed to accept office under Souvanna Phouma as Minister of Interior, an important post administratively but not in the formulation of major policy. Even this was too much for Kong Lae, however. He objected to Phoumi's inclusion. Phoumi himself remained in Savannakhet, pleading fear for his personal safety in Vientiane, but in fact working on those Americans, specifically members of the Central Intelligence Agency, known to favor his hard line against the Communists, and to strengthen his hold over the army. In both moves he was successful: but success in itself proved disastrous. On September 10th he and Boun Oum set up in Savannakhet a Revolutionary Committee which proclaimed the suspension of the Constitution. Soon American aid was channeled to Phoumi through Thailand. The official explanation was that since Phoumi still controlled a large section of the Royal Lao army, it would disintegrate if it did not receive its pay, food, arms, and ammunition. Another purpose, it was clear, was to cause the collapse of the Souvanna Phouma régime. Souvanna Phouma, who had been conveniently cut off from American assistance by a Thai blockade, was goaded into accepting Soviet aid, including military aid. On December 4, 1960, Soviet planes began flying gasoline, foodstuffs, and later guns from

Hanoi to Vientiane. The Communists had reached the Mekong.

Coups and countercoups occurred in Vientiane. Advised that Phoumi was at last marching on the capital, Souvanna Phouma went into voluntary exile in Cambodia, then into an alliance with Prince Souphanouvong, and, before the disaster was halfway through, into what appeared at the time to be the firm embrace of Peking and Moscow.

Vientiane fell to Phoumi on December 16th. Something might yet have been saved militarily if Phoumi's tactical skill had matched his ambition. Instead of sending even a company of troops to block Kong Lae's withdrawal from Vientiane, however, he tarried for two weeks before setting off in an often comic pursuit. This respite gave Kong Lae the chance to escape not only with the newly delivered Soviet aid but with all the reserves of trucks and field pieces delivered over a long period of time under the United States aid program.

Western military attachés who followed Phoumi's forces in the pursuit came back to Vientiane in dismay, with tales of Royal Lao officers crawling out of the brothels around noon each day, and ten miles or more behind the lines, while the troops they were supposed to be leading were left without leadership of any sort, and reacted accordingly. "It is impossible to exaggerate the incompetence—and frequently the cowardice—of the Royal Lao army," said one Western military observer in a report to his government.

Kong Lae reached Xieng Khouang without let or hindrance, linked up with the Pathet Lao, and immediately began to receive supplies through the Soviet airlift operating from Hanoi to the Plain of Jars.

The Right and Center were not merely divided now but represented by two opposing governments. Souvanna Phouma in Phnom Penh claimed to be legal Prime Minister, and Quinim Pholsena, his Minister of Information, who had gone with Kong Lae to the Plain of Jars, was recognized by Peking, Moscow, and Hanoi as his acting Prime Minister. Viet Minh forces entered the country both as technicians and in a fighting role, while in Vientiane, with increasing American aid, yet another government under the titular leadership of Prince Boun Oum and the domination of Phoumi prepared to continue the war in the name of Royal Lao.

For the South-East Asian Treaty Organization the hour of

crisis had come. It caught its feet, stumbled, and fell over one word in Article IV of the treaty. The word was "unanimous." "Each party recognized that aggression by means of armed attack in the treaty area against any of the parties, or against any state or territory which the parties by *unanimous* agreement may hereafter designate, would endanger its own peace and safety, and agrees that it will in that event act to meet the common danger in accordance with its constitutional process," Article IV laid down.

There was no unanimity about Laos when the Council Ministers met in Bangkok under the shadow of the Laotian crisis in March, 1961. Thailand, which saw itself sticking out like a sore anti-Communist thumb in South-East Asia, was for treaty action. It wanted to station SEATO garrisons in the Mekong River towns in Laos, thereby releasing Royal Lao forces for duty inland, while protecting, with minimum risk, the Mekong line. The British argument, in brief, was that this would have produced an immediate spread of conflict, that the Russians had indicated from the beginning that they would match the West measure for measure, that Chinese forces would then have made their appearance, and that soon the problem would have deteriorated into another Korea, or worse, with all the attendant risks of a major war.

To many the argument was convincing; but it did not dissipate the Thai-Filipino feeling that SEATO was fiddling while Laos burned. Between March 11, 1961, and the cease-fire agreement of May 3rd—while the British and Russian co-chairmen of the 1954 Geneva Agreement were deciding whether a cease-fire should precede another Geneva conference, which Prince Sihanouk of Cambodia had suggested, and which was greeted enthusiastically by the Chinese, the Russians, the British, and the French, and while SEATO was speaking in all solemnity about taking "whatever action may be appropriate in the circumstances"—the Pathet Lao, with Russian military aid and Viet Minh technical assistance, won the battle for Laos.

Beginning on March 11, 1961, when their forces seized the vital Vientiane-Luang Prabang–Xieng Khouang road junction, the combined Pathet Lao–Kong Lae forces began a series of operations that pushed the Royal Lao army out of the mountains into the foothills north of Vientiane. They planted themselves firmly only fifteen miles as the crow flies from the Royal capital of Luang Prabang and secured the command of the eastern flank of the Ho

Chi Minh trail. Although their regular units approached to within thirty miles of Thakhek on the Mekong, they were generally careful not to tread too heavily on Thailand's sensitive toes. Much more important in the Communists' plan was that the Ho Chi Minh trail was effectively theirs. Tchepone became a main staging and dropping base.

This offensive cannot be accurately described in conventional military terms. It was certainly coordinated. Planes seized in Vientiane in December, 1960, shuttled Kong Lae's troops to and fro: both Pathet Lao and Viet Minh forces continued to enter the country from North Vietnam. In some areas battalions and companies participated in attacks; in other places the Pathet Lao did little more than blow its trumpet and the Royal walls of Laos collapsed. In the breathless stories told by refugees platoons became battalions and battalions, armies. Though they exaggerated, the reality of the military situation was that Kong Lae, with perhaps 5,000 men, and the Pathet Lao, with about 15,000 backed by perhaps 10,000 Viet Minh, were in a position to take any, or all, of the Mekong River towns any time they felt so inclined. They were inhibited not by the Royal Lao army, now swollen from 25,000 to 50,000, but by the realization that their regular forces had advanced as far as international discretion admitted.

And so, on May 16, 1961, in circumstances that were ominously similar to those existing at the time of the first conference in 1954, the second Geneva conference met to guarantee the neutrality of Laos. Fourteen nations, including Britain, France, the Soviet Union, Communist China, the United States, and some of Laos's closer, and more immediately concerned, neighbors, sat down at the conference table. The conference was notable for its spirit of cooperation and compromise. From the outset the Russians insisted that they wanted nothing more than the creation of a truly neutral, sovereign, and independent Kingdom of Laos. Even the Chinese Communists did not allow their attacks on the United States to prejudice the prospects of a settlement. It is true that the Thais, who had disapproved of the conference, found none of their fears allayed by its deliberations: but the British, French, and Americans, delighted with the progress achieved, spoke in terms which suggested that their negotiations could lead to something even more important than a fruitful peace for a neutral Laos.

Only one significant element was lacking in this accord—Laos itself. For months progress at Geneva and regress in Laos were approximately equal. To diplomats anxious to extricate their countries from a complicated and dangerous mess, what seemed in Geneva an admirable solution was regarded by the Right-wing in Vientiane as no solution at all. The three Lao princes, Souvanna Phouma, Souphanouvong, and Boun Oum, conducted their own complementary and mostly unfruitful negotiations everywhere from Zurich to the banks of a jungle stream in Laos. In nearly a year they reached full agreement on only one point: that Souvanna Phouma should be named Prime Minister-designate. On the composition of the government and the distribution of the ministerial portfolios they disagreed violently. Geneva waited patiently, but seemingly in vain, for the arrival of the unified Lao delegation which was to put the seal of national approval on its international efforts.

Communist opportunism was the first cause of delay. The Pathet Lao wanted a cease-fire only when it had seized all the territory it could safely acquire without provoking that reluctant dragon, SEATO, into face-saving action. Later, when Souvanna Phouma and Souphanouvong had reached accord and all but minor sporadic military operations had ended, Phoumi began his one-man stand against the world to resist a coalition government in which the Rightists would, at best, be an equal minority party with the Communists.

Left to himself, Boun Oum might have succumbed quickly to the pressure now brought to bear. He was weak, a figurehead only. But Phoumi, lacking any popular support and with only indirect family connections, saw no future for himself or for the forces of the Right if he was divorced from the army in a coalition. Against the strongest of pressures, he fought the most remarkable and determined political rearguard.

An extraordinary, but by his own standards, effective figure in the behind-the-scenes maneuverings that went on in Vientiane at this time was John Addis, the British ambassador. Addis was an eccentric who devoted half an hour each day to two books—*Jane Eyre* and the Bible. He read and reread both and delighted in reciting long passages. He also played tennis every day—except Sunday—precisely at 4:30 P.M., neither a minute earlier nor a minute later.

Addis, who had served previously as chargé d'affaires in Peking, had two hates—Phoumi and the Central Intelligence Agency, which he blamed, not without some justification, for Phoumi's continued intransigence. His mission, as he saw it, was to break Phoumi's resistance, not by direct pressure but through the American Embassy, and, at a higher level, through the British Government. His most effective weapon was the suggestion that Phoumi and the Central Intelligence Agency rather than President Kennedy were dictating United States policy in Laos. Undoubtedly his pressure helped to prod the American Embassy into recommending the agonizing decision to break Phoumi first by delaying and then by canceling the $3 million monthly paycheck which was now required to keep the government in business.

Even so, Phoumi might have still caused an upset if the Royal Lao army had not failed more lamentably than ever before in the battle for Nam Tha. For Nam Tha was Phoumi's last card, and on it he staked everything he had left.

Nam Tha is a town and also a province in the far northwest of Laos, close to the Chinese and Burmese borders. Years ago an English couple drifted across the border from Burma and died there. For many years thereafter, to propitiate their spirits, the locals used to place cups of tea on their graves at 4:00 P.M. on the anniversary of their deaths. More recently Nam Tha became known because of Dr. Tom Dooley, who established his medical clinic there.

It is the center of an opium- and tobacco-growing area. The town itself, according to how you count, and where you stop, has a population of anything from 1,500 to 3,000. Though they had gathered up most of the rest of the north, and in particular, the provinces of Phong Saly and Sam Neua, the Pathet Lao had not bothered much about Nam Tha. Their interest began during the cease-fire, when both sides looked for soft spots in their opponents' armor and exploited them to the best of their ability.

Phoumi, against the advice of Americans who wished him well, built up Nam Tha secretly and strongly. By the beginning of May, 1962, he had eight battalions there, including his entire paratroop force of three battalions. On the morning of May 3rd, the Pathet Lao attacked and captured the town of Muong Sing, only seven miles from the Yunnan border. There was no fighting. Though its airport was vital to the defense of Nam Tha, Volunteer Company 138 of the Royal Lao army, which was charged with its defense, did not resist. An army Dakota, unaware that anything was amiss, attempted to land, and was promptly shot down. Its crew members were the only known casualties of this battle.

Deprived now of its only worthwhile airport, Nam Tha had all the ingredients of another Dien Bien Phu. Though it is misleading to mention the two "battles" in the same sentence, this is what, for Phoumi, it became. The French fought desperately and suffered fearful casualties at Dien Bien Phu. The Royal Lao army ran from Nam Tha as soon as the first shells started to fall. The Pathet Lao had assembled five battalions for the attack, but their main force was not needed.

Every officer in the Royal Lao army carries a swagger stick on which are inscribed various astrological directions for action or inaction, according to the time and date. The sticks suggested this was a good time for movement: the troops moved. In the van were the Nam Tha commander, General La Pathammavong, and the commander of the northern area, General Bounleuth. When junior- and middle-rank officers saw them running, they ran too. They ran so fast they did not bother even to block the road south to the Thai border, though at one pass a battalion could have held out for weeks. "They were thinking of it," said a disgusted American observer, "but someone fired a rifle and shouted 'Viet Minh,' and everyone ran."

First stop was the Mekong River town of Ban Houei Sai on the Thai border. The rabble paused here only to gain their breath before fleeing into Thailand with stories of Viet Minh and Chinese forces at their heels. The panic spread like a brushfire across the Western world. Thailand was about to be invaded! SEATO, with its unanimity stumbling block, was not consulted. The 7th fleet moved at action stations into the Gulf of Siam and United States marines streamed ashore to take up their stations in northeastern Thailand. The Australians and New Zealanders showed their solidarity by sending token detachments of air and ground forces. Even the reluctant British sent some air support. But Ban Houei Sai never did fall to Pathet Lao, and there is no evidence that they even got within twenty-five miles of it.

Territorially, the fall of Nam Tha was unimportant to Phoumi, and to the Royal Lao government. In every other way, however, it was Phoumi's last card. His armed forces were totally discredited. He was also at the end of his financial tether. United States dollar support had not been forthcoming during February, March, or

April. When the attack at Nam Tha occurred, he and Boun Oum were off on a tour of several friendly Asian countries in the hope that they might drop a million or two into the Royal Laotian hat. They did not. Though Phoumi said subsequently that the intention in evacuating Nam Tha was to draw the Pathet Lao into a trap and there to annihilate them, this was demonstrably untrue. It is equally improbable that he planned the crisis through in the way it developed in the hope that the reaction of his cousin, Field Marshal Sarit, in Thailand would cause Western intervention. What Phoumi wanted, and desperately needed, was a major break in the cease-fire and a chance to cause a last-minute upset at Geneva. Undoubtedly, a battle involving several thousand troops on either side would have caused this. When the bid failed, he was through.

Nothing now stood in the way of the second Geneva Agreement, and on July 23, 1962, the new accords were signed. SEATO's mantle of protection over Laos was finally discarded and neutrality laid down as a guiding principle: but there was nothing in the agreement to stipulate that Laos should not, if it chose, do what SEATO was set up to prevent—go Communist. The new coalition government stripped Phoumi of his post as Defense Minister, which went to Souvanna Phouma, who, in addition to the prime ministership, also held the portfolios of Veterans' Affairs and Social Action. Souphanouvong got Economy and Planning, and the senior vice-premiership. In all, there were nineteen Cabinet posts, of which the Neo Lao Hak Xat Party held four, and the Left-wing neutralists five. Phoumi led a group of four Right-wingers, with support from another four Right-wing neutralists, while the balance of power was held by Souvanna and his slightly Left-of-center colleague, Pheng Phongsavan, in the Ministry of the Interior. In all matters of major importance the unanimity principle applied. The Left could circumvent the Right and the Right could circumvent the Left.

I stood next to a Polish official on the staff of the International Control Commission at Vientiane airport the day Souvanna Phouma returned from Geneva to take up office. "How do you think this government will work out?" I asked him.

"Government!" he repeated. "This is not a government. This is a comic opera. It cannot possibly work."

Within a few minutes we were to see one of the reasons why. As the diplomats were arranged by protocol officers to greet

Souvanna Phouma, Liu Chun, the Chinese Communist chargé d'affaires, who had not yet presented his credentials, pushed the protocol officer aside, broke out of position, and stood next to the Russian ambassador. When the protocol officer reprimanded him, Liu answered, "I take no notice of protocol." The next incident occurred when Liu again stepped out of line, brushed past several ambassadors, and angrily prevented Souvanna Phouma from shaking hands with the Chinese Nationalist ambassador, Dr. Han.

As the official cars began to leave the airport, Laotian security officers under the direction of General Bounthieng, and in consultation with the protocol section of the Foreign Affairs Ministry, requested both the Chinese Communists and the North Vietnamese to remove their national flags from their cars. Both were informed that they had no right to fly the flags since they had not yet presented their credentials to the King.

They refused to remove the flags, and for more than two hours, while the rest of Vientiane had lunch and began its siesta, the Communists fumed in the sun. Once, when General Bounthieng was beginning to have some doubts, Liu Chun said that China was a nation of 650 million people and was not going to be told what to do by two million Laotians. Even Souphanouvong, who had been acting Prime Minister in Souvanna Phouma's absence, was angered by this. Eventually, Souvanna Phouma suggested a compromise: the cars could proceed to the delegates' homes with flags but would not be permitted to fly them again until after they had presented their credentials.

As everyone in Vientiane knew, however, Communist China was not likely to be defied for very long. Soon Liu Chun, who is president of the Central Nationalities College and also a member the United Front Work Department of the central committee of the Chinese Communist Party, presented his credentials. The Nationalist Chinese packed their bags and left. They were quickly followed by the South Vietnamese.

The Indian Samar Sen, who served as chairman of the International Control Commission until the end of 1961, used to be one of the more optimistic observers of the Laotian scene. But even he felt the most the West could hope for from its "neutrality" was that it would be "of the Austrian type in reverse;" in other words, whereas Austria faces West culturally and in every way other than by formal alliances, Laos would be technically neutral but effectively within China's sphere of influence. I put this proposition to Souvanna Phouma. At first he disputed the suggestion that he did not hope for true neutrality. Then, after reflection, he added that his country's position could not really be compared to that of Austria. "Austria is not next to the Soviet Union but only to its satellites," he said. "Laos is next to China, and we can't ignore the fact of 650 million Chinese."

Months later while I was sitting in Prince Souphanouvong's waiting room, I thumbed through a copy of *Extrême Asie*. It had a cartoon showing Mao Tse-tung as the driver of a steamroller about to crush a child marked "Laos," while an Indian member of the International Control Commission protested. "Réassurez-vous, brigadier, CIC, j'y vais doucement!" read the caption. I showed it to Prince Souphanouvong. Like Queen Victoria, he was not amused.

China does not need to crush Laos with a steamroller for the Communists to achieve their purpose. Many months after the second Geneva Agreement there had been no progress in setting up a workable government. Nothing had been done to halt the flow of men and materials along the Ho Chi Minh trail south of Tchepone and east of the Mekong River: and Thailand was in graver danger from infiltration than it ever was from aggression the day Phoumi's troops cried wolf at Ban Houei Sai and fled across the Mekong. The neutralists with Souvanna Phouma broke into hostile groups. Quinim Pholsena, Souvanna's Foreign Minister, died from a machine gun burst fired by one of Kong Lae's soldiers assigned to guard him and fighting broke out on the Plain of Jars between Kong Lae's neutralists and the Pathet Lao.

According to Phoumi, there are fewer than two hundred Communists in Laos today. No one disputes the figure. Communism did not conquer: the opposition to it collapsed. "You can't blame the American economists on the spot who had to work out a formula to suit the type of aid," said a Western diplomat. "But the policy that created the ridiculous 25,000-man do-nothing army was absurd. The peasants got nothing. What they wanted were access roads, education, improved farming techniques, and medical care. All aid should be directed to this. Everywhere you go these days people will tell you that the peasants are the water in which the Communists swim. It has been very true here. Some of the best people in the country have been attracted to the Pathet Lao because it offers the tradition of service without wealth. The *nouveau riche* of Vientiane and the army discredited themselves. They were both totally unacceptable."

I asked two senior Americans in Vientiane to comment on these opinions. One, an economist, replied: "He is quite right. What the peasants need is basic food, water, shelter, and clothing. Sometimes they have to walk three or four miles to get water, which they have to carry by hand. They want basic education, some training in agriculture, medical help, and access roads so that they exchange their surplus goods for money. Our $300 million have supplied very little of that."

"Where did we go wrong?" mused the American army officer. "We went wrong in pushing too much in here too quickly. The rich grew richer and the poor grew poorer. Well, the poor didn't grow poorer. They stayed as they had been for generations. The gap between the rich and the poor just grew wider. The army was a write-off. These people don't fight. Senior officials were maybe sergeants in the French army. They got their positions not because of capability but because of loyalties to Phoumi. Phoumi is a great anti-Communist but he has no executive capabilities at all. He is no leader and he hates to take advice. Maybe the original army wasn't too big at 25,000, but it was never properly trained. We should have taken, say, five hundred men to start with and given them some real training and worked out from that. We went about it in the wrong way. When aid is given as we gave it in such vast sums to a country that is not viable and has never really existed as a State but is just a collection of different peoples, then you have to keep a tight rein on the spending of that money. If advice is rejected or misapplied, the aid should be cut off. We did that here —but much too late."

Everywhere it was too late. In the closing year American officers responsible for the training of Meo tribesmen were thinking in terms that ran far beyond mere military effort. I have in front of me an order issued by Lieutenant Colonel John T. Little, who commanded the White Star training team. It is dated September 22, 1961, and is addressed to commanders of all field training teams, the White Star mobile training team, and the Military Assistance Advisory Group.

It reflects a deep understanding of the problem. Unfortunately, it is much too long to reproduce in its entirety here, for it goes into considerable detail in outlining a program designed, as its author puts it, "to beat the enemy at his own game—the winning of men's minds, emotions, and loyalty to the concept of freedom, justice, individual human rights, equality of opportunity, and a higher living standard."

The five introductory points are brief, however, and give an idea of what follows:

1. In an insurgency condition, the guerrilla is dependent on a sympathetic population. Counterguerrilla operations must, therefore, have as one objective winning the population's cooperation and denying the enemy their sympathy. This can be done by psychological operations in many forms.

2. An imaginative program of village assistance properly backed by the military and civil authorities is one form of psychological operation which will contribute significantly toward this objective and achievement of United States goals in Laos.

3. The attached outline for a civil assistance program which can be applied realistically by operational detachments is forwarded for team use in establishing a positive civil relations program. The ideas expressed have been field tested and are practical. Use them as a guide for your actions in the field. Start at once.

4. You are not in competition with other United States agencies, U.S.I.S. and U.S.O.M, you are the spearhead of these activities and a focal point for injection of these activities until Lao civil assistance teams are trained and in use. Your primary mission is training and operations with FAR (the Royal Lao army). This is secondary to that mission but has an important impact on it.

5. Those teams operating from villages in which U.S.I.S. and U.S.O.M. representatives are not permanently represented are expected to initiate action in this field and to keep this headquarters informed of progress.

Today the White Star and all other American military teams have pulled out, and in the Meo villages where they made a foothold by such wise and humane methods, the Pathet Lao have fought their way back to mete out their reprisals on those who collaborated with the "imperialists." It is a sorry chapter in an unfinished tale.

CHAPTER 14

Aggression
By
Seepage

COMMUNIST PLANS TO create a political base for a war of national liberation in northeastern Thailand are far advanced. For more than thirty years Communist organizations set up initially under the direct and personal leadership of Ho Chi Minh have been active in these remote and neglected provinces. Yet for most of this time Thai governments have shown no more than a casual concern over clandestine activities, Communist or other, in their border regions. From 1953, the central committee of the Malayan Communist Party directed the Malayan revolt from its sanctuary in southern Thailand; Bangkok officials virtually ignored it. Opium traffickers ran a business worth millions of dollars in the north; the police grew rich on the spoils. Communist agents moved in and out of the northeast from Laos; no one really cared.

Complacency turned into an apparently overzealous concern in 1961. Because Thailand was opposed to the suggested Geneva conference and its plans for Laos, Bangkok was suspected of crying wolf in the northeast. For a time, its revelations of plots and conspiracies were treated only half seriously. Today there are few scoffers. Pathet Lao military and political schools are known to have opened their doors to dissident northeasterners. Pathet Lao agents, some of them even using helicopters, have crossed into Thailand to bring money, medicines, blankets, and guns to their supporters, who include peasants, villagers, minor officials, Buddhist monks, and former members of parliament.

During May, June, and December, 1961, Thai authorities rounded up three hundred and fifty Communist agents and suspects in the northeast, including a former member of parliament who was tried and quickly executed. Others known to be more important simply moved across the river and joined up with the Pathet Lao, or went underground in one of the hundreds of northeastern villages where the authority of the Thai government exists in name only.

Both Western and Thai agencies in Bangkok believe that the arrests in 1961 helped to throw the Communists off balance. They do not think that they have destroyed the Communists' capability to move from political subversion to armed revolt. Though more than a hundred weapons, including carbines, Stens, and other submachine guns, were seized in the raids, Chinese and North Vietnamese arms have continued to go to the Pathet Lao since the Geneva Agreement and are ample to meet the needs of their allies in Thailand.

"We think a Communist revolt is a matter of timing," said a SEATO official, summing up the prospects in the northeast in the summer of 1962. "A premature revolt could damage the Communists' cause badly. The longer they leave it, however, the greater their difficulties will become. Our guess is that they will time it to coincide with a critical period in South Vietnam, probably within the next year or so."

For centuries the Mekong River, which separates Laos from Thailand, has been more of a highway than a border. In the early postwar years, when the Lao Issara revolted against the return of the French, the northeastern provinces of Thailand were a sanctuary and a source of supply for the rebel forces. When things got too hot in Laos, the hard-pressed Lao Issara and later the Pathet Lao could always cross into Thailand and find shelter in villages among friends and relatives.

Today the traditional trade and social intercourse between villages across the river goes on as usual. The war in Laos did not disturb it. In the morning, just after first light, fleets of slender Thai pirogues speed across the Mekong laden with pigs, chickens, and vegetables for the markets of the Laotian river towns. Though it stands on a rich alluvial flat large enough to grow all the food it needs, Vientiane's food comes from Thailand. Northeastern Thailand is, in fact, the Laotian market garden. All along the river the northeasterners find it easier to take a boat across the river than to make the long, difficult, and sometimes impossible trip over the rough trails that connect with inland Thai centers.

Nine million people, roughly a third of the total population of Thailand, live in the fifteen provinces of the northeast. Though most belong to the general Thai family, the overwhelming majority are Lao, in culture, custom, and language much closer to the people across the river than to the Thais of Bangkok. Living among them quite cheerfully, but proudly and openly for Ho Chi Minh, is a substantial Vietnamese minority.

The first Vietnamese came here more than forty years ago, fugitives from the French in Indo-China. Some settled permanently in the vicinity of Lake Nong Harn, the northeast's only rich rice-growing area. Here, in 1929, Ho Chi Minh founded the Overseas Vietnamese Association in Thailand and Laos for the Salvation of the Fatherland.

With its headquarters near the Laotian border, the organization profited from the ill-feeling that developed between the Thai and French forces and its wartime association with the Thai resistance movement. By the end of the Second World War it had become a state within a state. When the revolt against the French broke out in 1946, Vietnamese villages in the northeast raised and trained their own forces, which went off to fight for Ho Chi Minh.

Neglected by Bangkok in their hilly, dry, and barren lands, the indigenous northeastern peasants had little knowledge of, or sympathy for, the Thai government. One indigenous separatist movement ended abruptly in the early 1950's when General Phao Siriyanon, then police chief and a member of the ruling triumvirate, ordered the execution of its leader, a member of parliament named Tiang Sirrikhan. This put an end, at least temporarily, to talk of armed resistance, but did not halt the flow of pharmaceuticals, gold, and weapons into Laos and on to the Pathet Lao and Viet-Minh in exchange for raw opium and heroin.

Not until 1953, when the Viet-Minh "volunteers" swept into Laos to establish Prince Souphanouvong and his "government" at Sam Neua, did Bangkok show any real concern about these events in the northeast. Field Marshal Pibul Songgram, then Prime Minister, decided to make a personal investigation of the problem as a prelude to resettling the Vietnamese minority in less sensitive areas of Thailand. He abandoned both ideas in the town of Nong Khai when Vietnamese women lay down in the streets, blocking the ministerial motor cavalcade, while some even cut their throats in further protest.

Pibul went back to Bangkok, and things in the northeast went on in their own semiautonomous way. Two railway lines entered the area. One went as far east as Ubon, where it linked up with the road to the southern Laotian town of Pakse. A second had its terminus at Udon, fifty miles south of Vientiane. But the journey to either town was a two-day nightmare in trains that lacked seats and lavatories. Passengers in need of food had to fend for themselves. I made the journey once while suffering from a bout of dysentery, and survived on a diet of glutinous rice which wayside vendors sold neatly packaged in sticks of bamboo. Along the south and west banks of the Mekong French consumer goods sometimes appeared in Thai village shops. Elsewhere, the little that was offered for sale came from local cottage industries and was of the poorest quality.

The first Geneva Agreement of 1954 spurred some renewed interest in the northeast. The government at last began to give serious attention to the Vietnamese refugee problem, and with the prospect of picking up the freight on American commodity goods intended for Laos, the Thai government pushed the railhead to the south bank of the Mekong, opposite Vientiane. The rail journey became a comfortable air-conditioned overnight trip. United States aid built the ninety-two-mile "Friendship Highway," connecting Saraburi in the rich central delta with Korat, the gateway to the northeast. It also built a number of airstrips and helped to replace hundreds of dangerous timber bridges with new bridges of reinforced concrete.

These efforts combined with the United States–sponsored move to encourage crop diversification in the northeast helped to bring a new look to the principal towns in the region. Judging by the numbers of bicycles in the streets and the variety of consumer goods in the shops, it has also helped to bring about a near revolution in northeastern urban living standards. Some of these improvements also penetrated to the villages on or near the main roads. They did not have much effect elsewhere.

From time to time the Thai government published accounts of Communist activity in the northeast. These were often colorful but rarely accepted at face value, even by the Thais. The Sarit regime had not hesitated to use the Communist bogey for its own ends, especially in its early days. Crying wolf in the northeast seemed to be tailor-made to justify official policies.

That Communist participation in a Laotian coalition might pose some added security problems for Thailand was admitted, however, even by those who wanted a settlement in Laos at any price. In consequence, Western embassies in Bangkok began to take a serious interest in Thailand's remote border areas, especially the northeast. "Since we know that Chen Ping, the Malayan Communist Party leader, and some five hundred of his armed followers have been using southern Thailand as a sanctuary for the past ten years, it seemed reasonable at least to inquire about the situation in the north and northeast," said one ambassador. "What we discovered rocked us."

Among those who went into the northeast and returned convinced that the Thais were no longer exaggerating the Communist threat was the deputy chief of the Australian Security Service, who turned in a report described by those who read it as "hair-raising." He was followed early in 1962 by joint Thai–United States mobile information teams. Their object was not to probe deeply into Communist penetrations, or to launch an anti-Communist propaganda offensive, but by positive means to attempt to create a stronger sense of village association with Thailand and a greater sense of loyalty to the Thai government. A secondary object was to learn more about village conditions and needs and the sources of villagers' news, feelings, and opinions. Teams took along a doctor to give medical help, showed movies, distributed pictures of the King of Thailand, and gave some encouragement of better things to come.

The teams were mostly Thai, but in each case one or more Americans went along and the United States provided logistical and other support. They confirmed the worst reports of regional neglect. "There is no road to any village visited by the team—only rutted, eroded and meandering oxcart tracks inches deep in dust," the first team reported. "Transportation is so difficult in many areas that many people have never been to the *amphur* [district capital]. Buses ran to none of the villages and most people had never seen any kind of automobile.

"The only difference among the schools inspected by the team is in degrees of poverty. . . ." One village had 160 children and only one teacher. Others used temple buildings as schoolhouses, open on three sides to the wind and dust in the dry season and to the driving rains of the monsoons in the wet.

Water was scarce almost everywhere. One man was even found to have suffocated while trying to dig a deep-enough well. None of the villages had electric power. Health facilities were almost non-existent. And the only offers of help some had ever received had come from members of the Pathet Lao who crossed the Mekong bringing medicines, blankets, and money. They had singled out peasants to act as purveyors of Communist propaganda and to lead in the establishment of village cells. At one village, Umao, the Pathet Lao had even used a helicopter to ferry supplies and cadres. The team investigated this report thoroughly to make sure the information was not hearsay or rumor. Since it was confirmed by police, village officials, and individual peasants, there seems little reason to doubt its accuracy.

On its second trip the same team visited another twenty-four villages and made contact with about 15,000 people. As on the first trip, most of the villagers had never seen a movie or an automobile. While buses ran to some of the villages in the dry season, all except those on the Mekong River were completely cut off from outside communication during the wet season. In one district populated by thousands there was only one second-class health center staffed by one midwife. Lack of roads in most areas made it virtually impossible for the sick to get to the health centers and extremely difficult for the health workers to visit the villages. Malaria was endemic, and hepatitis, jaundice, liver fluke, and respiratory ailments, including pneumonia, very common. In less than three weeks the doctor who accompanied the team vaccinated about four thousand people and treated hundreds of others, "a service which was much appreciated," as the report put it, "except possibly by one young and attractive girl who asked him if he had any medicine for a broken heart."

Despite the dire poverty of many villages most had more than one radio set. The clearest signal, either short- or medium-range, in almost every village came from a Communist station. Peking and the Pathet Lao radio at Xieng Khouang both broadcast in Lao and Thai. Hanoi Radio also broadcast in Thai.

Neither this team nor others that followed into even more remote parts of the north and northeast wanted to press questions on Communist activity. Team members could not refrain from commenting on the lack of young men in the villages along the Mekong, however. While the rest of the villagers swarmed to look at the movies brought by the team, or to receive medical aid, the young men were conspicuous by their absence. "They're off working somewhere," was the standard reply to questions. No one would say where.

Yet at these night stops on the Mekong what the team described as a sizeable proportion of its movie audience crossed the river from Laos to see the show. Men, women, and children all came, and even some soldiers in the uniform of the Royal Lao army. "Except for the latter," the report noted, "it was not possible to distinguish by language or dress who was Lao and who Thai in the audience."

Herein lies the crux of the problem. The Communists do not have to march across the border: it is already dissolved. They do not ask the northeasterners to revolt against Bangkok but only to identify themselves with their kin on the other side of the river, to promote a separatist movement based on their racial and cultural affinities, and on the fact that the river is a means of communication and trade, not a barrier.

It is well to remember that none of the recent Communist, or quasi-Communist, uprisings in underdeveloped countries have begun as popular revolts. Their popularity has depended on the expedient, often non-Marxist, exploitation of local grievances, in particular peasant resentment against landlordism. And here in the northeast, in addition to the local sense of injustice created by years of governmental neglect, and the affinity of the people for the Laotians, only 30 to 40 percent of the peasants own their own land, compared with 80 percent in the much richer central rice lands.

It is no easy matter to separate fact from fiction in the northeast. However, Western intelligence agencies now accept as established fact that the Pathet Lao have established two political and military schools especially for the Thais, one at Mahaxay, due east of Thakhek and close to Nakorn Phnom, and the other north of Paksane, and that many people from the northeast have attended these schools and returned to spread their knowledge.

The situation in the northeast is roughly comparable with that which existed in South Vietnam in 1959. This time, however, instead of complacency there is a sense of urgency and alarm. Both the Thais and their Western allies are informed. The disease has been diagnosed in its relatively early stages. Perhaps there is still time to do something about it before the illness becomes fatal.

To a degree that goes far beyond the point of folly, however, all postwar Thai governments have been preoccupied with Bangkok. Power has not rested on the votes of the electorate, but on guns plus money. Both are concentrated in and around the capital. And on their manipulation by a small group of men, postwar Thailand has revolved.

It is almost axiomatic that men who gain power by *coup d'état* also fall by *coup d'état*. Much of the energies of the Thai leaders have always been spent, therefore, on the preservation of their positions.

When the Second World War came to an end, two Thais stood out above all others. One was Pridi Phanomyong, the son of a mixed Chinese-Thai marriage, the other Pibul Songgram, the son of a minor government official. Both had spent their student days in France and both had had leading roles in the *coup d'état* of June 24, 1932, which broke the absolute power of the Siamese monarchy.

Politically, Pridi favored the Left and Pibul the Right. Pridi wanted a system of State Socialism. Pibul fancied himself as a dictator of the Hitler-Mussolini type. In 1938 Pibul got his chance, becoming simultaneously Prime Minister and commander in chief of the army. He created generals, bestowed honors, and changed the country's name from Siam to Thailand, thereby making putative claim to the loyalties of the ethnic Thai groups in Laos, Burma, and southern China. Pibul, then acting as puppet Prime Minister, collaborated with the Japanese. Pridi, then acting as Regent, led the underground. After the war Pibul briefly went to jail on charges of collaboration, while Pridi, with the backing of the navy and marines, and the friendly encouragement of the West, became, for a brief period, Prime Minister.

In those early turbulent postwar years, the demand for guns

came from almost every quarter in South-East Asia. The Lao Issara wanted guns in Laos and were prepared to pay for them with such materials as Vientiane's water pump. The Viet Minh were in the market. So were the Indonesians. Instead of providing Pridi with the essentials of power, his guns went off to support the revolutionary fronts of the region, leaving the way open for Pibul, now released from detention, to make his comeback. He was helped both by the corruption of government officials, which had brought many civil leaders into disrepute, and the death in mysterious circumstances in July, 1946, of the young King Ananda. To his subjects the king was not far removed from a god, and his death in circumstances which seemed to preclude the possibility of accident, and pointed to murder or manslaughter, was staggering.

Almost alone among the Thai people, Pridi seemed to take the matter calmly, though he was greatly hurt by Pibul-sponsored rumors that he was in some way implicated. Not long after, pleading ill health, he resigned. His successor, Luang Thamrong, the Minister of Justice, did nothing to curb the activities of get-rich-quick officials who profited from early postwar shortages to line their own pockets.

With the help of the army, Pibul struck and overthrew the government on November 8, 1947. His intention was to establish himself as an overt dictator. When it became apparent that the United States and Britain were far from ready to accept him in such a position so soon after his wartime collaboration, he back-pedaled and designated himself commander in chief instead. Pridi sought refuge in the house of Captain Dennis, the British naval attaché, who subsequently became *persona non grata* with the Pibul régime, when, as British Consul in Songkla, in southern Thailand, he was discovered to be smuggling Pridi supporters out of the country in the boot of his car.

Dennis got Pridi out of Bangkok and aboard a tanker bound for Singapore. Pridi did not appear interested in suggestions put to him at this time that he should set up a rival government, or hoist the flag in a remote corner of the country with promises of British support. He was tired, disappointed, and beaten. But there was life yet in his followers. For the next two years Pibul ruled precariously. Scarcely a month went by that Bangkok was not swept by rumors of impending coups. Almost all had some substance, and one, in 1951, nearly succeeded when naval officers loyal to Pridi seized Pibul at a formal handing over of a river vessel under the newly instituted United States military aid program.

At pistol point, the officers took Pibul to the gunboat, H.M.S. *Ayuthia.* In the course of the fighting, which lasted for three days, the air force bombed and sank the gunboat. In the mêleé, Pibul dived overboard into the murky waters of the Menam, swam to the shore and, before the day was over, had broken the revolt.

The West was pleased. For now collaborator Pibul had become an ally. Malcolm Macdonald and United States Ambassador-at-Large Philip Jessup both worked on him to recognize the Bao Dai régime in Vietnam early in 1950. The *quid pro quo* was the first grant of American aid and the dropping of severe war damage claims against Thailand by Australia, Britain, and the United States. Two days after the Korean War broke out, Thailand again showed its solidarity with the West by offering troops, ships, planes, and rice for the United Nations effort in Korea. In return it received a substantial loan from the International Bank for Reconstruction and Development.

As Thailand moved internationally into the Western camp, the navy bowed out as an internal political force and the police bowed in. For the next six years Pibul balanced himself precariously between the new strong man of the army, General (now Field Marshal) Sarit Thanarat, and police General Phao Sriyanon, who was once described appropriately enough by Seni Pramoj, a former Prime Minister and leader of the Free Thai movement in the United States during the Second World War, as the "worst man in the whole history of modern Thailand."

Phao was thick-set, stolid, ambitious, and utterly ruthless. He had the heavy, expressionless eyes of the killer. His finances came from gold and opium rackets, and from minor racketeering in coffeeshops, vegetables, and ice. Far and away the most important was opium. Something like three hundred to four hundred tons of opium pass through Thailand each year to the world's underground markets. This includes opium in transit from Laos, valued perhaps at $30 million, opium from the Shan States of Burma, from Yunnan Province in China, and from the indigenous crops grown by tribesmen in the north. The profits are huge, and Phao's police enjoyed them.

Little effort was made to conceal the trade. Police provided escorts for opium trains, operated warehouses, and arranged the shipment abroad. Phao was, in fact, the Thai counterpart of General Le Van Vien, who, with the indulgence of the French and Bao Dai, ran both the police and the organized vice of Saigon in 1954.

But whereas Le Van Vien's authority did not extend far beyond the waterways around Saigon, Phao was a national figure. As the leader of the country's paramilitary forces responsible not only for internal security and normal police functions, but also for the protection of the border, he commanded an armed force of about 50,000 men equipped with tanks, armored cars, light aircraft, and the usual infantry weapons.

Phao had his own private intelligence service, with hand-picked followers in every police department to weed out those suspected of disloyalty to their chief. Members wore special gold rings with a red stone and a diamond in the center. They had direct access to Phao and were much feared inside and outside the force, using their special association with their leader to run their own private protection rackets in prostitution and extortion. Murder, intimidation, and bribery were all police weapons.

Sarit in those days looked much less formidable than his rival. Bloated and old in appearance beyond his years, he was a heavy drinker who suffered from cirrhosis of the liver and a kidney infection. Disgusted with the size of a drink offered him one night at a British Embassy, he sent an aide to his automobile to bring him a bottle of brandy and a tumbler, and with man-sized drinks he saw out the bottle and the evening.

What Pridi was to Pibul, Sarit was to Phao. A year older—he was born in 1909—they had been fierce competitors in their early days, with Sarit always holding a slight edge. Their paths in the army and in business ran parallel courses. Phao was Pibul's aide in 1939 and acted as his secretary during the Japanese occupation. Sarit was at Pibul's side during the 1947 coup. Both used Chinese financiers as counselors. Both amassed fortunes.

The collapse of the French position in Indo-China in 1954 invested Thailand with even greater importance in Washington's eyes. Between 1946 and 1949 it had received no more than token economic aid—a total of $6.2 million in grants. In 1949 and 1950, when Korea held the stage, it got nothing except military aid. Then, under the impact of the collapse of Chiang Kai-shek on the mainland of China, the mounting threat to Indo-China, and its own desire to throw in its lot with the West, it received a steady $8 million to $9 million each year.

With Dien Bien Phu, Thailand hit the jackpot. Suddenly it was cast in a new role, the center piece of the Dulles concept of containment in South-East Asia. Even if its leaders had quaint concepts of political morality (as seen through Western eyes), they were at least good anti-Communists. That was the principal thing. As Bertrand Russell once said, there is not a politician in the entire Western world who could hold office if all the facts were known about him. Why moralize, then, about our allies?

Thus, in the closing months of 1954 and early 1955, the half-Chinese half-Thai city of never colonized Thailand became the SEATO capital. American economic aid to Thailand shot up from $8.8 million in 1954 to $48.5 million in 1955. The Central Intelligence Agency, masquerading under the name of Sea Supply, took over the training and reequipment of General Phao's paramilitary police force, while JUSMAG (the Joint United States Military Aid Group) began to do a similar job for the armed forces. There was need of it. In principle the Thai army at this time consisted of five divisions. In fact, it had a total effective strength of about 60,000. Its equipment included some artillery and medium tanks and a mixed bag of American, Japanese, British, Swedish, and Danish weapons. About two-thirds of its total strength was permanently deployed around Bangkok, a counterpoise to Phao's police and, as such, a major instrument of internal political power.

Whatever its limitations as a deterrent to the Communist "aggression by seepage," as one United States ambassador calls the Communist tactic of fighting wars of national liberation, SEATO gave Bangkok a remarkable uplift. Its boom dates from the first Ministerial conference, when, to impress the visiting Foreign Ministers and their delegates, the Thai government turned the prostitutes, homosexuals, and the city's thousands of unfed, snapping, and woefully diseased dogs off the streets. City guidebooks discontinued the practice of recommending brothels and blue movies. Opium dens became hard to find. During the conference men with spray pumps on their backs invaded the hotels in the evening to pump the rooms full of an acrid smoke to discourage the mosquitos. Bangkok never looked back. Partly with American aid, it set off at a gallop to catch up with the cities of its Western allies.

Pibul, having delivered himself of some colorful descriptions of the Communist threat, set out to study Western democracy and to interpret it for Thailand. In his absence, Phao, who counted the Central Intelligence Agency representatives among his supporters, began to seek a way to oust Sarit, and to pave the way for his own accession to power. His father-in-law, Field Marshal Phin Chunhawan, had been chief of staff of the army, and Phao, of course, had his own contacts with the army.

Pibul's first task after his return was to cut Phao down to size. But he cut him so far that Phao did not recover, giving Sarit the main chance, which he was only too happy to seize.

Bangkok during the next two years was at once stimulating and depressing. The city was filled with new hotels, new roads, new shops, and a general air of prosperity that superficially seemed to make it a show window for SEATO. As time passed, however, it also became filled with even more corruption, vicious anti-Americanism, and a quite blatant determination to lay off some of the wagers involved in the country's alliance with the West. It was not so much a matter of hunting with the hare and running with the hounds but of walking up when the escalator was going down, so that irrespective of destination a case could be argued for intention.

The official pro-Western policy was vigorously denounced by newspapers under the patronage, or control, of members of the pro-Western Government. Under this "pushmi-pullyu" philosophy, Pibul declared his confidence in SEATO while one of his protégés editing the newspaper Sathiaraharb argued the case for closer ties with Peking. While American military aid, including tanks, artillery, and trucks, was giving a new look to the Thai army and through it much potential power to Sarit, who had taken over as commander in chief from General Phin Chunhawan, his newspaper, Sanseri, indulged in such pleasantries as a quarter-page cartoon showing Uncle Sam kicking John Bull into the sea and dragging off Thailand in chains. One of Sanseri's features was a comic strip, "The Shepherd's Message," which came free from Peking.

Of the twenty-four vernacular newspapers circulating in Bangkok at that time, Sanseri, the most virulent of all in its denunciation of the United States, had the largest circulation—about 50,000. Eleven others with a total circulation of another 50,000 were also anti-Western, neutralist, or in favor of closer ties with Communist China. Five with a total circulation of about 20,000 were anti-Government but not anti-West. Their views seemed to be fairly well reflected popularly when a USIS public information survey which took a sample poll among five hundred Thais found that neutralists and those generally favoring the Communists in such matters as SEATO outnumbered those advocating closer ties with the West in the proportion of three to two.

Sarit was the key anti-American figure. He detested the United States Central Intelligence Agency, which had turned Phao's elite border police into a small but efficient force, and was furious with JUSMAG when it advised against further increases in the strength of the army. Through his newspapers he blamed the United States for pushing Thailand into SEATO, for Thailand's failure to befriend Communist China, for not allowing the Thai people to visit China, for the failure to abrogate the anti-Communist Law, for obstructing his own plans to build an oil refinery at Farng, the Thai oilfield, and for interfering in Thailand's internal affairs.

The newspapers were not merely mildly anti-American. They spoke in Communist terms of "inperialist exploitation" and of "being a slave to the dollar god." Sea Supply was accused by Sarit's papers of direct involvement in the opium business, and one paper attacked it for allegedly bringing in sixty-nine cases of gold to buy Phao's opium as a means of keeping the régime in power.

All this time a façade of democracy had been maintained. In fact, Pibul had been so impressed with the soapbox orators of London's Hyde Park in his 1955 search for democracy that he even authorized a Leftist-dominated Hyde Park Movement, which lifted the lid off public criticism. But democracy as Thailand knew it now was a grotesque caricature. "This régime is pulling down the boa tree and planting thistles," said Seni Pramoj. "You think there's democracy here. I tell you it is already dead. They've built a monument to it."

Khuang Aphiwong, another former Prime Minister and then leader of the Opposition, was even more bitter. His candidates would have won six or seven of the nine Bangkok seats in the elections of February, 1957, if the ballots had not been loaded against him and if Phao's gangsters had not intimidated the voters.

Khuang was not one of the group who favored closer ties with Communist China, however. He believed China wanted to make use of Thailand as a stepping-stone to the rest of South-East Asia: but he was critical of American policy. "People dislike the government," he said. "They know it wouldn't stay in power for a day if American support were withdrawn. Therefore they blame the Americans. Everyone blames the Americans for helping the government, even though you know, and I know, that they are not doing it for the sake of the government but for the defense of the Far East. The Communists understand the situation and push the blame on the Americans. If aid is to be really effective, it must be directed toward helping the country and the people and not a discredited government."

He accused Max Bishop, the United States ambassador, of "driving Thailand into the arms of the Communists, just as American support for Chiang Kai-shek drove the Chinese into the arms of Mao Tse-tung." If Thailand fell, he said, it would be the Americans' fault.

In all countries where critical situations exist, Western diplomats, and Americans, especially in these days of Western leadership, find themselves confronted with the dilemma of supporting the government in power, while maintaining links with opposition groups and organizations. The more oppressive the government, the more it resents opposition. To consort with its opponents inevitably arouses official hostility. Far too often embassies take the easy way out and become wholly identified with unpopular administrations and lose all links with their critics. Often an ambassador will say, "My instructions are to give so-and-so my unqualified support, and this is what I am doing," even though "unqualified support" sometimes means gilding the lily and suppressing adverse comment within the embassy.

This was the error Bishop fell into. To this was added the mystery that-wasn't-a-mystery of the CIA masquerading as Sea Supply. To build up the Thai police was a legitimate undertaking that could have been accomplished overtly. The covert approach merely provided the opening for the Thai newspapers to invent stories that the CIA were in everything from counterfeit currency and opium rackets to the desecration of Buddhist images. Public resentment reached a peak when Kukrit Pramoj, editor of *Siam Rath* and Seni's brother, was arrested for writing an article in which he "insulted" Bishop.

The greater the outcry, the more Sarit's cause prospered. On August 21, 1957, the Thai army's "big three"—Sarit, Lieutenant General Thanom Kittikachorn, and Lieutenant General Praphas Charasathien—resigned from the Cabinet. The government's story was that they had resigned because Pibul had ordered his Ministers to choose between State and private interests. Sarit denied it. He said they had resigned because the government was not acting in accordance with public opinion, particularly in domestic affairs, and, in his own case, because of poor health. "If I want to maintain business benefits, it would be better for me to remain a Cabinet Minister, appoint other people to take my trade posts, sit quietly and let the profits roll in," he said.

The questions now were whether Sarit had really veered to the Left and become as he sounded, or whether he was merely moving expediently to ensure a united front against the discredited Pibul régime. The answers were not clear at the time. Seni Pramoj calls Thailand a country of invisible curtains, and the curtain of anti-Americanism was certainly used to good advantage by Sarit in the pursuit of power.

The time had come for Pibul and Phao to go. "We must take one step backward in order to take a hundred steps forward," said Sarit. The step was to move the 1st Division's tanks and infantry to the traditional *coup d'état* positions in Bangkok. Pibul got away in his Thunderbird to an east coast port and then on to Cambodia and exile, first in the United States and later in Japan. Phao was allowed to go to Switzerland, a decision the new régime was subsequently to regret when it wanted to bring him to trial for political murders. A natural death saved Phao from further worries. Pibul has played out his role in Thai politics. At sixty-five he is unlikely to return. And Pridi, according to latest reports, has arteriosclerosis.

Sarit's first act was to relieve Western embassies of their fears and doubts. There would be no change, he promised, in Thailand's foreign policy. Thailand would remain with the West. In a move designed especially to reassure Washington he named Pote Sarasin, a former ambassador to the United States and SEATO's obviously pro-Western Secretary-General, to take over the provisional government until an election could be held a couple of months later. The election gave the National Socialist Party, formed *after* the election by Sarit from among candidates who had enjoyed his backing, 220 out of 283 seats in the National Assembly. With his trusted and trustworthy coup follower, General Thanom, installed as Prime Minister, the way was clear for Sarit to leave for Washington for long-delayed surgery.

Thanom took the job with only the utmost reluctance. A soldier with a reputation for integrity and honesty, he did not fit easily into the command of the mixed team of Leftists, militarists, and opportunists who made up the new government. The police force, which oddly enough seemed to have developed a liking for Phao after his fall, was unhappy about the new Minister of the Interior and the third man in the triumvirate, General Praphas, and Washington, despite Sarit's assurances of continued support for SEATO and Western policies generally, was less than reassured by the presence in the Cabinet of avowed Leftists, including Major General Netr Kemayathin, Sarit's publisher, and Tim Buriphat, the deputy Minister of Education.

Before going off to the Walter Reid Hospital for his operation, Sarit was told plainly that continued American economic aid would depend on something more tangible than mere assurances of his goodwill, including, for example, a change of editorial policy on the part of *Sanseri*. Sarit cabled from America that the policy had to change. Netr's price for stepping down was popularly said to be three million *baht* (or slightly less than $200,000).

Nothing really worked while Sarit was away. No one knew whether he would survive an operation. Pridi, looking for a comeback, wrote to the Thai Press Association from China to revive an old Thai dream that a canal should be cut through the Kra Isthmus, in the narrows of southern Thailand. He proposed that the project should be financed by the sale of the Royal jewels. The letter, which was published at the time of a Royal tour of the north, backfired. Under the new government's encouragement, the quite genuine efforts of the King to make himself a useful symbol of Thai unity and the beauty and charm of Queen Sirikit had made the throne not merely revered but popular. At the same time, however, Thai visits to Communist China increased. The Soviet Union continued to feed propaganda to the newspapers and to spread it among students. Left-wing politicians tried to exploit disaffection among some three hundred army officers, apparently with a view to instigating another coup.

Sarit, though still ill, returned in June, 1958, in an effort to sort out the mess. He left again in August to continue his convalescence, this time in Britain. Thanom's attempts to find a solution to the border problems with Cambodia over the Phra Viharn temple were frustrated by General Praphas, who instigated a protest demonstration against Cambodia which eventually turned into a riot and had to be suppressed by his own police. Twice Air Marshal Chalermkiart Watanangkul, the commander in chief of the air force, flew to London to discuss the situation with Sarit. The result was the coup within a coup in October, 1958.

I arrived in Bangkok at this time from a somewhat more dramatic crisis in the Taiwan Strait, intending to leave the following morning for Phnom Penh. In the evening I phoned an old Thai friend and told him my plans.

"Don't go," he said.

"Why not?"

"I can't tell you," he replied, "but, whatever you do, don't go."

I phoned the airline, canceled my reservation, and the following morning set out on the diplomatic round. There seemed to be no hint of impending trouble. Seni Pramoj's invisible curtain was well in place.

That night, however, Sarit, responding to the further entreaties of the air marshal, left London secretly for Bangkok, where he arrived, again secretly, at 3:00 A.M. on Sunday, October 19th. He spent the entire day in conference with Thanom and Praphas at the headquarters of the First Army. The following morning he asked for an audience with the King. A Royal Proclamation was necessary to dissolve Parliament. The King gave his assent, and the coup within a coup moved into gear.

It was the quietest and gentlest of all coups. About eight o'clock that evening, having learned now of Sarit's return, I toured the traditional coup concentration areas in a taxi with Darrell Berrigan, editor and publisher of the newspaper *Bangkok World*. It was a wet evening, and few people were on the streets. Once we were halted when King Phumiphon and Queen Sirikit drove past on their way to a movie. "Let's see how the driver responds when the King goes past," said Berrigan. "I'm sure the monarchy has a real hold, but it will be interesting to see how someone like this reacts when no Thai can see him." Sure enough, as the King's car approached, the driver bowed his head, closed his eyes, and clasped his hands together.

Three hours later Berrigan phoned to say that the troops were in the streets and that Bangkok radio was alternately playing martial music and announcing government edicts in Thai and English. In rapid succession Sarit suspended the Constitution, dissolved the National Assembly, and declared martial law throughout the country.

The coup was conducted in the name of anti-Communism. In a sense it was. By closing down Leftist newspapers and arresting some scores of anti-Westerners, Sarit gave notice that the flirtations with Peking and Moscow were to come to an end. Essentially, however, he acted to consolidate himself in power.

While the Laotian storm clouds were gathering the following year, he pulled Thailand together. He seemed determined to store up merit in the next world and to make amends for his misspent youth by throwing himself wholeheartedly into the business of government. He fooled the doctors who predicted that his illnesses would inevitably prove fatal within a year or two. And he began a honeymoon with the United States.

Under his autocratic and sometimes heavy-handed rule he gave Thailand the most effective government it had known in the postwar period. Efforts to diversify the country's agriculture resulted in higher receipts from exports, and agricultural and mining production and manfacturing showed a steady increase. Except for the running squabble with Cambodia, which led in October, 1961, to Cambodia breaking off relations with Thailand, all was well with the world.

Prince Sihanouk, pausing in Tokyo on his way back to Cambodia after visiting the United States, told a press conference that Cambodia had to fight not so much against Communism as against pro-Western neighbors. Sarit quite properly interpreted this to include Thailand, and then gave it a twist of his own when he spoke at a meeting in Bangkok to celebrate the third anniversary of the 1959 coup within a coup.

"It is known and understood all over the world that he

[Sihanouk] alone would not be in a position to fight against Thailand," Sarit said. "The words thus uttered clearly indicate that there was a plan to serve as an intermediary or a bridgehead to induce the Communists to harm neighboring nations, which would be treacherous to the region of South-East Asia. The government has had to guard against danger on this front. At the same time, it has had to exercise restraint and to condone such arrogance by taking for consolation the old proverbial tale of a pig challenging a lion to a fight."

To ultrasensitive Sihanouk, Sarit had called him a pig. He broke off relations, closed the border, and kept his fingers crossed while the World Court deliberated the case of the temple of Phra Viharn. For Thailand, however, these were mostly noises off. Laos was the real storm. The French defeat in Indo-China in 1954 had colonial overtones that tended to conceal the Communist threat. Even in Indo-China, many anti-Communists thought it was better to get rid of the French first and to take care of the Viet Minh later. There was no such feeling about Laos. Almost everywhere among government officials in South-East Asia, including those whose vision we are apt to regard as myopic where Communism is concerned, the events in Laos portended something very close to disaster. "Laos is lost," said Dr. Subandrio, the Indonesian foreign minister. Sihanouk, who conceived the idea of the Geneva conference to solve the Laotian problem, concurred. The opinion was prevalent also in Manila, Singapore, Kuala Lumpur, and Saigon.

"Maybe Laotian neutrality will last a year or two, or even longer," was the Canberra assessment of the situation when the Geneva conference finally reached agreement. "The Communists don't seem to be in a hurry and it may suit them to play it that way. But they're playing with two-headed pennies and can't lose."

This allusion to the Australian coin-tossing game of "two-up" may be obscure to the uninitiated, but except apparently to the Western statesmen at Geneva there was little obscure now about what had happened in Laos, or what might conceivably happen in the future to its neighbors.

This was why official Western attitudes to the Geneva conference produced such a vigorous reaction in Thailand. It was not a case of hip, hip, hooray for peace, but hyp, hyp, hypocrisy for the Western pretense that served as a substitute for policy. The Thai anger was understandable. On December 11, 1961, for instance, Malcolm Macdonald, acting as the British co-chairman of the conference, opened the day's session with a brief review of past progress and future prospects. "We are, in fact, on the point of creating a practical and just system of international guarantees which will ensure to Laos neutrality, untroubled peace and sovereign independence," he said. A week earlier the acting leader of the United States delegation, William H. Sullivan, called it a "pattern for peace not only in Laos, not only in South-East Asia, but throughout the world."

In the long, sorry story of Laos these comments merit a special place. For what Geneva was, in fact, creating in Laos was calculated neither to assure its integrity nor its sovereignty, while the peace it promised was of the kind that Mao Tse-tung once said grew out of the barrel of the gun.

Their obvious dishonesty infuriated the Thai government, which had already proposed an amendment to the SEATO unanimity rules designed to prevent the British and the French using the veto to prevent treaty action. In Thailand, and also in the Philippines, Britain and France now became the objects of bitter attack. Both were publicly denounced as appeasers. Felixberto Serrano, then Foreign Minister of the Philippines, told me in Manila in July, 1961, that Britain would stop at nothing, including appeasement, to avoid becoming embroiled in military action in South-East Asia. He thought Britain and France ought to be encouraged to confine their interests to Europe and that a new NATO-type security organization should be formed around the United States, Australia, New Zealand, and interested Asian countries. "The situation is urgent, almost desperate," he said. "Even such a staunch anti-Communist nation as Thailand is once again considering neutrality. I have this from no less an authority than Thanat Khoman."

The South-East Asian tour of Vice-President Lyndon Johnson in the summer of 1961 mended few fences. Serrano said he had hoped for something more than the "exuberant reassurances" Mr. Johnson brought with him. And Thanat, with the United States obviously in mind, said bitterly about the reception that greeted Thai proposals at Geneva, "We learned from the Geneva conference that the country which claimed to be our great friend likes its foe better than its friends."

These statements may appear irresponsible. That is not the point. What mattered was the state of mind they reflected. Thailand wanted above all to keep the Communists away from its borders. It did not feel that the Geneva Agreement provided sufficient guarantees to ensure the maintenance of genuine neutrality by Laos.

Only firm United States pressure got Thailand to the conference table to sign the agreement. While the other signatories sent their foreign ministers for the occasion, Thailand sent an ambassador, a last small gesture of defiance. "In Thailand," wrote Theh Chongkhadikij, in the Bangkok *Post*, "there is a sinking feeling that the Laotian affair is not a case of the Western Powers not being aware of the Communist objectives in South-East Asia, or having forgotten Communist unfaithfulness of the past, but, possibly, one of trying gracefully to wash their hands of Laos."

This comment was an accurate reflection of Thai official feeling. It was also profoundly close to the truth. Washington, London, and Paris did not have the wool pulled over their eyes in Laos. "Of course we know that Laos's chances of neutrality are slight, but the more we say so the more difficult it is for the Americans," said a British diplomat in Bangkok. Laos *was* a bad place for a war, and, having decided against fighting, the bungling West had no alternative but to negotiate for what it could get.

Inevitably, however, the Laotian settlement revived some of the latent anti-Americanism in Bangkok. There were not only deep hurt and bitterness, but further talk of neutralism as a way out. Neither the feeling nor the talk were eliminated by the swiftness with which the United States rushed the Marines to Udon in northwestern Thailand, when Phoumi's forces fled from Nam Tha across the Mekong in May on the eve of the Geneva Agreement, and Thailand for a time seemed threatened by invasion from the Pathet Lao and Viet Minh. This move, in which Washington got token support from Australia, Britain, and New Zealand, but not from France, Pakistan, or the Philippines (which was almost as critical of the Geneva Agreement as Thailand and angry over the United States Congress's temporary rejection of its $73 million war damage claim), was political rather than military. Not even the Thais really believed that an invasion was imminent, though it suited Bangkok's temper to suggest that this was the case.

Partly mollified by the arrival of the forces, but angry again at their withdrawal without prior consultation, Thailand was even more inflamed by what it considered mischievous United States behavior in the Phra Viharn temple case. The temple stands on a platform jutting out from a hill across Cambodian territory. Drop a stone from the temple and it will land in Cambodia. The approach from the Cambodia side, however, is steep, difficult and, during the wet season, impassable, while a somewhat gentler slope makes it accessible at all seasons from Thailand.

To the Thais this was conclusive proof of ownership. Thus, when Dean Acheson, who is regarded by Bangkok as one of President Kennedy's closest advisers, accepted the Cambodian brief there was a predictable hullabaloo. When Cambodia won the case with the support of the United States vote, just as the Geneva conference was coming to a close, a new wave of anti-Americanism struck. Its most articulate expression came from Thanat Khoman and his immediate subordinates in the Foreign Office.

Neutralism has often been slightly disreputable in Thailand because it is recommended so strongly by Cambodia. But now it was openly canvassed in the form of an ultimatum. Either the United States conclude a bilateral mutual defense agreement with Thailand, or Thailand would have no alternative but to become neutral. "Of course, the signing of a mutual defense pact with the U.S. will bind Thailand more strongly to the U.S.," wrote Theh Chongkhadikij in his article which summed up much of what Thanat was saying privately. "Whether this is desirable is debatable. The long-term best interests of Thailand—of Thailand alone—have to be the deciding factor. If Thailand with uncertainty and instability near its border cannot get what it considers adequate and effective guarantees for the preservation of its independence, freedom and sovereignty, it may be forced into accommodating itself to the conditions surrounding it, in the hope that the Communists who are coming closer and closer will live and let live. In the absence of real safeguards, if Thailand stands firm against the Communists, it will do so at its peril because then the Communists will do everything to crush it—and they may be placed in a better position to do so as a result of the Geneva accords, it is felt here.

"The authorities in Bangkok are waiting to see whether the U.S. forces and the troops of the other allies stationed here are to be withdrawn, following the signing of the new Geneva agreements. If the troops are withdrawn without conclusion of a mutual defense pact with the U.S., the feeling that the Western Powers, after getting off the hook in Laos, are also going to foresake Thailand and the rest of South-East Asia may be strong enough to indicate neutrality as a wise policy for survival."

No doubt Vice-President Lyndon Johnson thought that by publicly nailing the United States flag to the South Vietnamese masthead he would lend encouragement to the forces opposed to Communism. But what he did, in effect, was to draw the line in Vietnam when the war was in Laos. This has raised doubts that cannot be dispelled easily and will predictably remain while Britain and France continue to have a voice in South-East Asian policies.

Several attempts have been made to persuade France that it would be better to withdraw gracefully from SEATO. It has indicated quite firmly that it intends to remain, while Britain can legitimately claim that it has made a notable contribution toward regional security by the wisdom of its Malayan and related policies, the contribution of the Thompson Mission to South Vietnam, which has had a significance out of all proportion to its numbers, and its solidarity when it came to contributing its token towards the reestablishment of Thai confidence in its Western allies during the border crisis in May, 1962. All of this is demonstrable, but the fact remains, as one Thai put it, that "recent history in this part of the world suggests that where Paris or London do not care to tread, Washington does not often walk."

For Washington to respond to Thai pressures for a mutual security pact would also sound the death knell of SEATO, which might not matter very much, though it would be a public confession of failure and an admission that Peking was right all along in calling it a "paper tiger." Whether a mutual security pact would really guarantee Thailand against "going Communist" is another matter. As we have seen in South Vietnam and Laos, the metamorphosis from political penetration to a full-blown war of national liberation, though it passes through phases which seem clear and well-defined in a post-mortem examination, has all the creeping characteristics of an incurable disease. You're just about dead before you know you're sick.

No one can say we have not been forewarned about the northeast. But what have we done about it? What have the Thais done about it? And what are we going to do?

The answer to the first two questions is "not much." Most United States economic aid goes to Thailand in the form of bulk petroleum products to generate *baht* for economic development purposes. A regional telecommunications system has absorbed some $17 million; the "Friendship Highway" (which was built primarily as a military road in the days when planning was in terms of overt invasions, but has contributed directly and potentially to improvements in the northeast), $19 million; a bridge replacement scheme (which had similar intentions and has had similar results), $13.4 million; improvements to the northeast highway, $4.2 million; a power plant for Bangkok, $2 million; aeronautical ground services to create a modern integrated system of ground facilities for domestic and international air traffic, $5.6 million; and Bangkok city planning another $2.5 million. Such nationwide and essential services as malaria eradication received more than $6 million, and a program to develop improved crop varieties more than $2 million. These and similar aid projects were undertaken with the economic development of Thailand clearly in mind. All of them were important.

In comparison with the volume of United States aid and technical assistance received by other threatened countries in the region, Thailand's share has been comparatively small. In the eleven-year period July 1, 1950, to June 30, 1961, it received $284.8 million. The contribution in financial year 1961 of $24.8 million was about average, therefore. But since Laos with less than one-twelfth of the population received $35.8 million in the same year, and South Vietnam, with about half the population, $151 million, Thailand, relatively speaking, did not get much. What it got was honestly spent, so much so that the retiring USOM director, Thomas E. Naughton, on July 13, 1962, claimed that "rigid auditing, and end-use checking of our own and outside experts have never revealed a case in which our funds have been dishonestly used, or willfully diverted from the purpose for which they were meant."

This would be a remarkable achievement anywhere, and it reflects highly on the conduct of the operations mission, especially in a country where members of the government, or their wives and partners, have engaged quite openly in private businesses ranging from the opium trade to haberdashery.

The fact nevertheless remains that United States aid to Thailand, like United States aid in so many other underdeveloped countries, had the effect of a rock thrown into a pool. It caused a big splash at the center but the ripples had disappeared well short of the villages that the joint Thai–United States teams "discovered" in their 1962 investigative tours, and well short, of course, of the areas in which the Communists first began to establish their cells and bases. The aid was not wasted. It did good things. But since it was clearly given to deny the Communists the sort of foothold they have obtained, it failed in its primary objective.

The situation now confronting Thailand, and the United States and its allies, in this critical area is that they have to begin at the very beginning. One policeman to about three thousand people is sufficient perhaps in a large town or city. But in the northeast one police officer and two men, with no means of transport other than their own feet, are often responsible for twenty or more villages. For months at a time the monsoons prevent them from making even routine inspections. Since there are no telephones and no means of radio communication, the Communists could take over one or more villages and Bangkok might never learn of it. However much he might want to report acts of treason or subversion to the police, the average northeasterner often does not have the physical capability. He does not need to be terrorized into keeping the silence.

Everywhere, not merely in the northeast, the government's administrative apparatus does not get below the district level. Villages, in effect, govern themselves beyond and below the ken of Thai authority. This is why the Vietnamese succeeded in establishing themselves so easily and so firmly in the past and, partly, why the Pathet Lao have found it so easy today. Much depends on a village headman. If he is won over by the Communists, then the task becomes virtually impossible for the police.

As a start, the Thai government with the assistance of USOM took twelve hundred district officers from the northeast to Bangkok for a week's sightseeing and training. This was followed by a similar excursion for eighteen hundred village headmen living within twenty to thirty miles of the border.

Training teams from the Ministry of the Interior have also begun to go into the field with the specific object of bridging the considerable administrative gap between the appointed district officer and the village chief. In a further, more widespread, effort to overcome this enormous handicap, USOM and the Thai government have sponsored a community development program. The idea is to foster the growth of local self-government, and assist the villages to secure and use the technical assistance they need from the various government services in carrying out projects in agriculture, health, sanitation, roads, local facilities. In so doing it is hoped to involve them progressively in an understanding of, and participation in, the six-point social and economic plan to "raise the living standards of the northeast to a level comparable with those in other regions, and to lay down economic and social infrastructures in the region" which the government announced in October, 1961.

This plan calls for the provision of water for consumption and home use and for agriculture and industry through the construction of impounding dams and irrigation tanks, the creation of fishing grounds, flood control and the improvement of natural water resources; the construction and improvement of the means of transport, including highways, feeder roads and railways; government assistance through agricultural services, irrigation and market expansion; the establishment of agricultural improvement units; a land tenure system based on private landownership (though avoiding land fragmentation); the creation of adequate power at reasonable prices; the encouragement of private industrial and commercial development; and the promotion of community development, public health, and education to a level not below that existing in other regions.

Regional hospitals will be built. By 1966 it is hoped to have 3,300 secondary schools in the northeast. A university for northern Thailand will become functional in 1964, and a university for the northeast two years later, amalgamating two faculties of agriculture and engineering and taking students from an institute of agricultural and mechanical sciences which is being set up as a priority project.

In an effort to stimulate area development, three to four urban centers are contemplated for each region. These will provide public and other utilities. The government also hopes to promote industrial investment. An entirely new system of "agri-metro" centers will be built to combine social, agricultural, and manufacturing development. The first of these will be at Khonkaen, a sizable town on the northeast highway connecting Korat with Nong Khai, on the Mekong.

The plans here call for the construction of a dam to develop both hydroelectric power and sufficient reserves of water to irrigate 100,000 acres. The area has a great potential for agricultural development. Rice, kenaf, cotton, maize, and castor beans all ought to do well. In areas farther south the "Friendship Highway" has already opened up virgin country for farming. Results have been excellent, especially since the United States–sponsored introduction of Guatemalan corn and Hawaiian sweet corn, which bumped up corn exports from $1 million in 1951 to $26 million in 1960.

Altogether the government plans to spend $190 million on northeastern development. Of this the storage and tapping of water resources will take $42.5 million, industry and power $14.5 million, transport $99 million, and agricultural credit $24 million. Since the local currency projected investment totals only $40 million, however, the financing of the rest of the project is left to the United States and others. As the Thai government notes, "Maybe only the foreign exchange part will be covered by loans and therefore the number of projects will have to be reduced." Maybe.

Yet the temptation to throw one's hat in the air is very great. For here at last, and even before the shots start being fired, there is at last a true appreciation of the nature and form of the Communist threat.

Realistically, however, even if the funds are available, the Communists have such a start that armed struggle can scarcely be avoided. We have evidence of intention. Given that, the opportunity for Pathet Lao guerrillas to reinforce the local agents even more easily than the Viet Minh came to the help of the Pathet Lao, and the fact that Laos is a ready-made sanctuary for the Thai rebels, just as once Thailand was a refuge for Laotians like Prince Souphanouvong, all are heavily in the Communists' favor.

The Thai border police force guards the frontier. It is well officered and equipped. But though it has the resources to supervise official border traffic, it cannot hope to cope with the covert along a thousand miles of border, or the innumerable pirogues that go backward and forward across the Mekong each day as casually as suburban housewives in other parts of the world use their automobiles to do the morning shopping.

Troops stationed in the northeast are mostly locally recruited, while the officers usually come from Bangkok. This is economical, but it does not make for better relations between officers and men.

Considerable Communist penetration of the rank and file is known to have occurred, but the system makes it difficult to determine exactly how much, since the loyalties of the locals are to each other rather than to the officer corps which has intruded from Bangkok.

The army itself is a questionable force. Its actual strength is about 80,000, though theoretically it is much larger. Since the commanders are responsible for paying the troops, there is profit in succumbing to the temptation to exaggerate the numbers. Unlike the Arvins and the Royal Lao army, the Thai army is not paid for by the United States. It operates, therefore, on a limited budget. The troops get only small wages, but they also receive rations for themselves and their families. The combined total is inadequate, however, to support both the men and their families if they are separated, and the army is therefore obliged to pay a field allowance when, and if, the troops are sent out on exercises. Since the army budget rarely can afford to meet such additional costs, the troops by and large get little field training. JUSMAG is training mobile groups but they have achieved very little tactically. It would be unwise, therefore, to expect too much of the army.

Ever present in the minds of some of the Thai leaders is the lurking suspicion that their close identification with the West is unwise, that perhaps neutrality is the right course after all. In September, 1962, General Praphas, who could easily be the successor to Sarit, was hinting once again about a radical change in Thai policy if the United States acquiesced in the Cambodian request to arm three additional battalions. This was more of a bribe than a threat; it will be interesting to watch, nevertheless, how the Thai leadership reacts when the thumbscrews start to turn in the northeast. Sihanouk has long advised the Thais to be smart and to play it the Cambodian way, since by persisting with their Western alliance they make Thailand an inevitable target for Communist subversive techniques that cannot be countered. The corollary is that by throwing off its Western alignment, Thailand, like Cambodia, will get the best of both worlds.

Since Peking's aim is not to shear off a lump of Thailand for the benefit of Laos, but, initially, to destroy United States influence in South-East Asia, there is no doubt that Thailand could buy off a revolt in the northeast by accepting a "neutral" status. China wants what it calls a "zone of peace" in South-East Asia. The "neutrality" of South Vietnam and Thailand would create it.

Conclusion

W<small>HAT WE ARE</small> up against in South-East Asia is a carefully prepared and skillfully executed plan to destroy Western power and influence by tactics which begin with subversion in remote and neglected areas, move into armed revolt, and proceed, so the Communists hope, to the conference table. By settling for something short of total victory, both in the field of battle and in diplomatic negotiation, the Communists emphasize the spirit of compromise and reasonableness. They fool the gullible and those who have no right to be gullible.

In all the angry discussions about whether Laos was the right or the wrong place to fight a war, or to seek a showdown with Hanoi, Peking, and Moscow, and all the nauseating hypocrisy at Geneva about the virtues of peace and neutrality which we claimed to be helping, there was distressingly little examination of the root causes of the fiasco. It was better, it seemed, to put on a bold face than to admit our own blunders.

Early in 1955, when the SEATO Ministers were gathering for their first Council meeting in Bangkok along with their military advisers and experts, a young Vietnamese who had fought first of all with Ho Chi Minh and subsequently with Prince Souphanouvong in the Lao Issara forces, sat down over a map with two Western officers. Their concern was the nature of the Communist threat to South-East Asia. One of the Westerners, conventionally trained in the best of military schools and well briefed on the topographical features of South-East Asia, took his crayon and drew a broad black arrow that came through the porte de Chîne on the China-Tongking border and split into two branches, one going into South Vietnam and Cambodia and the other directed through Laos to Thailand. "This is how they will come," he said.

"You are wrong," said the Vietnamese, taking the crayon and drawing a series of small circles with lines branching off them like the spokes of a wheel. "This is how they will come." By the time he had finished, the map was covered with interlocking lines.

"What are you doing?" asked an Australian. "Making cobwebs?"

"Yes," said the Vietnamese. "Cobwebs. That is it."

We lost Laos to these cobwebs. We are in danger of losing South Vietnam to cobwebs. We are threatened by cobwebs in Thailand. If we had embarked on the deliberate process of giving Laos away, we could scarcely have lost it more shamefully or more quickly. Everywhere our fundamental premise was that the challenge was purely military and could be answered only by bigger and better military formations. Thirty miles from Vientiane villagers had never heard of the Royal Lao government or the Royal Lao army. We held Vientiane, for most of the time, and we held Luang Prabang and the other Mekong towns, and we lost the countryside: and when we lost the countryside, we lost all. We got only what we deserved, though we might well ask ourselves if the Laotian people got what they deserved.

By the time it came to the second Geneva conference, the situation was hopeless. Even so, rarely have so many intelligent men, and men of stature, from so many countries indulged in so much political pipe-laying and diplomatic skulduggery. Western policy, as it was presented at Geneva, was based on the assumption that the Communists had made an exception of Laos, that they wanted nothing more there than a truly neutral State. This assumption sprang from Russian pledges made privately in Moscow and Geneva, coupled with the confidential note of urgency that we had to hurry up with the job to keep the Chinese out. Since previous policies had been based on the demonstrable fact that the Communists were working to take over the area, and that, especially in Laos, they were making considerable progress, the change, so far as Laos was concerned, was not merely in policy but at least in part in the premise on which the policy was based.

While there may have been good (if far from obvious) reasons for taking such assurances at face value, there were also some obvious reasons for doubt. Khrushchev's interpretation of peaceful coexistence at the time did not exclude revolutions of the Laotian type. The principal article in the April, 1962, issue of *International Affairs*, which is published by the Soviet Society for the Popularization of Political and Scientific Knowledge, dealt specifically with this point. It reaffirmed that both the Communist Party of the Soviet Union and the international Communist movement "consider peaceful coexistence as a form of class struggle on a world scale. They do not think that a devastating war is needed for the revolutionary transformation of the countries that have not yet taken the socialist road." It added that "revolutionary national liberation wars, like class struggles in any capitalist country, do not clash with coexistence, and can be brought to success only under peaceful coexistence." In short, the "neutrality" Khrushchev envisaged for Laos was not at all inconsistent with *International Affairs'* concept of a national liberation war "brought to success."

The article was published for all the world to read. Less publicized, but certainly well known to the Western statesmen in Geneva, were Khrushchev's activities in Havana and Djakarta at this time. Missile bases had not yet appeared in Cuba, but the buildup was well under way. In Indonesia, Khrushchev sought to create similar trouble. Long after Holland was ready to settle in West New Guinea on any terms that would have permitted its withdrawal with dignity, Khrushchev was continuing to press the Indonesians into military action.

Even on the assumption that Khrushchev was serious when he said he was concerned only to bring about a neutral Laos, what possible assurance was there, in view of existing relations between the Soviet Union and Communist China, that Peking had similar interests, or could be kept in order by Khrushchev? "At first sight the split between Moscow and Peking seems very encouraging," said a Vietnamese official, "but if it means only that the Russians can disclaim responsibility every time the Chinese grab more territory, the result is not going to be very helpful for any of us."

In any event, Russian influence among South-East Asian Communist parties had waned to the point where none was prepared to antagonize Peking. Hanoi moved slowly but surely to the Peking side. The move first became apparent when the Lao Dong Party sent a message of congratulations on the twentieth anniversary of the Albanian Party and also published an article entitled "Brilliant and Victorious Twenty Years of the Albanian Workers' Party" in the party newspaper *Nhan Dan*. By the end of 1962 there was no longer any doubt. The Thai, Burmese, and Malayan Communist parties had also expressed their approval of the Albanian leadership, thereby deliberately aligning themselves with China. D. N. Aidit, leader of Indonesia's two million Communists, not only supported the Chinese position but also canvassed for the creation of an Asian Communist international secretariat to coordinate regional policies. It now goes almost without saying that Peking, not Moscow, would have the strongest voice in such a secretariat.

So far as South Vietnam is concerned, the substitution of the United States for France and Diem for Bao Dai in the anti-Communist lineup in the current phase of the war poses problems for the Viet Cong and Viet Minh that did not exist before 1954. The United States has not really begun to fight in Vietnam yet. Its great resources have scarcely been tapped. Instead of a hundred helicopters, it can deploy a thousand, if need be. There is still much room for military maneuver short of large-scale intervention by American forces.

Nor is there any basis for comparison between the Vietnamese forces and leadership of the 1950's and the Vietnamese forces and leadership today. Diem is resolute; Bao Dai was irresolute. Diem is tough; Bao Dai was weak. Diem will fight; Bao Dai would not. But Diem, with an in-built resistance to what he regards as demagogism, is incapable of turning himself into a popular leader. If his administration was effective, that would matter less, at least so far as the war is concerned; but the administration is ineffective. There is no government but Diem and his family and what one Vietnamese called his accomplices. If Personalism has any appeal to the masses, it is not evident. The army is frustrated. The intellectuals are frustrated. The peasants are harried.

Inevitably, the situation here invites comparisons with China in the closing days of the Civil War. Diem and Chiang are both Christians and Confucians, with the same conceptions of order and discipline and of their role in society. Diem has his Republican Youth movement, through which he hopes to control the young people; Chiang had his counterpart, the Three People's Principles Youth Corps. Chiang suppressed freedom of thought, association, and expression; Diem has followed his example. Chiang lost the support of the intellectuals; Diem has also lost their support.

The Chiangs' Society for Moral Endeavor and New Life Movement and the Ngos' morality laws and Personalism are all closely related. The New Life Movement planned to create a "new national consciousness and mass psychology based on the ancient virtues of *li, i, lien,* and *ch'ih,* or etiquette, justice, integrity, and conscientiousness. Personalism is based on Thành, which Diem interprets as "intellectual loyalty and noble morality, an acute consciousness and clear vision of the compass of one's duties toward the Creator, toward the country, and toward oneself as well as toward one's fellow man"; and Tín, "the sincere and courageous practice of all these duties, no matter how grievous." Like the New Life Movement, Personalism has been high in ideals and low in performance. But Chiang, despite his threats and promises to return to the mainland, is finished—what Ngo Dinh Nhu would call a "political cadaver." Diem, the last Confucian, is still a considerable force in the South-East Asian scene.

There are other significant differences. The corruption of the Chiang régime was an established fact; even those most maliciously disposed against the Diem administration can produce nothing that can be described as evidence of *serious* corruption in Saigon today. Diem himself has no interest in material rewards. Under the influence of Ngo Dinh Nhu, however, the regimentation under the Diem administration goes even further than it did in China under the Kuomintang. His mass production of politically organized strategic hamlets is full of dangers. In the more or less secure areas their bamboo palisades may be good enough. Even with radios to call for helicopter support, however, those in more remote and red areas are extremely vulnerable. Malayan "new villages" were effective with double rows of barbed wire, and cleared and floodlit fields of fire. Village populations tended to be more heavily concentrated. The village perimeters were usually fairly small and not too difficult to defend. In Vietnam fences around the hamlets sometimes extend for miles, and, in far too many cases, present no problem at all to disciplined and determined attackers. Widespread guerrilla attacks on the hamlets coordinated with a switch to mobile war in the Truong Son could prove serious.

When General Nguyen Don is ready, this is the type of tactic Saigon must expect. It would be excessively optimistic to report that it is ready for it. It is even less ready to cope with the complementary "peace" campaign.

A military reverse would aggravate the already critical political situation in Saigon. It might also leave the highly regimented hamlets open for a Communist takeover. The substitution of one form of authoritarian control for another would pose no particular problem.

A day or two before the Viet Minh entered Hanoi in 1954, I watched a group of Viet Minh girls with long pigtails, white tunics and black trousers marching across a paddy field to the single beat of a drum. All over South Vietnam the girls have been organized by Madame Nhu. Blue is preferred to black in the uniform, Personalism to Communism in the ideology. But I wonder how many appreciate the difference.

Even by doubling the number of government men with guns, which is the current goal, it is improbable that the Viet Cong can be maneuvered into a position where their main battle corps can be brought to battle and defeat. In the delta, where the terrain is favorable, smashing attacks with thousands of troops have not succeeded in eliminating really significant numbers. The problem will be infinitely more difficult in the mountains. Even in the Maquis D, only thirty miles from Saigon, the Viet Cong for years have had a main base. Its general whereabouts are known, but the Arvins have not been able to take it out. It would take years to winkle out the Viet Cong from the Truong Son, years of hard slogging by forces which do not yet seem to have much stomach for such fighting.

On the other hand, I am not pessimistic enough to believe that a military defeat for Diem is inevitable or even probable. American assistance for Diem is much more effective than it was when the French were running the war. Some sort of stand-off is the likely *military* result unless the Viet Cong can make an earlier political breakthrough, or a *coup d'état* finally succeeds.

That there will be more attempted coups is certain. Saigon thinks and talks in terms of coups. Generals are shadowed when they go out to dinner. An air of tension is always present. It will increase in intensity as the war drags on. "Peace" and "neutrality" are highly appealing catch-cries already. The more popular they become, the more Diem will be pushed into repressive measures and the more the pressures will increase either to get rid of him or to settle the war by negotiation at the conference table.

The pressures will be both internal and external. Peking, Phnom Penh, and Hanoi and the National Liberation Front have long been advocating another Geneva conference and the creation of a South-East Asian "zone of peace." If the United States was so pleased about neutrality for Laos, what is wrong about a neutral South Vietnam? What is sauce for the goose is also sauce for the gander.

The pressures are not confined to the Communists or to their satraps. The British and the French are fearful of the depth of the United States military involvement in South Vietnam. They contend that substantially increased numbers of non-Asian troops would lend "coloration" to the Communists charges of colonialism and increase the danger of escalation.

There is some truth in these contentions: but implicit in them is the suggestion that it would be better to fight the war over the conference table.

With the assurance of even limited support from Australia, New Zealand, Thailand, and the Philippines, the United States might not be gravely embarrassed if, under grave military pressure, it had to embark on further ventures in South Vietnam or elsewhere in South-East Asia without the approval or help of its European allies. But the point is that military pressures are not likely to be grave—only persistent, and never fully identifiable as overt aggression.

The time may well come in South Vietnam when the United States may even hope for some sort of escalation, something to get its teeth into, something like the set-piece battle the French were always hoping for—until they got it. This sort of challenge is direct and readily identifiable and much easier to counter than a Laotian-type "peace" offensive.

Nothing presents itself as an easy way out. Total military victory does not seem possible, and the restoration of order, if that is possible, will take years. Diem will not broaden his government. He will not change his advisers. He will not accept outside advice.

Is the answer, then, that Diem must go? That the situation demands, and that the South Vietnamese people deserve, and need, something more effective and more enlightened in the way of government is obvious, but though there are many men of talent and sophistication who have not been used, the opposition is scattered, disunited, in jail, or Communist. Nothing about the army suggests that it would prove a proper alternative.

The probability is that the régime will go on, ever more isolated from the people, and that the Americans will meet the military challenge in whatever way it may develop until one day Diem either abdicates his task (a real fear among some Americans in Vietnam) or is removed by an assassin or a *coup d'état*. None of these possibilities is attractive; none holds a solution for South Vietnam or for South-East Asia.

If there is any consolation in this recitation of the reverses we have suffered, they are surely to be found only in the lessons to be learned. That Peking, in particular, intends to continue with the technique of promoting wars of national liberation of the Indo-China type is patent. Indo-China and Cuba are held up as examples. General Vo Nguyen Giap, for instance, feels that what happened in Indo-China is the best model of all for small countries.

"The victory of the Vietnamese people is that of a small and weak nation and possessing no regular army which rose up to engage in an armed struggle against the aggression of an imperialist country with a modern army and benefitting from the support of the American imperialists," he concluded in *People's War, People's Army*. "In the present international situation, a weak people which rises up resolutely to fight for its freedom is sure to triumph over all enemies and to achieve victory."

In South-East Asia we were transfixed by the stars when we should have been searching among the stones. We rode on horseback and saw only the flowers. We looked for figureheads when we should have been looking for the people. We conceded the mountains, the forests, and the paddy fields to the Communists and put our energies in the cities. We raised armies instead of living standards. Because someone once called the Chinese Communists agrarian reformers, even the idea of helping peasant villagers, who comprise 80 per cent, or more, of the population of the under-developed countries, seemed suspect. In the long haul, as we have seen in China, Communist land reform is a monstrous trick; but it is also true that in hundreds of villages all over South-East Asia the only people working at the grass roots for an uplift in people's living standards are the Communists. They are dedicated, hard-working and, in their own interests, successful.

As I have suggested in these pages, there are hopeful signs that we have at last learned the lessons of the Indo-China War. We shall deserve what we will surely get if we fail this time to remember them.

Index

Note: All persons listed in this index will be found under their family names. However, if a person is commonly referred to by his given name, he will also be found under that name. For example, the President of the Republic of Vietnam, Ngo Dinh Diem, is often called "President Diem." Therefore he is listed under "Diem," with a cross reference from "Ngo Dinh Diem."